VICTORIAN DEVOTIONAL POETRY

VICTORIAN DEVOTIONAL POETRY

THE TRACTARIAN MODE

G. B. TENNYSON

Harvard University Press
Cambridge, Massachusetts
London, England
1981

Library of Congress Cataloging in Publication Data
Tennyson, G   B
  Victorian devotional poetry.

  Includes bibliographical references and index.
  1. English poetry—19th century—History and criticism. 2. Devotional
literature—History and criticism. 3. Christian poetry, English—History and
criticism. 4. Oxford movement. 5. Poetics.
I. Title.
PR595.D47T4   821'.8'09   80-14416
ISBN 0-674-93586-1

To M.W.

"Where Patience her sweet skill imparts"

— Keble

Preface

A POSSIBLY APOCRYPHAL STORY from the days of BBC radio tells of a broadcast of an Anglican service from Westminster Abbey. A long silence in the ceremony is finally broken by the voice of the bishop saying in a stage whisper to the server, "Psst! Put my mitre on." Another pause. The same voice again, saying, "On *me*, you fool!" Apocryphal though it may be, the story sounds an appropriate cautionary note for one who would undertake to write about matters both religious and literary, especially when the religious matters involve the Anglo-Catholic movement in the nineteenth century when mitres mattered. There is some danger that one will put the mitre on the wrong head. Religious-minded readers are likely to think that too much attention is being given to purely literary, hence, purely secular, matters; literary-minded readers are likely to think the reverse is true. It is with an awareness of the perils of false emphasis, then, that I undertake the present study, for it involves in approximately equal measure matters religious and matters literary.

My aim in this work has been to give equal credit to the religious and literary dimensions of Victorian devotional poetry in the Tractarian mode, that is, to *share* the mitre. This aim reflects what I believe to be the real emphasis of the poetry itself. From the point of view of standard approaches to the Oxford Movement it will seem to lean too much to the literary side. From the point of view of standard approaches to Victorian literature it will seem to lean too much to the religious side. The final appeal must therefore be to whether this approach adds to our understanding of both the religious and literary phenomenon that was the Oxford Movement.

However the question of balance in the study is decided, there is no question in my own mind that my many debts to institutions and persons who have aided me in this work are fairly equally divided between the religious and the secular. I am happy to record them here.

My earliest, and still an enduring, indebtedness is to the John Simon Guggenheim Memorial Foundation for a fellowship in 1970-1971 to initiate the research that led to the present book. Without that support this book would not have been possible. I am also grateful to the University of California for a sabbatical leave in my Guggenheim year and in 1977-1978 to work on this study. Throughout the period of my research I have been greatly aided by support from the Research Committee of the University of California, Los Angeles.

The support of the institutions cited enabled me to consult hard-to-obtain works in various libraries, and I gratefully acknowledge the kindness of the librarians and curators at the following institutions: The Archiepiscopal Library, Lambeth Palace, London; the Bodleian Library, Oxford University; the British Library, London; The Catholic Central Library of the Franciscan Fathers of the Atonement, London; Dr. Williams Library, London; Edinburgh University Library; Honnold

Library, Claremont, California; Henry E. Huntington
Library, San Marino, California; Library of Keble College,
Oxford; Library of the Oratory of St. Philip Neri, Birm-
ingham; Firestone Library, Princeton University; Library of
Pusey House, Oxford; Sion College Library, London; St.
Deiniol's Library, Hawarden, Wales; Society of St. John the
Evangelist, Cowley, Oxford; Beinecke Library, Yale Univer-
sity; Department of Special Collections, UCLA Library; and
the Vatican Library, Rome.

Many individuals have aided me in various ways in my
researches on this topic, and I thank especially: Lionel Adey,
University of Victoria, Canada; Owen Barfield, Kent,
England; Father John Barker, Los Angeles; Ian Campbell,
University of Edinburgh; Raymond Chapman, London
School of Economics; Allan C. Christensen, Rome; Charles
Cox, Devon, England; Robert De Cordes, Long Beach,
California; the late Father Stephen Dessain of the Oratory,
Birmingham, who graciously let me examine Newman's per-
sonal library; Brother Dominic of the Community of the
Glorious Ascension, London; Peter Halliday, London; Father
Brian Horne, Kings College, University of London; Professor
K. J. Fielding, University of Edinburgh; Colin McDowell,
Rome; Philip T. Rand, Rome; and the following persons at
UCLA: Patricia Gilmore-Jaffe, Corinne Henning, Janet D.
Keyes, Patrick Pacheco, and Sharon Propas. I am especially in-
debted to Dr. Carol Lanham, UCLA, for help with Latin and
Greek.

I am grateful to members of several graduate seminars at
UCLA for their thoughtful responses to some of the ideas advanced in this study, particularly to Gordon Cheesewright,
Elliot Engel, Roger Hambridge, and Ina Rae Hark. For the
same reason I am grateful to members of the NEH Summer
Seminar in Victorian Critical Theory at UCLA in 1977,
especially to Michael Bright, Edward Cohen, Father James

Dorrill, Richard Freed, Robert Goetzman, and Sister Marcella Holloway.

I thank the following organizations and institutions for the opportunity to speak to receptive audiences on topics related to this study; Conference on Christianity and Literature, Western Region; Nineteenth-Century Studies Groups, University of Edinburgh; Thomas Aquinas College, Santa Paula, California; Victorian Division, Modern Language Association; Westmont College, Santa Barbara, California.

The manuscript was ably typed by the staff of the Central Stenographic Bureau, UCLA, under the direction of Ellen Cole. I am greatly in their debt for this and other typing services. I owe a special debt of gratitude to my wife, Elizabeth J. Tennyson, for compiling the index.

At one time I had thought this study should be dedicated to the memory of the originator of both the Oxford Movement and devotional poetry in the Tractarian mode, John Keble. It seemed also the right way to strike the balance between religion and literature, since Keble was both priest and poet. But I learned that inspiration from the past can be less important in the actual completion of a project than encouragement in the present. The existing dedication reflects that learning. It also sidesteps the issue of the relative weight to be assigned to literature and religion and gives the nod to the charity that should inform both.

G.B.T.

Los Angeles, California
On the Feast of the Transfiguration
August 6, 1979

Contents

xi

Illustrations

VICTORIAN DEVOTIONAL POETRY

Abbreviations

A   John Henry Cardinal Newman, *Apologia pro vita sua*, ed. Martin Svaglic (Oxford, 1967)

C   Isaac Williams, *The Cathedral* (London, 1838)

CY   John Keble, *The Christian Year*, ed. Walter Lock (3rd ed., London, 1904)

J   John Julian, *A Dictionary of Hymnology*, 2 vols. (1907; rpt., New York, 1957)

L   *Lyra Apostolica*, ed. H. C. Beeching (London, n.d.)

LP   John Keble, *Lectures on Poetry*, trans. E. K. Francis, 2 vols. (Oxford, 1912)

N   *The Works of John Henry Newman*, 39 vols. (London, 1898–1903)

O   John Keble, *Occasional Papers and Reviews* (Oxford, 1877)

T   *Tracts for the Times*, 6 vols. (London, 1834–1841)

I

Introduction

And help us, this and every day,
To live more nearly as we pray.
— *The Christian Year,* "Morning"

IN A CELEBRATED ESSAY T. S. Eliot argued that for most people religious poetry is a species of minor poetry and that in general Eliot himself agreed with this judgment.[1] He has held that most so-called religious poets enjoy a special but limited awareness of an aspect of life — the "religious or devotional" — that distinguishes them from even the great Christian poets, whose work encompasses a larger range of passion and awareness, to say nothing of the distance at which they stand from the great poets who may not be Christian at all. Even while taking issue with Eliot's judgment, at once so plausible and problematic, one can acknowledge its suitability as an introduction to Victorian devotional poetry. This poetry is both religious and minor, and for most people the connection would seem to be not accidental. But minor poetry has long been recognized as offering insights into its age, and frequently, even into the work of major figures that cannot easily be come upon from any other source. Minor poetry can offer aesthetic pleasures as well. I believe that the study of minor religious poetry discloses other insights and pleasures peculiar to it alone, and the study of such poetry may even challenge whether "minor" is a category inherent in a subject or simply in the limitations of a given poet.

In discussing religious poetry Eliot cited among his examples only one of the poets in any way involved in this book—Gerard Manley Hopkins—and in a subtle qualification, allowed for the possibility that he may be a major poet after all.[2] Otherwise, such poets as John Keble, Isaac Williams, and the Tractarian poets generally gain no mention from Eliot or indeed from most modern commentators on religious poetry. They are minor poets even among minor poets, and it has been many years since any stature whatsoever has been claimed for them as literary artists, although in their day each enjoyed considerable repute as a poet, and one at least—Keble—was held to be among the great religious poets of the language.

This book does not aim at a rehabilitation of these poets that would put, say, Keble or Isaac Williams among the immortals and the others among at least poets of the second rank, but it does aim at rehabilitation in some degree. All of the poets considered here have merit as poets greater than their present neglect would suggest, though I concede that these merits are difficult to extract from much that is simply inferior. Apart from the question of merit, however, the poetry the Tractarians wrote has considerable interest of a cultural as well as a literary-historical kind; it illustrates a sensibility of an age usually examined from other perspectives and thus not always justly assessed. Tractarian poetry and the aesthetic that it exemplifies constitute a concurrent tradition in the age alongside the better-known social and psychological ones, a tradition that goes far toward clarifying what the Victorian experience was.

Beyond the aims having to do with poetry and the age, this

book has another aim: to examine the nature of the religious sensibility at work in poetry. I have consciously called the poetry under discussion "devotional" rather than religious. Eliot used the terms apparently interchangeably, but as I considered the terminology for this study, it seemed to me time to strive for greater precision in the literary vocabulary. Indeed, I think much of the objection one might make to Eliot's remark about the minor character of religious poetry would be obviated by avoiding so comprehensive a term as religious poetry, which after all can readily be construed to include the most important work of such poets as Dante and Milton. It is unlikely that Eliot meant to include either *The Divine Comedy* or *Paradise Lost* in the category of minor poetry, but the imprecision surrounding the use of a term like "religious poetry" can easily lead to that sort of inclusion.

Current usage regarding "religious poetry" remains about as imprecise as that which prevailed in the Victorian age, when religion was not so separate a department of life as it is today. Then writers spoke equally of "religious," "sacred," and "devotional" poetry, though more often of the first two types than the last. A similar indefiniteness prevails today, except that the term "sacred poetry" is the one least often encountered. Nor is there any ready guide to distinctions among these terms, even in the vast body of contemporary criticism or in the numerous modern glossaries of literary terminology.[3] All the same, a kind of informal distinction seems to be emerging regarding the terms "religious poetry" and "devotional poetry," and in my use of them in this study, I shall try to formalize what I perceive this distinction to be. To begin with the most comprehensive definition of religious poetry, we can take that offered by Dame Helen Gardner as both a theoretical definition and as one that guided her in the practical task of determining which poems to include in an anthology of religious verse. As near as one can phrase it, her definition is that of poetry that demonstrates a commitment to an unseen power.[4] Such a definition is broad indeed. My own inclination is to narrow this concept somewhat and take religious poetry to be that in which a commitment is made or implied to an established belief, or system of ideas, or body of faith, that is, to a religion. It is such a definition that I think most readers would understand by the term "religious poetry." If it excludes anything that Gardner's definition would include, it is only poetry, more properly called philosophic or reflective, and the anomalous kind of poetry, included in the Gardner anthology, expressing a *rejection* of commitment or belief. "Religious poetry," then, is the term I shall use for all poetry of faith, poetry about the practices and beliefs of religion, poetry designed to advance a particular religious position, poetry animated by the legends and figures of religious history, and poetry that grows out of worship. Using the term "religious poetry" in this large designation comprehends devotional poetry and sacred poetry as well as the verse of hymns. I take all these to be more or less recognizable subdivisions of religious poetry, mindful of course that such subdivisions can often overlap one another.

Following what seems to me a tendency, but only a tendency, of the Victorians, I shall generally restrict the term "sacred poetry" to narrative verse on biblical and early Church topics, normally retellings in verse of Bible stories but including also elaborations of such stories and tales of the first Christian era. By this definition *Paradise Lost* would be sacred poetry. That may seem to some unduly restrictive for a poem of such magnitude; if so, they must find objective ways to distinguish it from its nineteenth-century echoes like Henry Hart Milman's *The Fall of Jerusalem* (1820) and Robert Montgomery's *The Messiah* (1832) or the series of Oxford Prize Poems on sacred subjects, all of which are most often referred to in the age as sacred poetry.[5]

"Hymns" I take to be that verse, normally in common measure written for congregational singing as adapted to various musical settings: in short, the poetry of communal worship. This is itself a large area of literary endeavor, somewhat neglected by literary critics partly because the verse of hymns is difficult to disentangle from the music.[6] The study of hymns has therefore been left to musicologists and ecclesiastical historians. Hymns are, however, the closest of the subdivisions of religious poetry to what I call devotional poetry. Hymns may be considered as in the main the devotional poetry of Protestantism, though there are of course Catholic and High Church hymns as well. Although some of the poetry I discuss was adapted for use in hymns, most of it was not, and virtually none of it was written with hymn use in mind. It is a testimony to the affection in which poems like Newman's "Pillar of the Cloud (Lead, Kindly Light)" were held that they have found their way into hymnals; most of them are far from ideally suited for such use, as anyone who has endeavored to sing that hymn can testify. At the same time, the close connection between devotional poetry and hymns is made clear by the extent to which Tractarian devotional poetry stimulated a whole new development in hymnody and modified even the well-established Evangelical tradition.

The term "devotional poetry" that I have applied to the great bulk of poetry in this book is the term that has come into increasing use in twentieth-century criticism, sometimes as a general term for religious poetry but more often in connection with the religious poetry of the seventeenth century. Eliot, in speaking of religious or devotional poetry, cites the names Vaughan, Southwell, Crashaw, Herbert, and Hopkins, testifying to the prominence of seventeenth-century writers in contemporary thinking about devotional poetry. Without restricting the term to the seventeenth century, I readily acknowledge that seventeenth-century poetry is paradigmatic for understanding the idea of devotional poetry as I am using the term. Such poetry exhibits an orientation toward worship and a linkage with established liturgical forms, especially forms associated with High-Church Anglican or Roman Catholic religious practices. By devotional poetry I mean, therefore, poetry that grows out of and is tied to acts of religious worship. If sacred poetry is exemplified by poems ranging from *Paradise Lost* to the *Fall of Jerusalem,* and hymns by such well-known verse as "O God, Our Help in Ages Past" and "Abide with Me," devotional poetry is best illustrated by Herbert's poetry in *The Temple* and, as we shall see, by Keble's in *The Christian Year.*

Although I intend to adhere to the terminology cited above, I must acknowledge that it is only approximate. In an area so little discriminated by critics there cannot be as much precision as in areas more fully examined and classified. Moreover, the usefulness of any generic designations is limited. One could, for example, consider "poetry of meditation," as identified by Louis Martz, as yet another subdivision of religious poetry alongside sacred poetry, hymns, and devotional poetry.[7] I prefer to think of the poetry of meditation as a particular emphasis within seventeenth-century devotional poetry. Whether a kind, a subdivision, or an emphasis, it is in any case peculiar to the seventeenth century, except for its possible reappearance in modified form in the poetry of Hopkins. One could also cite something broadly analogous in Keble's and Isaac Williams' meditations on scenes in nature, but this practice owes more, I think, to Wordsworth than to the seventeenth century and is of course a much freer and less structured undertaking than the techniques of meditation in seventeenth-century poetry.

Further, one could make a case for something called "liturgical poetry," a type of poetry that can be found in

medieval Latin office hymns and antiphons, and in the ver-
nacular in some Anglo-Saxon Cynewulfian poems.[8] This too I
consider an emphasis within devotional poetry, one revitalized
by the Oxford Movement. It is, however, but one of the ways
in which the devotional impulse is channeled into poetry
rather than a fully developed genre or subgenre of poetry.

There are, then, continuing problems in precision of definition in the area of religious poetry. The present study will not
solve them, but I hope it will bring the general subject into
sharper focus.

What I am calling Victorian devotional poetry is intimately
connected with the Oxford Movement and chiefly with the
early or Tractarian phase of that movement. Insofar as it is
considered at all by modern commentators, this poetry has
been seen as a kind of by-product of Tractarianism. It is my
contention that something closer to the reverse is the case, or
at least that cause and effect here are almost impossible to
disentangle. The chief reason for seeing Tractarian poetry as
incidental to the Movement is the understandable dominance
in our eyes of Newman as the architect of the Movement and
the consequent emphasis on theological and polemic aspects of
the Movement. Dean Church's still standard history, *The Oxford Movement*, bears the telling and Newman-like subtitle
"Twelve Years: 1833-1845,"[9] which is as much as to say that
the entire movement began and ended with Newman. But increasingly in the twentieth century, commentators have tended to view the Movement as a phenomenon of greater range
and duration than the twelve Newman years, and modern terminology reflects this larger view. Thus it is now more and
more common to restrict the term "Tractarian" to the early
phases of the Movement, or to those features that were
especially marked in the early phases, and to consider the
Movement overall as having survived Newman's departure,

eventually to become synonymous with the Anglo-Catholic Movement that endures to this day in the Church of England. Raymond Chapman's study of the literary influence of the Oxford Movement[10] extends as far as William Morris and J. H. Shorthouse, neither of whom had been born when Keble delivered the Assize Sermon in 1833; so, in a parallel way Victorian devotional poetry can be taken to apply to a very large body of poetry in the nineteenth century that derives from the Oxford Movement, and devotional poetry in the Tractarian mode, as this book is subtitled, can be taken to encompass the poetry of the early phase of the Movement that provided the seedfield out of which the later poetry grew.[11] Concentrating on Tractarian poetry, then, is comparable to concentrating on the first phase of the Oxford Movement, but it need not imply that the Movement or the poetry associated with it ceased to exist after 1845.

Although the importance of the Oxford Movement is everywhere present in this study, I have not sought to retell the story of the Movement as a whole but only to relate aspects of the story to the poetry. The full story of the Oxford Movement has been told frequently and well in the abundant literature on the subject that began almost from the moment the Movement was recognized as having a distinct identity. Readers unfamiliar with the main outlines of the Movement can turn to Newman's *Apologia* and Church's history for the story of the first phase; for the larger view of the Movement readers should look to the many twentieth-century studies, from Ollard to Chapman.[12] To aid in relating matters treated in the present study to the Movement as a whole, I have included a table of dates in an appendix.

Where this study departs from most treatments of the Oxford Movement is in my conviction that the literary expression of the Movement, and the poetry in particular, is as much cause and symptom as it is result of the Movement. For the most part, historians of the Movement have concentrated on the public events—the Assize Sermon, the publication of the *Tracts for the Times,* the trauma of Tract 90, the departure of Newman—and on the theological ideas advanced by the chief spokesmen for the Movement. We have come to see the Oxford Movement as an ecclesiastical and theological phenomenon, often rendered as the dramatic story of Newman's progress from Evangelicalism to Roman Catholicism. Of course it was all these things, and it cannot be understood apart from them. But, as the more thoughtful students of the Movement (beginning with Newman himself) have long noted, the Oxford Movement was something else as well. It was the religious manifestation of a change in sensibility, a new kind of awareness made possible in large part by the European-wide phenomenon of Romanticism.[13] Newman's citing of the importance of the works of Sir Walter Scott for the Movement—and the subsequent century-long reverence for Scott by the Tractarians and their successors—is one of the earliest notices that, at bottom, the Oxford Movement was an affair of the heart and spirit. Such matters touch aesthetic sensibilities even before they reach expression in ecclesiastical and theological forms. Beneath the *odium theologicum* of arguments about the apostolicity of the Church of England or the reintroduction of the mixed chalice lies a religious and an aesthetic perception of what apostolicity means and what a sacrament is. It is in this aesthetic sense that Newman was speaking when he said the heart is commonly reached not by reason but by dogma, for to Newman and the Tractarians dogma was not the dead, dry forms of the schools but a living and aesthetically apprehended insight into the life of things. To see again into the sensibility that could so construe dogma we should look less to the formal theological disputations of, say, the Hampden Affair, or Tract 90, and more to the purely literary undertakings of the participants in such controversies.

Insofar, then, as this work is a contribution to the study of the Oxford Movement, it comes at that Movement from the aesthetic and literary side rather than the theological or ecclesiastical, even though the Tractarians were not disposed to separate these sides as sharply as we do. Writing in 1963, A. M. Allchin noted that "in the sphere of worship, prayer and spirituality" the influence of the Oxford Movement "has been wider than anyone could have imagined fifty years ago," and that in liturgical matters the Tractarians were pioneers "in something much bigger than they themselves ever knew."[14] I believe that similar, if less grand, claims could be made about Tractarian poetry, which is very much an aspect of "worship, prayer and spirituality."

Recent studies in nineteenth-century critical theory generally and Tractarian critical theory in particular have greatly enlarged our understanding of the aesthetic background against which the work of the Tractarians must be set. In many respects indeed, the greatest literary achievement of the Tractarians, apart from Newman's prose, was the formulation of a full-scale poetics.[15] Accordingly, I shall give as much attention to Tractarian critical theory as to the poetry itself. But the two are finally inextricable. Not only was the poetry written for the most part concurrently with the theoretical speculations about literature (hence it colored as much as it reflected those speculations), but it was also the poetry that reached an audience far beyond the readership of works like Keble's *Praelectiones Academicae,* and even beyond the fairly extensive readership of the *Tracts for the Times.* It was Tractarian poetry that did the most to make the Tractarian ethos available to those who were not themselves part of the small Oxford circle that actively participated in the Movement. It seems to me not at all farfetched to argue that *The Christian Year* has had a greater impact on the character of English-language Christian worship in the past century and a half than any other single influence, and that the poetry of Isaac Williams is as much responsible for the nature of ecclesiastical architecture during the same period as the activities of the various Camden societies.

It is the aim of this study to make Tractarian poetic theory, Tractarian poetry, and the Tractarian ethos these exemplified more accessible to a public now largely unacquainted with any of these aspects of the most important religious undertaking of the nineteenth century.

II

Tractarian Poetics

Wouldst thou a poet be?
And would thy dull heart fain
Borrow of Israel's minstrelsy
One high enraptured strain?
      — *The Christian Year*, "The Circumcision of Christ"

THE *TRACTS FOR THE TIMES*, which gave the name Tractarian to the religious movement of 1833, ran to ninety numbers before being suspended at the request of the Bishop of Oxford. The great bulk of the Tracts deals with such theological issues as the authority of the Church, apostolicity, faith, the wisdom of the Fathers, the sacraments, holiness, sanctification, and the like.[1] This theological emphasis has long been recognized as a leading feature, indeed *the* leading feature, of the Oxford Movement, so much so that it has at times obscured other features equally important. Not the least of the obscured features is the Tractarian concept of literature, a dimension of Tractarianism evident in the Tracts themselves and in the critical writings of the principal Tractarians before, during, and after the eight years' run of the *Tracts for the Times*. Several such documents stand out: Keble's and Newman's literary essays, some of the Tracts themselves, and above all, Keble's *Praelectiones Academicae*, the series of lectures he delivered as Professor of Poetry at Oxford during the years 1831-1841. All these, along with various statements and reminiscences by the Tractarians, constitute a self-consistent and coherent aesthetic theory that explains the kind of poetry that was begotten of the Tractarian sensibility.

That Tractarian poetic theory was to some degree absorbed in the age, however infrequently it may have been the subject of specific examination, is evident from the sympathetic criticism of such writers as J. C. Shairp, or Walter Lock, or R. W. Church, and others of the post-Tractarian generations who were to a greater or lesser degree affected by the Oxford Movement.[2] Yet so pronounced has been the shift in this century away from the Tractarian outlook that the rediscovery in the early 1950's of Keble's literary theory by Alba H. Warren and M. H. Abrams came as something of a novelty.[3] Their treatments stood as the definitive, and almost the only, assessments of Tractarian poetic theory, until several recent studies brought a still greater depth of understanding to Tractarian views on art.[4] For perhaps the first time since the days of the Tractarians themselves, we are now in a position to see just what they thought literature and its function to be.

The Tractarians were, of course, children of their time (Keble, for example, was born in the same year as Shelley), and it is not surprising to find in them many assumptions of the Romanticism that characterized the first quarter of the nineteenth century. But only recently has the extent of Tractarian indebtedness to Romantic theory been very much examined. Stephen Prickett sees the Tractarians as part of what he calls in his subtitle "the tradition of Coleridge and Wordsworth in the Victorian Church." It is that tradition, so little explored even in the mammoth secondary literature on Coleridge and Wordsworth, that forms a necessary background to the understanding of Tractarian poetics. Accordingly, we need to look at the chief features of the Romantic inheritance of the

Tractarians before considering Tractarian poetic theory in its own right.

The Tradition of Wordsworth and Coleridge

It is a commonplace of writings on the Oxford Movement that Tractarianism was in some important way a product of Romanticism, even as it was also a product of renewed reverence for antiquity, apostolicity, and the particular Anglican spirituality associated with the High Church tradition of the seventeenth-century divines. The locus classicus for the idea of a Romantic impulse behind the Oxford Movement has always been Newman's statement in the *Apologia* crediting part of the rise of the Movement to "the literary influence of Walter Scott, who turned men's minds to the direction of the middle ages" (A, p. 94). Commentators on Tractarianism have noted the persistence of the esteem for Scott throughout the course of the Movement in the nineteenth century, and in so doing have seemed at times to consider awareness of Scott's influence as sufficient explanation of the connection between Tractarianism and Romanticism. It is worth looking again at the full passage from the *Apologia,* for it goes well beyond Walter Scott; moreover, the passage is Newman's reaffirmation in 1864 of sentiments he expressed at the height of the Tractarian movement in 1839 in an article entitled "The State of Religious Parties," published in the *British Critic,* the journal Newman was then editing as the organ for Tractarian ideas.[5] Indeed, on the matter of Romanticism, Newman in the *Apologia* does little more than quote passages from his 1839 essay.

Newman first notes that the Oxford Movement was a "reaction from the dry and superficial character of the religious teaching and the literature of the last generation" (A. p.93); then he mentions by name five persons who stimulated the thinking behind the Oxford Movement and refers to one other not named. Of the total, four were literary figures: Scott, Coleridge, Southey, and Wordsworth, in that order. The other two were clergymen: Alexander Knox (1757-1831) and "a much venerated clergyman of the last generation," who remains unidentified by Newman but who was almost certainly Thomas Sikes, rector of Guilsborough (d. 1834).[6] It is an arresting and largely literary roster, even though Newman is speaking of the origins of the religious movement in general. Of Scott, Newman says he appealed to "the general need of something deeper and more attractive, than what had offered itself elsewhere," and that he "re-acted on his readers, stimulating their mental thirst, feeding their hopes, setting before them visions, which, when once seen, are not easily forgotten, and silently indoctrinating them with nobler ideas, which might afterwards be appealed to as first principles" (A, p. 94). These are large claims, but they seem to be borne out by the continued respect Scott enjoyed among Anglo-Catholics throughout the age.

At least as much to the point of Tractarian poetic-religious impulses is what Newman has to say about the other Romantics in the background of Tractarianism. Of Coleridge, Newman writes:

> While history in prose and verse was thus [through Scott] made the instrument of Church feelings and opinions, a philosophical basis for the same was laid in England by a very original thinker, who, while he indulged in a liberty of speculation which no Christian can tolerate, and advocated conclusions which were often heathen rather than Christian, yet after all instilled a higher philosophy into inquiring minds, than they had hitherto been accustomed to accept. In this way he made trial of his age, and succeeded in interesting its genius in Catholic truth. (A, p. 94)

Southey and Wordsworth, Newman says, were "two living poets, one of whom in the department of fantastic fiction, the other in that of philosophic meditation, have addressed themselves to the same high principles and feelings, and carried forward their readers in the same direction [as Scott and Coleridge]" (A, p. 94).

The work of all these literary figures is coupled by Newman with the writings of Alexander Knox, who has been called by later commentators the Herald of the Oxford Movement, and with the utterances of Thomas Sikes, a clergyman of the old High Church tradition. Both of these men were concerned to awaken churchmen to the riches available but largely unnoticed in the Church of England. Sikes prophesied the time when "those great doctrines, now buried, will be brought out to the light of day, and then the effect will be fearful" (A, p. 94). Knox, along with John Jebb, Bishop of Limerick, engaged in reflections on the nature of the Church that have a Coleridgean ring. He and all the clergy of the old school looked to the Book of Common Prayer and the lessons of antiquity for guidance in understanding the character of the Church of England. By referring to Knox and Sikes, Newman is acknowledging the impact of the continuing High Church tradition, represented most prominently among the Tractarians themselves by John Keble, a tradition long regarded as a main source of the Movement.

From Newman's treatment in the *Apologia* it is clear that to him the forces behind the Oxford Movement were simultaneously literary (or, more properly, aesthetic) and religious, and, on the basis of sheer numbers cited, literary by a margin of two to one. But the key concepts are always intertwined and not distinguished as sources of influences. It was, for example, in reaction to the aridity of the "religious teaching and the literature" of the previous generation that the Movement arose. And the literary figures are spoken of in the same terms used for the clerical ones: Scott "indoctrinated" his readers by setting before them "visions"; Coleridge instilled a "higher philosophy"; Southey and Wordsworth both addressed themselves to "high principles and feelings"; Alexander Knox wrote of the "rich provisions" of the Church for "habits of a noble kind"; and Sikes spoke of "those great doctrines" that had lain neglected. With such language one cannot separate the specifically religious from the literary, and it seems clear that Newman in 1864, as in 1839, felt no need to do so.

Of course the Movement was not simply these six figures alone. It was, as Newman goes on to say in the *Apologia*, still quoting from his *British Critic* article, "not so much a movement as a 'spirit afloat;' it was within us, 'rising up in hearts where it was least suspected and working itself, though not in secret, yet so subtly and so impalably, as hardly to admit of precaution or encounter on any ordinary human roles of opposition'" (A, p. 95). It was, in short, the spirit of Romanticism at work in the Church.

Sir Walter Scott may enjoy pride of place among those cited by Newman as disposing the mind of the age toward what was to become Tractarianism, but the two most influential figures in the formation of Tractarian poetics were surely Wordsworth and Coleridge. The former indeed enjoyed consistent public homage from the Tractarians, culminating in Keble's Creweian Oration honoring Wordsworth in 1839 when the poet was presented with an honorary degree at Oxford.[7] Four years later, Keble dedicated to Wordsworth his own *Praelectiones Academicae,* hailing Wordsworth as "true philosopher" and "inspired poet."[8] Keble and the Tractarians were necessarily more guarded in the respect they accorded to Coleridge, for, as Newman made clear in the *Apologia,* Coleridge "indulged in a liberty of speculation which no Christian can tolerate."[9] Despite this public discomfort with the later Coleridge, Coleridgean ideas permeate Tractarian thinking on aesthetic subjects and, except on the question of nature, probably color Tractarian poetics more than those of any other single figure.

The main point of contact between the Tractarians and Coleridge lies in their disposition to regard religion and aesthetics as kindred fields. In Coleridge's thinking such a disposition is of central importance, though students of literature have historically somewhat neglected it;[10] among the Tractarians this disposition is the very bedrock of their thinking on aesthetics. For understanding Tractarianism, the special virtue of Stephen Prickett's study of the Coleridge-Wordsworth tradition in the Victorian Church lies in his demonstration of the need to approach Coleridgean (and Tractarian) discourse from simultaneously aesthetic and religious perspectives. Prickett has shown that Coleridge was working in an aesthetics not only Romantic and German (the question of borrowings here is unimportant), but also traditionally Christian, and that consequently it is necessary to include religious concepts in any study of Coleridge's aesthetic position, and especially of his language. The same is true for studying those who follow in the Coleridge tradition; Prickett rightly takes students of theology to task for ignoring the literary dimension in English Victorian ecclesiastical history. He writes: "One of the things the literary critic who reads theology rapidly discovers is that modern theologians often seem curiously unaware of the literary premises from which such men as Hare, Maurice, Keble, and Newman begin. Anyone who has read both literary criticism and theology in the Victorian period soon comes to realise how deeply the two are intertwined" (p. 7). Prickett's cautionary word to theologians could equally well be applied to those students of literature who have approached the Tractarians without sufficient sensitivity to the religious dimensions of their writings on literature. In both cases the proximate source for the intertwining of literature and religion is Coleridge.

Coleridgean language, as Prickett sees it, is more than a mélange of terms originating in related disciplines like philosophy, theology, and literature; it is rather an attempt at synthesis whereby literary concepts are recognized to be aspects of a larger philosophical and theological unity. Coleridgean language, Prickett says, "was seen as metaphorical. 'bi-focal,' or 'stereoscopic,' and in Coleridge's special sense of the word, 'symbolic'" (p. 7). We can also apply here Owen Barfield's concept of "polarity," which in Coleridge's thinking expresses the dynamic character of all life as a unity of contending forces, each working against, but also with and by virtue of the other through a unifying power inherent in the relationship of the poles. "Two forces of one power," Barfield puts it.[11] Such a view as seen in Coleridge, Prickett notes, perceives "no break between the 'natural' and the 'supernatural.' Though they stand in a dialectical relationship to one another, they are, nevertheless, the two ends of an unbroken continuum" (p. 56). The consequences of this kind of thinking for Coleridgean terminology are extremely far-reaching, as the much discussed philosophical dimensions of Imagination and Fancy have shown. Less frequently noted but at least as important are the religious implications of this terminology. Nothing in Coleridge has been so much quoted or so little pondered as the religious dimension of his definition of the imagination. Most commentators seem to think that Coleridge *likened* the imagination to the infinite act of creation, whereas Coleridge said the Imagination was the *repetition* in the finite mind of the eternal act in the infinite mind. That is to say, the human mind in its limited sphere recapitulates, because it participates in, the divine mind in its infinite sphere. The imagination, then, that most fundamental of Coleridge's literary concepts, was defined by Coleridge in religious terms. Here is the basis for a religiously based aesthetic, ultimately developed by the Tractarians. Such is the case with virtually all of Coleridge's literary discourse.

In addition to the Coleridgean "high" view of the imagination as an aspect of the divine creating word, the Tractarians also inherited from Coleridge a more or less specific vocabulary, but one they modified in their own way. In it, Prickett notes, "poetry" becomes the paradigmatic artistic form and hence frequently the term to signify art in general. *Poetic* in turn becomes the adjective signifying not only that which exhibits the best qualities of poetry or art, but also that which is "imaginative" in a Coleridgean sense and "mythic" in a modern sense (p. 118). Thus, when the Tractarians speak of poetry and the poetic, they are usually speaking of art and the imaginative, focused, to be sure, most often on poetry or verse, but not confined to it. Again Prickett has pinpointed the character of this language as it comes from Coleridge, noting that Keble and Newman, speaking about the Church, have in common with Coleridge a language that

> draws its imagery in a very particular way from aesthetic criticism. It speaks of the Church in terms that are ultimately those of a work of art, and of the relationship between artist and public. One of the most puzzling aspects of nineteenth-century Anglican writing to the modern reader is the uses of the word 'poetic' which...is used by Keble and Newman in contexts far removed from 'poetry.' We shall, I think, have great difficulty with this word until we see that it is used in a sense very close to the modern meaning of 'myth.' As it is used by modern critics the word 'myth' is intended to convey no suggestions of being literally 'untrue' or being anti-historical; it is simply the word for a story that contains for its teller and hearers many levels of meaning that are inseparable from the framework of the story itself, and which cannot, therefore, be put in any other way. (p. 68)[12]

None of this should be taken to imply a wholehearted or conscious Tractatian adoption of Coleridge's later speculations, about which there were more rumors than facts at the time the Tractarians were formulating their views. Rather, Coleridge contributed significantly to Newman's "spirit afloat" in bringing together aesthetic and religious concepts and terminology and in reopening minds to what had been held in earlier times to be the close relationship of art and religion.

The Tractarians also inherited the nature worship so long associated with Wordsworth, the chief poet of the age of their formative years, but this too they fitted into a religious framework; indeed, they perceived Wordsworth himself as having approached nature in a religious way, and there is in the Tractarian reverence for Wordsworth none of the concern for orthodoxy that marks their attitude toward Coleridge. In the Tractarian view, Wordsworth was virtually a Tractarian, a designation even now not entirely inappropriate for the later Wordsworth, though the Tractarians saw all of Wordsworth in this light. Whether this distorts or evades an ambiguity in Wordsworth is of little moment for understanding the Tractarian vision. What is important is that the Tractarians saw Wordsworth responding to nature as they did, seeing in it the signs of the Creator. The later arguments over Wordsworth's "pantheism" have no parallels in Tractarian thinking. As Prickett notes, reflecting a modern perspective, "Keble's idea of Nature has not the ambiguity of Wordsworth's. Nevertheless, it does share with Wordsworth the overwhelming sense of a universe that is essentially 'poetic' in Keble's special sense of the word; as not an inanimate order, but a living, active, organic whole charged with divine meaning inseparably binding man and Nature" (p. 104). It is important to add also, as Prickett does elsewhere, that for Keble and the Tractarians the response to nature was conditioned as much by Bishop Butler's *Analogy* as by Wordsworth's poetry. We shall return to Butler, but here it is sufficient to note that Butler was also a favorite of Coleridge, so that for the Tractarians, a religiously sanctioned linkage between Coleridgean theory and Wordsworthian practice was at hand.

With such a clear joint indebtedness to Coleridge and

Wordsworth it may seem uncharitable of the Tractarians to have approached the former with such caution and the latter with such unqualified enthusiasm. Two factors explain their attitude. Coleridge was probably less directly known to the Tractarians than Wordsworth; certainly he was often mediated to them through Wordsworth. In any event, Keble largely formed his views on poetry well before he could have known much Coleridge criticism. By the 1820s—a more decisive decade for Newman's intellectual development than for Keble's—the writing of Coleridge of the middle years would have been more available, but the rumors about the later Coleridge would have made men like Keble and Newman uneasy. And that is the other factor in the Tractarian attitude: orthodoxy. The Tractarians sincerely resisted the excessive liberty of Coleridgean speculation, and even more, they shrank from the thought that the imputations of heterodoxy from which the later Coleridge suffered might be attached to *them.* Hence they freely honored the orthodox Wordsworth and regularly qualified their references to Coleridge. Today, when the tables have been turned, when Coleridge is praised and Wordsworth condemned on the grounds that the Victorians used to praise Wordsworth and condemn, or at least question, Coleridge, the Tractarians suffer if anything from imputations of excessive Wordsworthianism.

However the relative influences are assessed, it seems clear that the Tractarians were willing recipients of a Romantic aesthetic heritage that concerned itself with the nature of artistic creativity, and hence the nature of the artist; that invested art with a special authority because it derived art from the divine; and that linked especially the idea of love of nature with the poetic, the imaginative, the aesthetic. At the same time, Tractarian aesthetic theory is, as we shall see, more than a simple continuation of Coleridge and Wordsworth; it is rather Romanticism in a new key. The role of religion,

powerful in Coleridge and compatible with Wordsworth, is
pre-eminent in Tractarian poetics.

Pre-Tractarian Poetics

Where Coleridge's aesthetic speculations are tied to a
religious perception of the world, and where Wordsworth's
nature worship is at least patient of a theistic interpretation,
Tractarian poetics insists on an explicit linking of art and religion. So closely wedded are the two in Tractarian thinking,
and so visible is the Tractarian religious commitment otherwise, that there is an almost irresistible temptation to say that
the fundamental principle of Tractarian poetics is the subordination of art to religion. Some commentators have said as
much. But perhaps to say that much is to say almost too
much, especially if one is mindful of the long history of seeing
everything Tractarian from a purely religious viewpoint. If
pride of place must be assigned between art and religion, the
Tractarians would assign it to religion. But the Tractarians
did not conceive of the two on a collision course. They saw
them rather as allies in the joint task of salvation. Here the
concept of polarity might well be applied, though it has not in
the past been directed to Tractarianism, which has been seen
as so single-mindedly religious that any notion of a com-
plementary force has been excluded. But when we look at
both what the Tractarians said and how they said it, the conclusion is inescapable that what is at work is the joint and
mutually reinforcing activity of both religion and art. For
every explicit Tractarian assertion of the primacy of religion,
there is a counterbalancing, implicit approach to religion
through art. Aesthetic concepts so tinge the religious one as to
make it a nice question which is primary. What is clear is that
the one inevitably calls forth the other.

It is with Tractarian poetics that John Keble at last comes
back into his own as the premier Tractarian after a century and

a half of being overshadowed by Newman, for it is Keble who discoursed at greatest length on aesthetic subjects and who has left the largest body of writing on such subjects, even in the face of Newman's much greater literary output. What Keble said, moreover, is broadly consistent with what Newman and the other Tractarians said, as well as with what they all did when they turned their hands to original composition, whether literary or more obviously religious. Keble simply said it earlier, so early, in fact, that later commentators, even including Prickett, have not perceived how highly developed Keble's views on poetry were long before the start of the Oxford Movement. A consideration of Keble's pre-Tractarian writings not only makes the case for his priority as the Tractarian theorist, it helps to make clear why all the Tractarians, including even Newman, always regarded Keble as the true begetter of the Movement. Keble was a Tractarian two decades before the word had been coined.

As early as 1814 (when Newman was thirteen years old, but five years after Keble had discovered Wordsworth) Keble sounded several characteristic notes of what later became the Tractarian poetic position.[13] He was writing on Edward Copleston's *Praelectiones Academicae,* that is, Copleston's lectures on poetry delivered in his capacity as the Oxford Professor of Poetry during the period 1802-1813. The association is instructive. Though a member of the theologically liberal group known as the "Oriel Noëtics," Copleston was one of the unconscious forebears of the Tractarian movement by virtue of his contributing to the intellectual rigor and high moral tone of Oriel College, the original home of the Tractarians. He was also one of Keble's predecessors in the post of Professor of Poetry, and Keble's own most extensive writing on poetics would come some thirty-odd years later when he delivered his own identically titled *Praelectiones Academicae* while serving in the same post as Copleston. The 1814 essay on Copleston anticipates a number of points Keble was to make in his later, better-known work. The most prominent of these is Keble's assertion of the relation between poetry and religion: "It is to the awakening of some moral or religious feeling, not by direct instruction (that is the office of morality or theology) but by way of association, that we would refer all poetical pleasure" (p. 152). Not only does Keble thus sweepingly attribute all poetic pleasure to moral or religious feeling, but he further asserts that poetical pleasure itself is not confined narrowly to what is conventionally called poetry, thereby establishing what would become the Tractarian use of "poetry" and "poetical" as broad terms of aesthetics. He writes that some may object that he is

extending the empire of poetry too far, inasmuch as moral and religious associations are produced not only by writing, but by statues, pictures, melodies, even by numberless objects of common life. We readily grant that they are; nor have we the least objection to apply the term poetry to *every such case*. Nay, we have no doubt that the observation, if proved in detail, would confirm our position, by shewing that no subjects of the arts, or of common life, are fit for poetry, which do not immediately or circuitously produce some such effect. If all this be allowed, we see nothing absurd in calling the same result by the same name, whatever be the sensible instrument whereby it is produced. Be it addressed to the eye, ear, or mind only; be it a song of Handel, a painting of Reynolds, or a verse of Shakespeare; if it "transport our minds beyond this ignorant present," if it fill us with the consciousness of immortality, or the pride of knowing right from wrong, it is to us, to all intents and purposes, poetry. Nor is it anything uncommon in language to apply the term to these arts. We hear of the poetry of sculpture, the poetry of painting: and we have been led to our present conjecture, partly by an attempt to find out what it was in each case whereby they were imagined to partake of their sister's nature. (O, pp. 152-153, italics supplied)

Keble even anticipates the objection that his religious definition of poetry and art would appear to exclude too much that is regarded as poetry both from pagan antiquity and from contemporary non-Christian art and literature. "The answer," writes Keble, "is ready: we do not ask that [the poet] should profess religion or morality, but only that he should use ideas and language calculated to raise religious and moral associations. It is very evident that he may do this unconsciously even while he is preaching atheism or misanthropy, and that the images thus introduced into the mind may be so fascinating as completely to withdraw its gaze from the monstrous forms which lurk behind them." Pagan art and non-Christian art, then, are still art to the extent to which they raise, even if in spite of themselves, "religious and moral associations." That is the essence of "poetical pleasure," which is to say aesthetic pleasure.

Later in the essay, Keble commends Copleston's treatment of "the affections and of imagination," for here he found "less that seemed inconsistent with [my] own poetical creed." He then clarifies that creed, "sympathy and phantasy, the one chiefly employed on moral, the other on religious associations, divide between them the regions of verse: the one warning against selfishness, the other against despondency; the one staying our steps in the course, the other pointing to the goal; the one telling us of our duty here, the other of our reward hereafter." The affections, then, are those elements in our nature that Keble ascribes to earthly and human concerns, and these are primarily moral. Hence affections, or sympathy, need to be disciplined and tamed. That, he says, is the point of the Aristotelean concept of tragedy: "to purify the affections by terror and pity is the final cause of tragedy, and we are not aware of any reason why it should not be extended to all poetry." It is a stern and highly Tractarian view of the moral function of art.

The part of Keble's poetic creed concerning the affections, that is, his romanticizing of Aristotle, he takes to be self-evident; such a view has been, he says, "for these 2000 years an axiom in criticism." The other part of the creed, that which concerns the imagination, he thinks requires more explanation. And he offers the following:

All the pleasures of poetry, as the term is commonly apprehended, imply the embodying something visionary, the presenting something absent, the bettering something imperfect: their very being lies in the consciousness of some such operation. Now what (excepting in a mind thoroughly diseased and depraved, wherein imagination and reason too are slaves of the body) what can tend more strongly to make man feel his own dignity; to disencumber him of earthly affections, and lift him nearer what he once was, and what he may be again, than the exercise and invigoration of a power so totally independent of material things, so much at variance with the sense as this is. If, then, all the honest pleasures of the imagination have this high kindred, and if we may boldly exclude as unpoetical such as are corrupt and sensual, what hinders but that the poetry of the imagination, as well as that of the heart, be owned to have its beginning and end in religious and moral associations? (O, p. 158)

Keble is positing a kind of polarity in poetry and art between the earthly and the heavenly, between morality and religion. A polarity, it should be noted, not a conflict. The moral dimension of art is designed to purge the affections, the imaginative to exalt the mind to something higher. The formulation has obvious affinities with the ancient concept that art teaches and delights, but Keble's emphases and understanding of these terms show the effect of both romanticism and religion. The teaching dimension of art is moral, even as historically it had largely been, but in Keble without any admixture of mere instruction or addition to factual knowledge;

and the morality to which Keble points is insistently Christian. Art is thus firmly planted in the same soil from which sermons grow. (It was Keble who later uttered the memorable sentiment: "All sermons are good.") But at the same time art has another pole which exerts its power as a complement to moral instruction. That is the pole of the imagination as Romanticism had defined it. All poetic pleasure implies "embodying something visionary, the presenting something absent, the bettering something imperfect." That "something visionary" is no conventional Romantic escapism, but an aspiration toward God. In Keble's romanticism, *die blaue Blume* is none other than the divine source of all things, and in poetry, as in religion, one can make contact with the divine. Hence poetry has its "beginning and end in religious and moral associations."

Here, then, as early as 1814 are enunciated some of the most persistent Tractarian views on art. Poetry has its origin and its end in religion and morality. It is sister to morality and theology, but not by direct instruction. Aesthetic pleasure stems from the awakening of these moral and religious feelings, so that earthly affections are tempered and disciplined and human beings can be nearer to what once they were (before the Fall) and may be again (through Christ).

There are also precursors in Keble's 1814 essay of two ideas that will figure in Tractarian poetics—the concept of Reserve and the question of the ultimate cause and source of poetry and art. Keble speaks of "indirection" in the poet's expression of the religious aspect of poetry, anticipating the concept of Reserve; and, in citing Aristotle's concept of purgation he anticipates what will become the Tractarian idea of poetry as intense self-expression. Both of these notions are developed further a decade later in his essay "Sacred Poetry."[14]

Like the Copleston essay, "Sacred Poetry" was ostensibly a review, in this case of Josiah Conder's *The Star in the East*

(1824), but typically it concerns itself more with the general subject raised by Keble's approach to the volume, that is, sacred poetry overall, than with Conder's work as such.[15] Keble tends to treat Conder's poetry somewhat patronizingly as at once too Protestant and too contrived. His chief praise for Conder is for those poems in the collection that appear to have been written with no regard for publication and thus are free "from the pretension of authorship." Since by this time Keble himself had long been writing and privately circulating the poems that would constitute *The Christian Year,* one is warranted in seeing in his praise for Conder's private effusions a justification of his own hesitation in committing his verse to the public. Certainly his preference for that part of the work that "bears internal evidence, for the most part, of not having been written to meet the eye of the world" (O, p. 81) is an expression of his feelings of delicacy and reserve in approaching religious subjects. Yet more telling in establishing the Tractarian attitude to consciously religious poetry is Keble's virtual apology at the outset of the piece for presuming to subject sacred poems to literary criticism at all. If religious poems, he says, appear to be written with "any degree of sincerity and earnestness, we naturally shrink from treating them merely as literary efforts." To do so is to interrupt the "current of a reader's sympathy" and "to disturb him almost *in a devotional exercise"* (O, p. 81, my italics). But Keble does proceed to consider sacred poetry as a literary type and to examine the history of sacred poetry in English literature.

Keble goes farther in "Sacred Poetry" toward identifying the type with religion *tout court* than he had done in the essay on Copleston. His model is the Psalms. These, he says, are entirely free from any striving after effect or originality. A reader otherwise unacquainted with the Psalms would take them up and exclaim: " 'This is something better than merely attractive poetry; it is absolute and divine truth.' " Then Keble adds: "The same remark ought to be suggested by all sacred hymns" (O, p. 81). The reason for such a close identification between sacred poetry and divine truth stems from the nature of the source of all poetry: "It is required . . . in all poets, but particularly in sacred poets, that they should seem to write with a view of unburthening their minds, and not for the sake of writing; for love of the subject, not of the employment." Unburdening the mind points to poetry as release for the surcharged spirit, the theory that Keble was to express more fully in the *Praelectiones* and that has since become identified with him, as well as somewhat distorted in modern interpretations. I shall consider the theory at greater length later; here I point out only that Keble links at once the idea of unburdening and love of subject to classical "rapture and inspiration" (O, p. 91) and not to twentieth-century psychiatric concepts. He couples the unburdening of the enraptured mind with the notion of restraint:

> If grave, simple, sustained melodies—if tones of deep but subdued emotion are what our minds naturally suggest to us upon the mention of sacred *music*—why should there not be something analogous, a kind of plain chant, in sacred poetry also? fervent, yet sober; awful, but engaging, neither wild and passionate, nor light and airy; but such as we may with submission presume to be the most acceptable offering in its kind, as being indeed the truest expression of the best state of the affections. To many, perhaps to most, men, a tone of more violent emotion may sound at first more attractive. But before we *indulge* such a preference, we should do well to consider whether it is quite agreeable to that spirit, which alone can make us worthy readers of sacred poetry. (O, p. 91)

He goes on to allow that there must be "rapture and inspiration," but that in sacred verse "the true Prophet," that is, the poet, "speaking to or of the true God, is all dignity and calmness" (O, p. 91).

In "Sacred Poetry" Keble is almost as concerned to justify the endeavor of writing sacred poetry as he is to characterize it. Accordingly, he devotes a good deal of his effort to refuting the sentiment that religious poetry is an inappropriate and indeed impossible literary type. His antagonist is, of course, Samuel Johnson and the strictures Johnson expressed against religious poetry in his *Life of Waller,* but, as Keble notes, such a view is not confined to Dr. Johnson alone. It is "not uncommon among serious, if somewhat fearful believers," and so Keble takes it upon himself to correct the error. In so doing he addresses himself to what he sees as the four main points of Johnson's argument against religious poetry, and he answers each in a way that illuminates Tractarian ideas on poetry, especially on religious poetry.

Dr. Johnson's four arguments proceed from typical eighteenth-century deductions based on the nature of poetry, of devotion, of God, and of man. Keble does not argue against the method, but he does contest Johnson's understanding of the nature of each of the things he cites. Thus Johnson argues that the essence of poetry is invention and that the topics of devotion are few, so devotion by its nature is not suited to poetry. Keble replies: "How can the topics of devotion be few, when we are taught to make every part of life, every scene in nature, an occasion — in other words, a topic — of devotion" (O, p. 92). Butler's *Analogy* and the sacramental system would seem here to be in Keble's mind. Dr. Johnson's objection that poetry operates by suppression and addition to real life and therefore cannot be applied to religion, which can tolerate neither suppression nor addition, is met by Keble with the response that Johnson has confused doctrine as such with poetry. The former cannot indeed suffer suppression or addition, but the latter is designed to work upon "the human mind and heart." Since these are differently constituted in every man, and yet it is the business of the religious poet to "sympathise with all, [the poet's] store of subjects is clearly in-exhaustible and his powers of discrimination — in other words of suppression and addition — are kept in continual exercise" (O, pp. 93-94).

Dr. Johnson's most celebrated objection to religious poetry, perhaps because it is the most Johnsonian in its orotundities, concerns the nature of God: "Omnipotence cannot be exalted; infinity cannot be amplified; perfection cannot be improved." Therefore, Johnson argues, poetry cannot treat God at all. Keble has a fitting reply that also subtly reproves Johnson's faulty concept of the deity. Keble allows that all perfection "is im-plied in the Name of God," but insists that it is the "very of-fice of poetry" to develop and display the particulars of such a complex idea and that Dr. Johnson's objection would apply just as strongly against "any kind of composition of which the Divine Nature is the subject." Moreover, even if such an ob-jection applied to natural religion it would hardly hold against Christianity, "the object of whose worship has condescended also to become the object of description, affection, and sym-pathy, in the literal sense of these words." Thus Keble corrects Dr. Johnson's almost deistic notion that absent omnipotence is a sufficient reflection of the fullness of God and records his own awareness of the overriding importance of the Incarna-tion, an idea that was to exercise much appeal in nineteenth-century devotional poetry. Typically, however, Keble im-mediately says, "But this is, perhaps, too solemn and awful an argument for this place" (O, p. 94).

Finally, Keble opposes Johnson's view that in "pious meditation" man is confined to faith, thanksgiving, repen-tance, and supplication, pointing out that in the present essay he has already sufficiently noted the variety of "devout affec-tions," or modes of meditation, to refute the notion. But he cannot pass on without singling out Johnson's "invidiously put" statement that "Repentance, trembling in the presence of the Judge, is not at leisure for cadences and epithets." Repentance, Keble observes, is not confined to trembling before the Judge; on the contrary, the very function of sacred poetry and sacred music is to "quiet and sober the feelings of the penitent—to make his compunction as much of 'a reasonable service' as possible." The echo of the Prayer Book is followed by arguments from the "sacred volume" that teach us to address ourselves to God "in all the various tones, and by all the various topics, which we should use to a good and wise man standing in the highest and nearest relation to us" (O, p. 95).

These arguments justifying sacred poetry as a fit endeavor for the poet also serve to show the extent to which the Tractarian mind brought religion into a wider and deeper relation with all life, including of course the literary life. God is not for Keble a series of unapproachable abstract concepts—omnipotence, infinity, perfection. The Incarnation alone makes such a view untenable. Nor for Keble is poetry an activity set to one side of religion. The Church and its historical teachings that we should make "every part of life, every scene in nature" an occasion of devotion, justify occupying our thoughts and talents in religious pursuits, including the writing of poetry. It is this comprehensiveness of religion that so marks the Tractarian sensibility and that makes its poetics so inextricable from its worship.

The remainder of the essay, though largely given over to Keble's assessment of the history of English sacred poetry, also contains some ideas that will later surface in Tractarian aesthetics. Keble is led to consider the history of English sacred poetry because of a distinction he makes between those poets who openly avow the devotional character of their writing (thus reaching a smaller audience, such is the state of English culture) and those who "veil...the sacredness of the subject—not necessarily by allegory, for it may be done in a thousand other ways—and so deceive the world of taste into devotional reading." The notion of veiling is a common one among Tractarians and ultimately becomes linked with Reserve and also with the fondness for nature imagery so evident in Keble and others; nature affords a way of veiling and speaking of sacred things by indirection. In the history of English sacred poetry, pride of place for poets of the veiling type goes to Spenser, for poets of the avowedly religious type to Milton. Insofar as the two are comparable, Keble gives the nod to Spenser, for though Milton's *Paradise Lost* is "the great epic poem of our language," it suffers from various defects and blemishes (including too sympathetic a portrait of Satan, probably because of Milton's unconscious sympathy with the "haughty and vindictive republican spirit"). The poet we might expect to find at the head of Keble's list, Herbert, is indeed there, but like Christ in Keble's earlier discussion of the nature of God, "Herbert is a name too venerable to be more than mentioned in our present discussion" (O, p. 105).

As always, Keble well represents the Tractarian sensibility even before it is defined as such, and the essay on sacred poetry, like the earlier essay on Copleston, illustrates how the poetics growing out of that sensibility was being articulated in the teens and twenties of the nineteenth century, when Keble's personal influence at Oxford was at its height. The hallmarks of Keble's poetics are the high conception of the office of poetry as something akin to or part of religion, and the view of the poet as unburdening himself of profoundly religious impulses by exercising the imagination. Such exercise must always be done with the utmost circumspection and reserve, most often acheived through an indirect expression that includes allegory and other veiled modes of utterance. This is already the essence of Tractarian poetics, but it receives expansion and elaboration as the Oxford Movement itself takes form.

Between Keble's 1825 essay on sacred poetry and the next

Figure 1. *John Keble, by George Richmond, 1863.*

explicit statement of the Tractarian aesthetic, Newman's 1829 essay on poetry, occurred the publication of Keble's *The Christian Year* in 1827. That volume in itself constitutes a contribution to Tractarian poetics, but it does so by example rather than precept. Accordingly, I will consider it in its own place as the first, and in many ways the most important, fruit of Tractarian aesthetic practice. Here we should note, however,

Figure 2. *John Henry Newman, by George Richmond, 1844.*

the brief remarks in the "Advertisement," or preface, as forging another link in the chain of Tractarian aesthetic theory.

Keble's preface runs to just over two hundred words, but in that brief span he strikes two characteristic Tractarian notes (CY, pp. xxxv-xxxvi). "Next to a sound rule of faith," he begins, "there is nothing of so much consequence as a sober standard of feeling in matters of practical religion." And his concluding remarks are in praise of "that *soothing* tendency in the Prayer Book, which it is the chief purpose of [*The Christian Year*] to exhibit" (Keble's italics). The key words are *feeling* and *soothing;* both are deeply involved in religion and in poetry. One should not be misled by the typically Keblian "sound rule" and "sober standard" into thinking that the Tractarian attitude towards religion and poetry is high and dry; precisely because the power of the feeling is intense, the Tractarians insist strongly on its being tempered and soothed. Much the same is said two years later by Newman.

"Poetry, with Reference to Aristotle's Poetics" was a contribution in 1829 to the just-founded *London Review* and was Newman's only lengthy discourse on aesthetics during his Anglican period. It has received relatively scant attention from literary critics, but Alba H. Warren looked at it in detail in his study of early Victorian poetic theory.[16] Warren was inevitably led to remark that the essay was not itself Aristotelian but Platonic, and in truth Newman devotes a good deal of his time to opposing Aristotelian formalism and exalting instead feeling, intuition, and original genius. Warren finds Newman's approach "neoplatonic and Coleridgean" (p. 43). Today we can add that it is also indebted to Keble and is highly Tractarian.[17] Warren concludes that Newman's essay, "as far as one can make out, was quickly buried and forgotten; it had no influence" (p. 45). We have to modify that judgment as well. The essay was not, then or later, the subject of great attention in itself, but as expression of characteristically Tractarian views about poetry it takes its place as part of an outlook that gained very widespread attention and as part of an aesthetic that had far-reaching consequences. Moreover—and Warren should have recognized this—Newman's views have much in common with general Victorian views on art.

The first part of Newman's essay is devoted to his disagreements with Aristotle. These are almost total, for Newman feels that Aristotle emphasizes "ingenious work-

manship" over "free and unfettered effusion of genius,"
that he praises the "unintentional result of the poet's feeling
and imagination" rather than as the "direct object of his care"
(pp. 7-8), and he tries to illustrate Aristotle's errors by considering some specific dramas. But this is all preliminary. He is
really concerned to move a general doctrine of the nature of
poetry, and this concern forms the larger part of the essay.

Although Newman declares Aristotle's doctrine of poetry
to be "most true and philosophical," Warren is right in thinking that Newman's explication of it transforms it into
something very un-Aristotelian, something Platonic, Romantic, and Tractarian. Poetry "provides a solace for the mind
broken by the disappointments and sufferings of actual life;
and becomes, moreover, the utterance of the inward emotion
of a right moral feeling, seeking a purity and a truth which
this world will not give" (p. 10). This is very much what Keble had made of catharsis in his essay on Copleston. Catharsis
here is moved back in the first instance to the poet himself,
who in composing poetry is seeking release for a profound inner emotion. The inner emotion that is purged is not so much
pity and terror as a yearning for something beyond. Newman
also follows Keble in saying that poetry "speaks the language
of dignity, emotion, and refinement," and he follows him further in appropriating the term *poetic* as a general term of praise
for a desirable aesthetic quality: "There is an ambiguity in the
word 'poetry,' which is taken to signify both the gift itself and
the written composition which is the result of it. Thus there is
an apparent but no real contradiction in saying a poem may be
but partially *poetical;* in some passages more so than in others;
and sometimes not *poetical* at all" (p. 11; my italics).

There are other typical Tractarian notes. In discussing
descriptive poetry Newman writes: "It is the charm of the
descriptive poetry of a religious mind that nature is viewed in
a moral connexion. Ordinary writers, for instance, compare

aged men to trees in autumn—a gifted poet will in the fading trees discern the fading men" (p. 12). He footnotes this remark with a stanza from Keble's poem in *The Christian Year* for All Saints' Day, although he does not identify the stanza as Keble's:

> How quiet shows the woodland scene!
> Each flower and tree, its duty done,
> Reposing in decay serene,
> Like weary men when age is won.
>
> (CY, p. 268)

But the most Tractarian element of Newman's essay is his theorizing on the nature of poetic creativity, especially as it differs from mere talent. Originality, Newman says, is "originality of right moral feeling," and poetry is "originality energizing in the world of beauty; the originality of grace, purity, refinement, and good feeling. We do not hesitate to say that poetry is ultimately founded on correct moral perception; that where there is no sound principle in exercise there will be no poetry; and that, on the whole (originality being granted), in proportion to the standard of a writer's moral character will his compositions vary in poetical excellence" (p. 21). This is, once again as in Keble, the assertion of an essential link between art and morality and a link between the character of the artist and the worth of his art. Both positions are fundamental to Tractarian poetics and become so for Victorian aesthetics as a whole.

To make clear just what he means by "right moral feeling" and "correct moral perception" as related to the character of the individual artist, Newman develops a train of thought we have already encountered in the early Keble. Not all poets will necessarily display "virtuous and religious feeling," but all must have it as the source of their poetry: "A right moral state of heart is the formal and scientific condition of a poetical mind" (p. 21). Still, even a bad man can write good poetry, but only insofar "as the traces and shadows of holy truth still remain upon it" (p. 22). The greatest poets will occupy most fully the "moral centre" (p. 22). Among such poets, Newman cites Milton, Spenser, Cowper, Wordsworth, and Southey, adding with some qualifications Scott, Shakespeare, and Homer. "All these poets," he claims, "are religious" (p. 22). Like most Tractarians, Newman does not hesitate to generalize about the character of poets on the basis of their writings, both where biographical data is available and where it is wanting. He is perhaps on biographically safe ground in saying that Hume and Gibbon "had radically unpoetical minds," and even in deploring Dryden's *Alexander's Feast* as "intrinsically unpoetical in the end to which it is devoted, the praises of revel and sensuality," or Byron's *Manfred* as a work from parts of which "the delicate mind naturally shrinks"; however, he is certainly adducing solely from the poetry when he says of Lucretius "his work evinces that his miserable philosophy was rather the result of a bewildered judgment than a corrupt heart" (pp. 22-23). Thus *poetic,* as Newman colors the term, means not only "imaginative," "aesthetic," "mythic," in Coleridge's and Prickett's sense, but also "moral" and "religious" in Keble's. As if to confirm such an interpretation, Newman follows his discussion of the intimate relation between right moral feeling and true poetry with the assertion (which becomes a standard Tractarian position) that religion itself is the truest poetry:

> According to the above theory, Revealed Religion should be especially poetical—and it is so in fact. While its disclosures have an originality in them to engage the intellect, they have a beauty to satisfy the moral nature. It presents us with those ideal forms of excellence in which a poetical mind delights, and with which all grace and harmony are associated. It brings us into a new world—a world of overpowering interest, of the sublimest

views, and the tenderest and purest feelings. The peculiar grace of mind of the New Testament writers is as striking as the actual effect produced upon the hearts of those who have imbibed its spirit. At present we are not concerned with the practical, but the poetical nature of revealed truth. With Christians, a poetical view of things is a duty—we are bid to colour all things with hues of faith, to see a Divine meaning in every event and a superhuman tendency. Even our friends around are invested with unearthly brightness—no longer imperfect men, but beings taken into Divine favour, stamped with His seal, and in training for future happiness. It may be added that the virtues peculiarly Christian are especially poetical—meekness, gentleness, compassion, contentment, modesty, not to mention the devotional virtues; whereas, the ruder and more ordinary feelings are the instruments of rhetoric more justly than of poetry—anger, indignation, emulation, martial spirit, and love of independence. (p. 23)

To read such a passage makes wholly understandable Newman's remark in the *Apologia* that the year 1829 marked the period by which he had come under Keble's influence (A, p. 26).

Newman concluded his essay on poetry with several paragraphs on a topic not much vented in Tractarian critical theory, and from Newman's remarks on it we can see why. It is the issue of the technical and practical side of writing poetry. To Newman and the Tractarians this was not a subject of great interest, even though Newman himself was a painstaking stylist and even though the Tractarian poets may justly be thought to have expended some considerable effort on the construction of their works. But a concern for technique appears to have been held to be indecorous, almost certainly because it did not seem fitting for exponents of Reserve to parade a concern for apparent superficialities. Thus Newman says that "the art of composition is merely accessory to the poetical talent" (p. 24). Of course the character of each poet will fix itself on the style, but the nature of the poet leads to "contemplation rather than to communication with others" (p. 24), especially in lyric poetry, which is almost always the paradigmatic form for Tractarians. The poet "will be obscure, moreover, from the depth of his feelings, which require a congenial reader to enter into them—and from their acuteness, which shrinks from any formal accuracy in the expression of them" (p. 24). Newman concedes that technical skill ("dexterity in composition, or *eloquence*") is necessary in all literary composition, and he enumerates some of the technical skills desirable in a poet: power of illustration, power of unfolding meaning in an orderly manner, and the ancillary "power of arrangement," and of course "command of language." But all of these are to be cultivated as means to an end, for these are "the sole outlet and expression of intense inward feeling," the "poetical mind" being one that is normally "overpowered by a rush of emotions" (p. 25). There is, in short, a Tractarian distrust of excessive concern with technique, as though the poet who does so thereby betrays a want of feeling, a want, one might say, of sincerity: "A talent for composition, then, is no essential part of poetry, though indispensable to its exhibition. Hence it would seem that attention to the language, for its own sake, evidences not the true poet, but the mere artist" (p. 25). To put the case in more familiar terms we could say that the true poet works from the Imagination, not the Fancy.

The Tractarian Years

The Oxford Movement is traditionally supposed to have begun with Keble's Assize Sermon of July 14, 1833, this being the date consecrated by Newman in the *Apologia:* "I have ever considered and kept the day, as the start of the religious movement of 1833" (A, p. 43). From many points of view, not least that of Tractarian critical theory, the Movement may be considered underway by the late 1820s, certainly by the time of the publication of *The Christian Year* in 1827. But from the point of view of strict terminology, the term "Tractarian" is most properly applied to events occurring after the first issuance of the *Tracts for the Times.* These were initiated by Newman and Hurrell Froude, the firebrand of the Movement and the man who considered his one certain good deed in life to have been bringing Newman and Keble to understand one another. The first, slender four-page Tract, written by Newman, appeared in September 1833; the last and most famous, also by Newman, the ninetieth in the series, was issued in 1841. The additional four years of wavering by Newman, until his final departure to Rome in 1845, make up the classic twelve years of Tractarianism proper.

The Tracts, with their sometimes ponderous disquisitions on theological and ecclesiastical subjects, have long been recognized as a major repository of the thinking of the Movement. The issues of Apostolicity, the authority of the Church, the sacraments (especially Baptism and the Eucharist, the two Dominical sacraments), faith, sanctification, the character of the Church of England as the *via media,* and related issues — occupied the minds of the writers of the Tracts, chief of whom was Newman. The ferment they stirred among the Tractarians themselves (quite apart from their reception in the world at large) generated yet further literary activity. Newman's lecture series of 1838, later published as the *Via Media,* can be seen as an elaboration of ideas from the Tracts, and the ambitious "Library of the Fathers" undertaken by Keble, Newman, and Pusey in 1838 and extended to 1855 clearly grew out of the heavily patristic character of many of the Tracts, especially out of the technique of publishing *catenae patrum,* or chains of quotations on a particular topic from the Fathers and other historic authorities of the Anglican Church. Likewise, the "Library of Anglo-Catholic Theology," begun in 1841, and the series "Lives of the English Saints," begun in

1843, are part of the Tractarian literary and propagandistic enterprise.

Each of the Tracts makes a contribution to an understanding of the distinctive Tractarian *ethos*,[18] to use the word domesticated in English by John Keble, and thus the ninety Tracts taken as a whole are relevant to an understanding of the Tractarian approach to literary topics. But a few of the Tracts address topics so immediately pertinent to Tractarian poetics that they require special mention. Those that stand out are, not surprisingly, contributions by the two premier poets of the Oxford Movement, Keble and Isaac Williams, and they deal with two quintessential Tractarian aesthetic concerns, Analogy and Reserve.

Isaac Williams' Tracts 80 and 87 (1838 and 1840) are both titled "On Reserve in Communicating Religious Knowledge," for the two are actually one treatise published in two parts.[19] The appearance of Tract 80 caused one of those skirmishes that marked the course of the Oxford Movement. Opponents, especially Evangelicals, seized upon the Tract as proof that deviousness was a very principle of the Movement, and this charge in turn fed the fears about Romanizing and superstition that had become attached to the Movement from an early date.[20] Leaving aside the historic conflict about the Tract, we can see in it nevertheless an explicit enunciation of an attitude about religion and poetry evident as early as Keble's first published essay. By the time Isaac Williams writes Tracts 80 and 87 we are entitled to speak of this attitude as the Doctrine of Reserve.

The concept of Reserve itself is of ancient provenance and was a standard practice in early Church, which alone would have commended it to the Tractarians. Clement and Origen are especially associated with the doctrine, and Bishop Butler may be credited with continuing its currency in Anglican circles. The idea of Reserve is closely tied to the theological concept of Economy, a term also frequently on the lips of the Tractarians.[21] Briefly, the idea of Reserve is that since God is ultimately incomprehensible, we can know Him only indirectly; His truth is hidden and given to us only in a manner suited to our capacities for apprehending it. Moreover, it is both unnecessary and undesirable that God and religious truth generally should be disclosed in their fullness at once to all regardless of the differing capacities of individuals to apprehend such things. God Himself in His economy has only gradually in time revealed such things as we know about Him. Both the sacredness and the complexity of the subject of religious truth are such that they require a holding back and a gradual revelation as the disposition and understanding of the recipient mature. One practical application of this doctrine can still be seen in the traditonal order of worship of the Mass. The early portion of the Mass, including the reading of the scriptural passages for the day and up to the beginning of the consecration, was traditionally called the Mass of the Catechumens; the second part of the Mass was the Mass of the Faithful. In the early Church the catechumens withdrew prior to the Eucharist proper, leaving behind only those who had been confirmed. This application of the doctrine of Reserve in the early Church gave rise among non-Christians to extravagant speculations and charges about the nature of secret Christian worship just as the Tractarian advocacy of the doctrine of Reserve was to give rise to charges of deviousness, popish conspiracy, and worse. Such charges paralleled, with similar undercurrents, those that swirled about the Tractarian reintroduction of auricular confession.

In his study of the concept of Reserve in Newman, Robin Selby says that on the question of Reserve Newman was Origen to Keble's Clement, indicating that Keble's attitude toward Reserve was that of the traditionalist who had received the doctrine and always adhered to it, whereas Newman's was that of the more speculative and adventurous mind that seized upon the doctrine as discovery and refined and developed it.[22] This may be but another way of stating the dynamic character of Newman's mind as opposed to the more static character of Keble's. Certainly Reserve in Newman seems a more supple doctrine, giving his style an intensity lacking in Keble's,[23] but whatever the differences in emphasis among the Tractarians, all shared the doctrine and exhibited its effects in all they did, including their treatments of literature.

In his *Autobiography,* Isaac Williams explains that his first tract on Reserve (Tract 80) was written for and read to one of Pusey's Friday evening gatherings of Tractarian faithful.[24] Williams chose the subject because he had been reading deeply at that time in Origen and "there observed how much [Origen] alluded to a mysterious holding back of secret truth, such as I had always been struck with in the conduct of the Kebles."[25] The essay was first shown to Keble, who immediately wanted it for one of the Tracts, and it was subsequently given its title by Newman. Thus all of the principals of the Oxford Movement—Hurrell Froude having already died—had a role in the presentation of the tract on Reserve. The second part of the treatise, Tract 87, bearing the same title, was written to reply to the criticisms directed to the first part, chiefly by Evangelicals. Both Tracts, like all of the weightier ones in the series, were addressed *ad clerum.* The two Tracts together, totalling 226 pages, amount to a more than ample exposition of the Tractarian understanding of Reserve.

The doctrine of Reserve in Williams is of course the same as that we have already encountered among the Tractarians generally. Williams provides an abundance of evidence for the practice in the early Church, where he notes it was called the *Disciplina Arcani,* and, following Augustine, he derives its procedure from the nature of God's dealings with men and from the example of the life of Christ.[26] In his attacks on

Evangelical pulpit eloquence and Evangelical ostentation in talking of religious matters, both of which are contrary to the doctrine of Reserve, Williams also makes clear that the doctrine is a principle of the moral life in general. As Williams presents it, there is a distinct connection between reserve as a social attribute and Reserve as a principle for approaching and teaching sacred matters. The example of the Kebles was certainly very much on his mind.[27]

From the point of view of poetics, Williams' treatment of Reserve is arresting because he makes explicit the connection between Reserve and the other great Tractarian principle, Analogy. Seeing that the ancient Church interpreted Scripture and sacred matters as being "figured and shadowed out by an infinity of types," Williams concludes that "the Almighty has hid this vastness of Analogy and types in His word and His works" (Tract 80, p. 46). He cites St. Augustine as having said that Reserve characterizes not only the word of God but His works also, nature and heaven themselves "serving for a covering to hide God from us, by this means to lead us on to the gradual knowledge of Him" (Tract 80, p. 62). In other words, Analogy is God's way of practicing Reserve.

As for poetry, it is the product of "that reserve or retiring delicacy, which exists naturally in a good man, unless injured by external motives, and which is of course the teaching of God through him. Something of this kind always accompanies all strong and deep feeling, so much so that indications of it have been considered the characteristic of genuine poetry, as distinguishing it from that which is only fictitious of poetic feeling" (Tract 80, p. 53). Whenever Reserve is cast aside "there is a want of true and deep feeling," which we know Tractarians saw as the source of poetry. Scripture itself points the example: "Many parts of it consist of poetry, none of oratory; and it is remarkable that the former partakes more of this reserve, the latter less so" (Tract 87, p. 76).

Williams' treatment of the Movement, from God's dealings

with men and the hidden and secret nature of Christ in the Incarnation, to the reserve and analogy characteristic of scripture, and thence to the reserve practiced in the early Church
and enjoined by the Fathers, shows how the doctrine of
Reserve made possible a concept of the Church that is
peculiarly Tractarian: the Church itself as a work of art. The
Church is "entirely a system of reserve" (Tract 87, p. 83): in
the sacraments and in the episcopal and priestly succession
there is "something *that hideth itself,* something like the personal presence of our LORD in His incarnation, surrounded
with difficulties to the carnal mind, withdrawing itself, and
leaving excuses for the Divine Power being denied" (Tract 80,
p. 65). The sanctity of the house of God, the sacraments,
Church ordinances and practices: all of these are part of a
system of Reserve. Williams does not here make explicit the
parallel between the Church and a work of art, as Newman
was to do later in prose and as Williams was himself to do in
verse, but his line of reasoning shows how the Tractarians
were able to make such an identification and why it is that
their concept of art is so consistently bound up with their concept of religion and of the Church. Williams' two Tracts on
Reserve are the fullest statement of the doctrine itself and,
before Keble's Tract and lectures, of its intimate connection
with the doctrine of Analogy and the concept of the Church
as a work of art.

The year of Williams' first Tract on Reserve was also the
year in which Newman published two volumes of Breviary
Hymns, the first from the Parisian Breviary, the second from
the Roman. Newman had already in Tract 75 (1836) written a
paean to the Roman Breviary; now he was offering the hymns
from that volume. The hymns presented are beyond our pur-
view, but it is noteworthy that Newman is, as always, in the
forefront of Tractarian outreach toward forms of devotion.
The pursuit of ancient hymns and prayers was to become a

minor industry among the successors of the Tractarians. Also
noteworthy are a few of the remarks about the nature of
hymns Newman makes in his preface to hymns from the Parisian Breviary, for they cast some oblique light on Tractarian
attitudes and Newmanian practice.

Newman claims that the "Apostle directed as appropriate"
only three kinds of poetry for use in Church: psalms, hymns,
and spiritual songs or canticles. The distinctions Newman
makes among these are rather subtle and certainly difficult to
apply with any rigor. Psalms he defines as "converse with the
powers of the unseen world," and songs or canticles as "a kind
of psalm written for particular occasions, chiefly occasions of
thanksgiving." Hymns, however, he conceives of as direct addresses of praise to God and as particularly problematic to accommodate in religious services, for they tend to be too long
and repetitious. The Church of England, having discarded the
ancient hymns at the Reformation, has in Newman's view
wisely not adopted Methodist and Evangelical hymnody, and
though Newman would like to see "sacred poets" supply the
lack, he thinks it unlikely because of present "unhappy circumstances" that they will do so. Therefore "thoughtful
minds naturally revert to the discarded collections of the ante-
reform era."[28]

Newman's observations reveal both the continued High
Church disapproval of Evangelical hymnody and the Tractarian inclination toward poetry that aspires to the condition
of prayer. The expression "converse with unseen powers" suggests not only the necessary element of mystery in poetry and
prayer, but may conceal as well a yearning to make the Communion of Saints approach as closely as allowable the invocation of them, especially since Newman is later at pains to point
out that he has "purified" some of the hymns. The ones he
changed are those in which the invocations to the saints "are
of such a nature as to be, even in the largest judgement of

charity, not mere apostrophes, but supplications" (p. xvi). The emphasis in the preface on the desirability of brevity and severity in poetic form seems a justification of Newman's own style rather than a description of Tractarian practice generally.

In the same year as Williams' first Tract on Reserve and Newman's Breviary Hymns, Keble published a lengthy review of Lockhart's *Life of Scott.*[29] The review marks yet another contribution to Tractarian poetics, for approximately half of it is devoted to broad aesthetic questions before Keble turns his attention to Scott and the Lockhart biography proper. Again, Keble expresses ideas by now familiar to those who have followed the development of the Tractarian aesthetic position, but he also makes several salient points having to do with the nature of artistic creativity, the vocabulary in which Tractarians regularly express their views, the relationship of poetry to the other arts, and poetry as a safety-valve for the over-burdened spirit.

In the Scott essay, Keble offers (in his own italics) a forth-right statement of his view of poetry: *"Poetry is the indirect expression in words, most appropriately in metrical words, of some overpowering emotion, or ruling taste, or feeling, the direct indulgence whereof is somehow repressed"* (O, p. 6). He follows this with the observation that his present paper does not allow the full development of this idea. At the time he wrote he was also engaged in delivering his lectures on poetry, in which the idea of poetry as emotional expression is given full development. The directness of this statement and the importance Keble attaches to it by setting it in italics shows how central and explicit it had become as a Tractarian poetic principle.[30]

Keble again offers evidence of the primacy that the words *poetry* and *poetical* had come to assume in Tractarian thinking. He engages in lengthy discussion, reminiscent of the Copleston essay, on the use of these terms applied to aspects of everyday life, to action, to external nature, and to the visual

arts, seeking to isolate in such use the quality being desig-
nated. He concludes that it is the *expressive* character of certain
acts, of certain scenes, and of the other arts that is meant by
calling them poetical. This expressiveness he likens to Aristotelean imitation, "provided we understand that term with
the two following qualifications: — 1. That the thing to be
imitated or expressed is some object of desire or regret, or
some other imaginative feeling, the direct indulgence of which
is impeded: — 2. That the mode of imitation or expression is
indirect, the instruments of it being for the most part, associations more or less accidental" (p. 16). It is hard not to see in
this definition something more Romantic than Aristotelean,
something close to a doctrine of the imagination, and hard not
to see in Keble's *poetry* and *poetic* a use we should today reserve
for the word *aesthetic.*

In the course of adducing the essence of the quality called
poetic, Keble also treats the relation of poetry to the visual
arts. He finds sculpture more poetical than painting because it
gives one, "more than painting does, the notion of a full
mind, struggling to express, with inadequate materials, some
idea with which it labours" (p. 14). For the same reason Keble
holds that ancient subjects are inherently more poetic than
modern ones, "as being more out of reach," but he allows that
many "inferior subjects may prove sources of poetry to this or
that individual, in such measure as they fill his whole mind,
and set his imagination at work in default of realities" (O,
p. 15).

In the Scott essay Keble also expresses his idea of poetry as a
safety-valve, or poetic madness as a form of inspiration, and
his concept of primary and secondary poets corresponding to
the distinction between *ethos* and *pathos.*[31] All of these ideas are
more fully treated in the Academic Prelections. Keble touches
as well on the sacramental element in the writing of the
Fathers that he develops more fully in his 1840 Tract on

mysticism, which would be the last major Keble contribution to Tractarian poetics before the *Praelectiones.*

Keble's Tract 89 (1840), "On the Mysticism Attributed to the early Fathers of the Church,"[32] is, after Isaac Williams' Tracts, the other extensive statement (a total of 186 pages) among the Tracts of a theological position that is also an aesthetic one: it is of course the doctrine of Analogy. The concept of Analogy had been central among the Tractarians from the start, evident from Keble's early writing and from the repeated Tractarian homage to Bishop Butler's *Analogy of Religion* (1736).[33] The *Analogy of Religion* was the work most frequently cited and recommended by Tractarians, and, although it had been required reading for candidates for ordination in the early nineteenth century, Tractarian devotion to it kept it alive in the Victorian age. To his reading of Butler in about 1823 Newman attributes his awareness of the idea of analogy and the related idea of probability in belief that was to become one of Newman's own theological themes. Newman writes that "the very idea of an analogy between the separate works of God leads to the conclusion that the system which is of less importance is economically or sacramentally connected with the more momentous system" (A, p. 29). When he read Keble's *Christian Year* he felt that it brought home to him the same two "main intellectual truths" that he had learned from Butler, that is, Analogy and Probability. Of Analogy Newman writes that it "was what may be called, in a large sense of the word, the Sacramental system; that is, the doctrine that material phenomena are both the types and the instruments of real things unseen, — a doctrine, which embraces in its fulness, not only what Anglicans as well as Catholics, believe about Sacraments properly so called; but also the Article of the Communion of Saints; and likewise the Mysteries of the faith" (A, p. 29). Butler's teaching on Analogy has been summed up by W. J. A. Beek as a belief in "the close correspondence between the natural and the moral world, in other words between natural and supernatural reality."[34] Butler's exposition of the idea of Analogy led naturally to the early Fathers; the Analogy of Religion, Newman notes, begins with a quotation from Origen. Keble's treatment of the Mysticism attributed to the early Fathers is thus a Tractarian gloss on the patristic and Butlerian concept of Analogy. Keble praises the Fathers for exhibiting "not a merely *poetical,* or a merely *moral,* but a *mystical* use of things visible" (Tract 89, p. 144; Keble's italics).

What Keble means by mysticism is very much what we today would understand by the allegorical method and what the Tractarians understood by Analogy. By using the term "mysticism" Keble adopts a term of abuse directed against the Fathers by Protestant opponents: "By the term Mysticism. . . I understand to be denoted, a disposition, first, to regard things as supernatural which are not really such; and secondly, to press and strain what may perhaps be really supernatural in an undue and extravagant way" (p. 4). The Tract is given over not to a denial that this disposition existed in the Fathers but rather to right understanding and defense of it in order to show that supernatural interpretation is enjoined by scripture and by the example of Christ. Taken as a whole, the Tract is the most thoroughgoing defense of patristic exegesis and the symbolic mode of seeing the world that can be found after the Renaissance, and it disproves the notion sometimes held in modern scholarly circles that the rediscovery of the allegorical method is a wholly twentieth-century affair.

To see how this Tractarian defense of Analogy relates to critical theory we need to turn to the final third of the Tract, which is concerned with "Mysticism as applied to the Works of Nature, and generally to the external World." Here the connections with poetry are made very plain. The key texts for Keble in this regard are St. Irenaeus' *"Nihil enim otiosum, neque vacuum signo, apud Deum*" (For there is with God nothing useless and no empty sign), and St. Paul's "The invisible things of Him are understood by the things which are made" (pp. 149, 152). He also makes extensive levy on the interpretations of Nature offered by St. Basil and St. Ambrose. As a check against idolizing mere factual or scientific knowledge Keble commends the Fathers' analogical interpretation of Nature, which he defines as "the way of regarding external things, either as fraught with imaginative associations, or as parabolical lessons of conduct, or as a symbolic language in which GOD speaks to us of a world out of sight: which three might, perhaps be not quite inaptly entitled, the Poetical, the Moral, and the Mystical, phases or aspects of this visible world" (p. 143).

The distinction here made between Poetical, Moral, and Mystical might seem to argue against my claim that Tractarians frequently used the term "poetic" as almost synonymous with "moral," and "moral" as synonymous with "theological," but I think in fact it confirms it. These three are "phases or aspects" of the same mode, hierarchically structured from lower to higher. Keble's expansion makes this clear:

Of these, the Poetical comes first in order, as the natural groundwork or rudiment of the two. This is indicated by all languages, and by the conversation of uneducated persons in all countries. There is every where a tendency to make the things we see represent the things we do not see, to invent or remark mutual associations between them, to call the one sort by the names of the other.

The second, the Moral use of the material world, is the improvement of the poetical or imaginative use of it, for the good of human life and conduct, by considerate persons, according to the best of their own judgment, antecedent to, or apart from all revealed information on the subject.

In like manner, the Mystical, or Christian, or Theological use of it is the reducing to a particular set of symbols and associations, which we have reason to believe has, more or less, the authority of the GREAT CREATOR Himself. (p. 143)

The linkage of the three is unmistakable. One implies the other, though of course the final and highest of the three aspects is dependent upon revelation. In this way it is possible for even pagan and non-Christian poetry to partake of truth, though not of course of the fullness of truth, for non-Christian poetry exhibits only the first stage of a movement from imagination to morality to theology. Keble drives home the divine character of poetry in yet a further expansion of this idea:

If we suppose Poetry in general to mean the expression of an overflowing mind, relieving itself, more or less indirectly and reservedly, of the thoughts and passions which most oppress it: — on which hypothesis each person will have a Poetry of his own, a set of associations appropriate to himself for the works of nature and other visible objects, in themselves common to him with others: — if this be so, what follows will not perhaps be thought altogether so unwarrantable conjecture; proposed, as it ought, and is wished to be, with all fear and religious reverence. May it not then, be so, that our Blessed LORD, in union and communion with all His members, is represented to us as constituting, in a certain sense, one great and manifold Person, into which, by degrees, all souls of men, who do cast themselves away, are to be absorbed? and as it is a scriptural and ecclesiastical way of speaking, to say, CHRIST suffers in our flesh, is put to shame in our sins, our members are part of Him; so may it not be affirmed that He condescends in like manner to have a Poetry of His own, a set of holy and divine associations and meanings, wherewith it is His will to invest all material things? And the authentic records of His will, in this, as in all other truths supernatural, are, of course, Holy Scripture, and the consent of ecclesiastical writers. (p. 144)

It would be hard to find even in Keble's other writings or

among the other Tractarians a more concentrated expression of the essential Tractarian aesthetic. Everything from the overflow of emotion to Analogy and Reserve is there, with the bonus of seeing God and His works, duly interpreted, that is, through the Church, as ultimately poetry. All that is lacking is an explicit expression of Nature itself as sacramental, and that is not far to seek in this Tract. In elucidating some of the ancient interpretations of nature, Keble says:

> If one were to call these latter, of the sun and the stars, examples of a symbolical or sacramental view of nature, it would perhaps be no improper mode of expressing the fact here intended; viz. that the word of GOD in creation and providence, besides their immediate uses in this life, appeared to the old writers as so many intended tokens for the ALMIGHTY, to assure us of some spiritual fact or other, which it concerns us in some way to know. So far, therefore, they fulfilled half at least of the nature of sacraments, according to the strict definition of our Catechism: they were pledges to assure us of some spiritual thing, if they were not means to convey it to us. They were, in a very sufficient sense, *Verba visibilia.* (p. 148)

After much further discussion of specific examples of signs and symbols from the visible world and a defense of the concept of typology in scripture,[35] Keble concludes with the affirmation that Christian antiquity was "far more scriptural" than we might at first think "in the deep mystical import, which it unreservedly attributes to the whole material world, and to all parts of it." Tractarian Analogy means quite simply that the entire universe is a symbol of its creator. The tract closes with a "(*To be continued*)" never to be realized, for this was Tract 89; it was followed by Newman's Tract 90 and the abandonment of the Tracts altogether.

Academic Prelections

To come at last to Keble's *Praelectiones Academicae* may convey at first an air of anticlimax, for this work is in large part a restatement of what had already been expressed in the earlier writings of Keble himself and the other Tractarians. But there are good reasons for directing attention to the *Praelectiones.* First, Keble's lectures still constitute the fullest, the most explicit, and in fact the only full-length statement directed exclusively to Tractarian poetics. Moreover, Keble draws out the implications of the Tractarian position, carrying it about as far as it can go. Almost equally important as a reason for examining the *Praelectiones* is that they have been for most modern commentators on Tractarian critical theory the only source considered or known. As a result, some misconceptions or misplaced emphases have characterized modern assessments of Tractarian aesthetics that see the *Praelectiones* enunciating a peculiar, or peculiarly Kebelian, position. In order to give Keble's work its due and to place it in a fuller Tractarian perspective, we need to consider it here as the capstone of the longtime Tractarian concern with the nature of art.

The *Praelectiones* are Keble's forty lectures as the Professor of Poetry at Oxford, a position he held for two terms running from 1831 to 1841. Thus the lectures were delivered during the height of the first phase of the Oxford Movement concurrently with the Tracts and the other literary endeavors undertaken in the years of greatest Tractarian intellectual ferment. They were begun before the *Tracts* themselves got underway and they came to an end in the same year the *Tracts* ceased, 1841. Keble's own Tract 89 and his essay on Walter Scott are properly seen as issuing from his chief literary work of the period, the preparation and delivery of the lectures. It can hardly be doubted that all of those involved with the Movement heard the lectures when delivered or knew of them. That they were presented in Latin would have offered no difficulty to Keble's auditors. When first published in 1844 they appeared only in Latin, and they did not see an English translation until 1912, which probably accounts for the paucity of reference to them later in the century and for the sense of their uniqueness or even oddity among modern literary students of the Oxford Movement. Had Keble's godson Matthew Arnold adhered to tradition and delivered his lectures as Professor of Poetry in Latin, and had they remained untranslated for almost fifty years after his death and more than seventy after the time of presentation, we should today have a very altered and restricted view of Arnold as a literary critic.

While the *Praelectiones* affirm the familiar Tractarian positions—art as the overflow of emotion, and the concepts of Reserve and Analogy—they present these positions at greater length than anything previously offered, and they explore their implications more fully. This is especially true of the concept of art as the overflow of emotion and of the nature and purpose of poetry. The *Praelectiones* also develop the Tractarian view of the relation of poetry to other arts, and they offer assessments of different kinds of poets and poetry, and a thorough treatment of Nature poetry relevant to Keble's own practices as a poet. Each of these positions needs examination in the light of the Tractarian vision of poetry.

The *Praelectiones* repeatedly affirm Keble's contention that poetry has its source in a powerful emotion natural to all men, an emotion that rises up to seek expression and in expression finds relief. That emotion is religious: it is the desire to know God. All art has such an upwelling of emotion as its source, but poetry is pre-eminently designed to give relief to this emotion, hence the title given the published lectures, *De Poeticae vi Medica.* Throughout the lectures Keble refers to poetry as a catharsis for the artist, a "divine medicine" for relieving the "over-burdened" mind, for "soothing emotion," for providing "release." He even speculates on how such a mode of release may first have been developed, thereby offering a theory of the origin of poetry. Men found, more or less by accident, which was really Providence, that words uttered under pressure and stress "shape themselves into cadence" and that the cadence has the power to soothe; so they repeat the process, and finding it again soothing, they adopt it as a mode of relieving intense emotion. Either by that providentially accidental discovery or by "express relevation of the Deity," mankind came to have poetry. The "express revelation," like the providentially accidental discovery, came before recorded history. It occurred to the first poets and was passed on as a gift. This is close to the idea of poetry as a kind of Ursprache, though Keble does not carry it quite so far. Nevertheless, since the accident or revelation occurred so long ago, the possession of poetry is now universal and poetry has become in effect another name for religious emotion.

The concept of poetry as the overflow of emotion is the idea from the *Praelectiones* that has most arrested the attention of contemporary students of Keble and of Tractarian thought on poetry. Both M. H. Abrams and Alba H. Warren were struck with Keble's heavy emphasis on the expressive character of art, and both recognized it as the essence of Keble's position. But both critics, perhaps in an effort to make Keble's theory accessible to the modern mind, have rather misapprehended Keble in crucial areas. Abrams likens Keble's theory to Freud's, recognizing of course that Keble and Freud make otherwise strange bedfellows. But Abrams explains it thus:

It may seem odd that this radical, proto-Freudian theory, which conceives literature as disguised wish-fulfillment, serving the artist as a way back from incipient neurosis, should come out of the doubly conservative environment of High-Anglicanism and the Oxford Chair of Poetry. But the very fact that Keble was more a theologian than a critic goes far to explain the nature of his poetics. Ideas, which in theology have become matter of course and inert, may become alive and drastically innovative when transferred—as Keble patently transferred them—into the alien soil of aesthetics.[36]

Alba Warren writes not dissimilarly of Keble on poetic enthusiasm that "Keble here seems to be somewhat closer to
Freud than to Aristotle."[37] Of Keble's theory as a whole Warren says: "Keble's theory of poetry is strongest in its statement
of value, weakest in its handling of form, and most interesting
in its psychological basis."[38] The real problems with these
assessments is the transference of Freud and modern
psychology into the alien soil of Tractarianism. For all the excellence of their summaries of Keble's statements in the *Praelectiones* both Abrams and Warren have been led to mispercep-
tions of Keble's actual position by what the Tractarians would
have called reading in the wrong spirit. It is true that Keble
reiterates almost wearisomely the notion of the overburdened
spirit, the repressed emotion of the poet, and the "healing
relief" of poetry. But it is not true that these torments are
psychological repressions as we understand such terms. Context in the *Lectures* and knowledge of the previous writings of
the Tractarians make clear that what is moving the poet to artistic expression (as it moves all men to their limited degrees of
"poetry") is the yearning for God. If this yearning is the
transformation of anything, it is a theologized, not a
psychologized, romantic *Sehnsucht.*[39] Even when Keble speaks
of poetry as preserving the poet from mental disease, we must
be careful not to read such an expresion in twentieth-century
terms. The mental disease is here a sickness of spirit to which
one is liable when the yearning for God is stifled. Terms like
"repression" and "neurosis" in such a setting are subversive of
what Keble was trying to convey, although they may convey
the modern critic's attitude to Tractarian theory. Keble's exercise of the doctrine of Reserve restrains him from citing God
as the object of the emotion as frequently as he speaks of the
emotion itself, but he makes it clear often enough (poetry is
"religious feeling," LP, I, 44; poetry is the "handmaid of
Goodness," I, 348).[40] Moreover, as Prickett's study and, I

hope, this book make clear, aesthetics and theology do not in the nineteenth century grow in alien soils; they are branches of the same tree.[41] It was precisely the aim of Tractarian poetics to point out the correspondences and not merely to sport with concepts from unrelated disciplines.

Likewise, for critics to transform Analogy and Reserve into "disguised wish-fulfillment" is to misapprehend what the Tractarians at any rate understood by restraint and indirection. These were required by the nature of the undertaking and the yearning. Both Abrams and Warren also subtly transform Keble's frequent references to madness and insanity in poets into another anticipation of Freud. But we have seen Keble linking madness to catharsis as early as 1814 in his essay on Copleston; by the time of the *Lectures on Poetry* it is clear that Keble's idea of madness and insanity in poets is a Tractarian adaptation of the ancient idea of divine inspiration and not an anticipation of Freud's notion of art as neurosis. Keble links madness to prophecy and inspiration, finding in it "the presence of a more than human power" (LP, II, 345). It is rather a case of God's coming down to man than of man's sinking into the beast.

Warren writes of Keble's theory: "The end of poetry in its psychological aspect is *catharsis,* which means relief and delight, perhaps delight in relief, at any rate delight. But poetry also has its moral aspect in which the end of poetry is truth, and especially Christian truth." Later, "Ultimately, then, the function of poetry is moral and religious." And in conclusion, "The final lecture in the long series stresses the interrelationship between poetry and religion."[42] While all this appears to give due weight to the religious character of Keble's theory, it subtly separates that character from the "psychological" and implies that religion has been grafted onto psychology, whereas in Keble there is not separation but gradation, from "poetical" (not "psychological," a work Keble does not use) to "moral" to "mystical," as he set it forth in Tract 89. The governing framework for Keble is theology, not psychology, and it is from the theological perspective that his theory must be viewed.

To read Keble's ideas in the *Praelectiones* in a Tractarian spirit is to see how self-consistent they are. The religious emotion that generates poetry must ultimately be seen as an analogy of God's "emotion" in creating the world ("the repetition in the finite mind of the infinite act of creation"). In this, Keble goes beyond even the equation of poetry with Imagination, which Prickett has discerned, to suggest an equation of poetry with religion itself. And since the Creator restrained and veiled the truth of His own creation in the symbolic vesture of the analogical world, so too must the poet restrain his expression and veil it by indirection, analogy, and allegory. For Keble, a century before the Abbé Brémond,[43] poetry is prayer: "For those who, from their very heart, either burst into poetry, or seek the Deity in prayer, must needs ever cherish with their whole spirit the vision of something more beautiful, greater and more lovable, than all that mortal eye can see. Thus the very practice and cultivation of Poetry will be found to possess, in some sort, the power of guiding and composing the mind to worship and prayer" (LP, II, 482-483). And poetry is sacramental:

And in this regard it is marvellous how Piety and Poetry are able to help each other. For, while Religion seeks out, as I said, on all sides, not merely language but also anything which may perform the office of language and help to express the emotions of the soul; what aid can be imagined more grateful and more timely than the presence of poetry, which leads men to the secret sources of Nature, and supplies a rich wealth of similes whereby a pious mind may supply and remedy, in some sort, its powerlessness of speech; and may express many things more touchingly, many things more seriously and weightily, all things more truly, than had been possible without this aid? Conversely, should we ask how, pre-eminently, 'came honour and renown to prophetic bards and their poems', it is Religion that has most to be thanked for this. For, once let that magic wand, as the phrase goes, touch any region of Nature, forthwith all that before seemed secular and profane is illumined with a new and celestial light: men come to realize that the various images and similes of things, and all other poetic charms, are not merely the play of a keen and clever mind, nor to be put down as empty fancies: but rather they guide us by gentle hints and no uncertain signs, to the very utterances of Nature, or we may more truly say, of the Author of Nature. And thus it has come to pass, that great and pre-eminent poets have almost been ranked as the representatives of religion, and their sphere has been treated with religious reverence. In short, Poetry lends Religion her wealth of symbols and similes: Religion restores these again to Poetry, clothed with so splendid a radiance that they appear to be no longer merely symbols, but to partake (I might almost say) of the nature of sacraments. (LP, II, 481)

It is in the light of these far-reaching claims from the *Lectures* that Keble's other ideas and judgments must be viewed. Some of these are well known, especially the division into Primary and Secondary poets, others less so. All fit into the overarching concern of Keble as a theorist for the harmony between poetry and religion. We need to pause briefly on the other ideas to put them in proper perspective.

Since the *Lectures on Poetry* is also the statement of a full aesthetic position, it is not surprising that Keble makes allowance for the other arts. These are all defined in terms of their relation to poetry, which is always taken as the primary art form, and they are valued to the extent to which they approximate poetry as the expression of religious feeling. The closest are not the other literary forms. Rhetoric and prose in Keble's view have much in common with poetry, but they err by saying too much. Keble's own prose may be taken as an ex-

ample of writing that is consciously restrained in order that it
not have the coarse quality of the more obviously declarative
literary forms, hence Keble's indirections and qualifications
that are more than mere scholarly caution. Hence too the
misunderstanding of Keble's position by those who do not pay
sufficient attention to the operation of Reserve in his writing.
Keble finds closer to poetry the arts of painting, sculpture, and
architecture in ascending order; architecture especially
resembles poetry because it finds expression in religious
buildings, a connection not lost on Isaac Williams. Sculpture
and painting too approach poetry by allowing for the expression of the artist's own feeling. But it is music that is the
"twin sister" to poetry because it "draws out the secrets of the
soul" through harmony and sequence. As in the larger doctrine of poetry as religion, in this assessment of music we have
the seeds of that Aestheticism later in the century according to
which art becomes self-contained and aspires to the condition
of music.[44] Not only are the other arts ranked in terms of their
approximation to poetry, but all expression can be viewed in
this way. Thus the unlettered have a poetry of their own; it
resides above all in country people in their feelings for nature
and their attachment to particular places and in the spon-
taneous reverence of simple people for religious relics. Here
poetry is operating as a term that comprehends both imagination and religion.

Keble's division of poets into Primary and Secondary is an
aspect of the *Praelectiones* that has received some attention, if
only as a curiosity. But this division is nothing less than
Keble's effort to account for poetic merit, certainly a necessity
in any full-fledged poetics. Keble's primary-secondary division
roughly parallels Coleridge's distinction between the Imagination and the Fancy, but Keble also harmonizes it with his
larger theory of poetry as religious expression. Seen in that
light, his rankings make perfect sense. The primary poets are

those who write poetry to relieve a powerful (religious) emotion; the secondary poets are those who merely imitate the former.

Virtually all of Keble's examples of poetry are taken from the classics (at one point he even translates Burns into Greek in order not to break the classical texture of his discourse!), and in such a context it might seem difficult for Keble to apply his intensely Christian aesthetic to the question of merit among the ancient poets. But he has little difficulty, for here he can call on the doctrines of Analogy and Reserve. The ancient primary poets are those who most effectively express — that is, with greatest Reserve and most telling Analogy — their intense religious emotions. These poets were ordained by God to keep alive thoughts of holier things in the pagan mind; they were unconscious heralds of the coming Christian dispensation. Secondary poets merely imitate such primary ones as Homer, Aeschylus, and Pindar, and in modern times Dante, Spenser, and Shakespeare. Dryden, Burns, Byron, and Shelley are numbered among the secondary poets. Despite the understandable reservations Keble's rankings evoke among modern readers (his downgrading of Sophocles to second rank, for example, in which he is at one with Newman), and despite the suspicion that historical and biographical considerations have played an undue part in his choices (his dislike of Milton's politics, for example), critics have not pointed out that Keble's rankings in the main do not depart very much from evaluations reached by other, more conventional systems. Nor do critics see the modernity of Keble's sidestepping the traditional genres. By borrowing from Quintilian (who borrowed from Aristotle) the concepts of *ethos* and *pathos* (roughly, literature expressing character and literature expressing intense feeling), Keble devised a method of assessing literary works that can be profitably applied without regard to genre. Thus Keble's approach should make him attractive to an age like our own that has seen the radical modification or even abandonment of the traditional concept of genre, both in literary criticism and in literary practice.

None of the foregoing means that Keble's theory is absolutely airtight or that there are not some inconsistencies and wanderings in so ambitious and heavily elaborated a presentation. But the main thrust of the *Praelectiones* is not so much toward the ranking and classification of poetry, albeit a good deal of time is spent on such matters, as it is toward harmonizing poetry with religion. In so doing, and bearing in mind the classical literary background of his audience, Keble devotes what seems to us inordinate attention to bringing classical literature into line with his theory in order to show its universal and pre-Christian validity, even though it is a theory that would have been impossible to advance before Christianity and the patristic age. It is hard for the twentieth-century reader not to regret that Keble's references to Christian literature are so relatively few, and that his treatment of poets of his own age is so largely incidental. But Keble's concentration on the ancients shows that he did not shrink from the harder challenge of accommodating pagan poets to his scheme rather than concentrating on known Christian poets who could be ranked in accordance with straightforward orthodoxy. His position is typically and boldly Tractarian. Hence it is perceived by modern critics as both radical and conservative, as at once backward looking and proleptic. Christian orthodoxy is always perceived in this paradoxical way, for it is both radical and conservative at the same time.

As noted earlier, Keble's lectures were dedicated to Wordsworth as "true philosopher and inspired poet, who by the special gift and calling of Almighty God, whether he sang of man or of nature, failed not to lift up men's hearts to holy things," and who was "a chief minister, not only of sweetest poetry, but also of high and sacred truth" (LP, I, 8) — a dedication that hardly leaves any doubt about Keble's linkage of poetry and religion and poet and priest. Although Wordsworth himself figures only slightly in the pages of the *Lectures on Poetry*, nature poetry is given considerable attention. Nature poets are categorized as belonging to two types, each represented by a classical author. The first is the nature poet who seeks after the hidden truths of God through Analogy. Such a poet was Lucretius. The second is the nature poet who turns to nature chiefly as an escape from care. Such a poet was Virgil. Keble's discussion of both of these poets is lengthy and complex,[45] but it is of less moment than his insistence throughout the *Lectures* on the importance of nature and nature poetry. It is in nature poetry that Keble finds the operation of both Analogy and Reserve compellingly at work.

As we have seen from the *Tracts,* Reserve and Analogy for the Tractarians are twin aspects of religion and poetry. They also characterize the way in which God speaks to men. And as we have seen from Keble's earliest writings, Nature is the paradigmatic example of God's speaking. The Pauline text Keble had used in Tract 89 and earlier to preface his poem for Septuagesima Sunday in *The Christian Year* constitutes the bedrock of his view of Nature as an analogue of God: "The invisible things of Him from the creation of the world are clearly seen, being understood by the things that are made" (Romans, 1:20). The mysticism of the Fathers was for Keble a reinforcement of this Pauline text. The external world of Nature is God speaking by Analogy, yet speaking with Reserve. The poet, who is in effect recapitulating the infinite act, can do no better than to take as his subject Nature itself, for in this way he writes poetry that is doubly religious: religious in the first instance because the very impulse to create is religious; religious again because Nature poetry treats as its subject that which already bears the imprint of God and which reveals God by analogy.

From such a perspective it is easy to see why nature poetry commended itself to Keble and many Tractarians for their own writings and why the Tractarians could see even in the early Wordsworth a religious impulse wholly in keeping with their own views. By making explicit the religious dimension of nature, Keble is not only drawing out implications in Wordsworth but also making clear to later times why virtually all nineteenth-century nature poetry carries such a heavy weight of spiritual meaning, whether the author is Wordsworth, Tennyson, Arnold, or even Meredith. We who have concentrated on finding the ambivalences and uncertainties of the nineteenth-century response to nature run the risk of overlooking how spiritually charged nature was to even the secular mind. Keble's may be an extreme view, but it is not out of harmony with a broadly shared view of nature as a repository of a special kind of meaning and of something akin to grace that characterized the age in general. As I have written elsewhere, the later Wordsworth himself appears to have embraced a more or less Tractarian view of nature, and in the "Ecclesiastical Sonnets," to have been writing what could almost be called Tractarian poetry.[46] The dedication of the *Lectures on Poetry* to Wordsworth, then, was not merely a respectful nod from the younger poet to the Laureate, but the assertion of a close kinship in poetic practice and outlook between the two, a kinship that one can now see was not wholly forced on Keble's part.

In Keble's view in the *Lectures*, nature was not only in itself an especially fit subject for poetry, but it was especially fit for the present age, for it was an age "weak in faith," an age more likely to be receptive to God by indirection and analogy than by direct statement. Thus he could write that the ancient Hebrews had little nature poetry because they had God direct and such was also the case in the Middle Ages (LP, II, 268-269). The modern age, however, with its sick hurry and

divided aims, needed the balm of nature poetry both as an escape from care in the Virgilian manner and as a means of approaching religious truth in the Lucretian.

As already noted, by the end of the *Praelectiones* Keble has
affirmed that poetry itself partakes of the nature of a sacrament. The passage in which this claim is made is also heavy
with references to Nature as an especially appropriate means to
attain sacramental grace through poetry. Keble does not claim
that Nature alone offers such an avenue for poetry, but he does
insistently emphasize how peculiarly well suited to poetry
Nature is. In so doing he is justifying what he had already
demonstrated in practice with his own poetry in *The Christian
Year*. And he is offering a rationale for the practice of other
Tractarian and post-Tractarian poets, most of whom were
Keble epigones.

By 1844 and the publication of the Latin *Praelectiones*, the
Tractarian position is, it should be clear, fully articulated. Of
course the position develops further as the Tractarian sensibility moves into the age following Newman's submission to
Rome in 1845, into the post-Tractarian and ritualist periods.
Even among the Tractarians proper, no two poets or works
exhibit exactly the same features. Thus, despite blanket asser-
tions from some critics about High Church hymnody (itself
usually a misnomer when applied to the Tractarians), differences mark the poetry of Keble, Newman, and Williams.

What the Tractarian poets have in common, however, is as
striking as what they do not share. They all approach poetry
as a mode of religious experience. At first blush this seems to
link them with Romantic predecessors like Herder, and Victorian successors like Carlyle and Arnold, among those in the
nineteenth century who see poetry replacing religion. The
Tractarians follow no such ignes fatui, or perhaps they follow
different ones. Poetry is not a replacement of religion but the

handmaiden of religion; it complements the religious impulse proper. Here is where the Tractarian theological emphasis plays its rightful part. Poetry is not the only means or even the primary means of aspiring to the Almighty. It is, to be sure, an act of devotion, but in Tractarian theory it is not an alternate or substitute act for the conventional act of worship. If anything, it is subordinated to the conventional act of devotion. Keble expressed the attitude best in the "Advertisement" to *The Christian Year*: "Next to a sound rule of faith," he wrote, "there is nothing of so much consequence as a sober standard of feeling in matters of practical religion." I have already suggested that the idea of "feeling" was central to Tractarian poetics; so, at the same time, especially for Keble, was the "sober standard." The sober standard of feeling was always and everywhere designed to complete a "sound rule of faith." Developments in the practice of poetry, even among the Tractarians, to say nothing of those who followed after them, tended to diminish the element of sobriety in the feeling expressed in poetry, although not in favor of poetry as an autonomous form or at the expense of religion. The danger in Tractarian poetics was that of religion replacing poetry. That too is anticipated by Keble in the *Lectures on Poetry,* and his formulation well sums up the Tractarian position: "Thus the very practice and cultivation of Poetry will be found to possess, in some sort, the power of guiding and composing the mind to worship and prayer" (LP, II, 482-483).

The Tractarian poetics that we have been examining, especially as summed up in the *Lectures on Poetry,* is immediately relevant to the poets of the Tractarian phase of the Oxford Movement—Keble, Newman, and Isaac Williams—but we must remember that all these pronouncements on poetry did not appear in a vacuum; they appeared side by side with the major literary works of the Tractarians. They are thus the fruit of practice as well as of reflection. In the actual development of the Tractarian outlook and its reception by contemporary readers, the poetical works of the Tractarians played a more visible part than the theoretical ones. For every reader of the *Tracts for the Times,* for example, there must have been dozens of *The Christian Year*; and for every reader of the *Praelectiones Academicae* (available only in Latin) there must have been hundreds or even thousands of *The Christian Year*. That is the volume that brought home to the age the literary practice of Tractarianism.

III

Keble and
The Christian Year

Now through her round of holy thought
The Church our annual steps has brought
    — *The Christian Year,* "Sunday Next before Advent"

KEBLE'S MODERN BIOGRAPHER, Georgina Battis-
combe, uttering a general sentiment, has observed that *The
Christian Year* has become for twentieth-century readers the
obstacle rather than the avenue to an understanding of Keble.[1]
One could add that *The Christian Year* has become for
twentieth-century readers the obstacle to an understanding of
The Christian Year. Few volumes of poetry so influential in
their own day can have fallen into such obscurity and even
disrepute in aftertimes as the volume that helped launch the
Oxford Movement and profoundly colored a large body of
poetry for more than two generations. Today it exists only in
the spectral half-life of footnotes, along with Marmontel's
Mémoires and Senancour's *Obermann,* except that too frequently the footnotes identifying *The Christian Year* are in error.[2]
Recent scholarship has gone some way toward rehabilitating
Keble, especially in his role as shaper of and spokesman for
Tractarian critical principles.[3] But recent scholarship has

treated gingerly or not at all Keble's chief claim to fame in his own day and his chief contribution to the practical application of Tractarian poetics— *The Christian Year.*

Victorian laudations of *The Christian Year* are legion and come from all levels of society and churchmanship, but such modern assessments as exist have generally relegated the volume to a low place on the scale of poetic excellence. Critics find apparent support from Wordsworth, who praised the work backhandedly by remarking that it was so good he only wished he could have written it himself to make it better.[4] Likewise, A. E. Housman's praise for the volume seems to us appropriately tempered by his conviction that what "devout women" admirers of it really like is not its poetry but its piety and that "good religious poetry, whether in Keble or Dante or Job, is likely to be most justly appreciated and most discriminatingly relished by the undevout."[5] The not infrequent acerbity of Hoxie Neale Fairchild seems to the modern mind for once justly evoked when he writes of *The Christian Year,* "Let no critic accuse me of praising Keble's pious nature-poetry because it is so unromantic: I think it is rubbish."[6] Modern critics are convinced that the Victorians were responding to the "sweetly pretty,"[7] pious sentiments of a volume that extolled the conventional beauties of nature and the primacy of domestic virtues. Modern readers conceive of a mentality rather like that ridiculed by Matthew Arnold in speaking of the Victorian idea of heaven as "a kind of perfected middle-class home, with labour ended, the table spread, goodness all around, the lost ones restored, hymnody incessant." It comes, then, as a surprise to find Arnold immediately thereafter quoting Keble as an apparent ally in opposition to such sentiments: " '*Poor fragments all of this low earth!*' Keble might well say."[8] Arnold is citing a line from *The Christian Year* to ridicule what twentieth-century critics take to be the essential appeal of the work itself.

Arnold's invocation of Keble to censure the middle-class vision is not a sign of Arnold's misapprehension of Keble's position; rather, it is a sign that Arnold understood Keble's uncompromising orthodoxy better than modern critics and that Arnold understood the point and purpose of *The Christian Year* better than those who take their cue solely from the conventional Victorian middle-class image of the work. Keble, of course, would not have rejected the gushing Victorian response that comes across to us as a kind of condemnation, nor would he have taken issue with Housman's "devout women" responding to the pious sentiments rather than to the poetry, but even more certainly Keble would have been pleased to find his godson Arnold quoting *The Christian Year* in a way that uses it to direct the mind to eternal things rather than things of this world. For Keble wrote *The Christian Year* from an aesthetic quite at variance with our own exaltation of the literary artifact as an autonomous world of its own; he wrote *The Christian Year* as an act of religious devotion rather than as an act of literary self-sufficiency.

Donald Davie[9] has rightly chastised modern readers for a disinclination to entertain religious poetry unless it is very far removed in time, generally as far as the seventeenth century or earlier. If, as he argues, this militates against serious reading of Watts and other eighteenth-century poets, it does so even more strongly against Keble and the Victorians. I hope the previous chapter has provided the necessary background against which to view Keble and his fellows, for in order to understand the appeal of *The Christian Year,* what it was to its more thoughtful admirers, and how it exercised its extraordinary literary, religious, and social influence, we must consider it, not in the light of its later status as the standard confirmation gift or Sunday School attendance prize (these are, after all, the proof of that influence), but in the light of the poetic principles that govern its poetry and its form. Then we can see how it exerted its impact on the Tractarians and their successors.

The Form of *The Christian Year*

The Christian Year is, first of all, a work of devotional poetry, that is, a literary work designed to enhance devotion, to advance Christian truth in a form appropriate to its august character. It is the work of the quintessential Tractarian poet-priest "seeking the Deity in poetry or prayer." The best way to understand *The Christian Year* as a Tractarian work is to see it in relation to the worship it was designed to enhance, and that requires an understanding of its most visible, and most overlooked, feature—its subordination to the liturgical year generally and to the Book of Common Prayer specifically. The linkage of poetry to the annual cycle of worship is the premier achievement of *The Christian Year.* Today this linkage can scarcely be sufficiently emphasized, so far are modern readers from familiarity with the Prayer Book. Yet in a very real sense *The Christian Year* is its form; without it, it is simply an uneven collection of poems, all of them religious, many on nature, but only a few rising to a high level of poetic distinction. Seen in terms of its form, however, *The Christian Year* is a highly original poetic document that caused a quiet revolution in prayer and poetry in the Victorian age.

The outward shape and form of *The Christian Year* came to be taken for granted by mid- and late-Victorian readers, but it will strike most modern readers with even greater novelty than it presented to readers of the earliest editions. That outward form is wholly dependent on the Book of Common Prayer. The Book of Common Prayer in turn is the specifically Anglican formulation of Christian worship based on ancient and medieval practice and organized chiefly around the liturgical year developed over the Christian centuries. In a time of widespread liturgical experiment coupled with even more widespread liturgical ignorance like the present, it is well to remind ourselves of the main outlines of the historical liturgical year and also to look at its presentation in the Book of Common Prayer as received by Keble and others in the nineteenth century.[10]

The most accessible points of contact with the liturgical year for the contemporary mind are the organization of the year into weeks and the two great festivals of Christmas and Easter. These three features are still generally familiar and are the irreducible elements in the elaborate structure of the annual sequence of Christian worship. Of the three, the most central, indeed, the anchor of the church year, is the annual recurrence of Easter. This has been so since the very beginnings of Christian worship. Because Easter is linked to the Jewish Passover and hence to the lunar calendar, it is a movable feast, and the changes in its date cause some variation annually in the number of Sundays in other seasons before and after Easter. Moreover, it is the Easter events that constitute the essence of the Sunday eucharistic worship, so that the week itself is seen in terms of a re-enactment every seven days of the central event of Christian history. As Keble wrote in his poem for Easter: "Sundays by thee [that is, Easter] more glorious break / An Easter Day in every week." The very existence of the seven-day week, although of great antiquity in the east, was in the west a product of Christianity and did not become universal until the late fourth century. It was in the fourth century too that the fixing of the date of Christmas gave the liturgical year its other anchor. From that period on, the weeks of the church year have been disposed and often named in terms of their relationship to one or the other of these two festivals. In time, other festivals also gave their names to liturgical seasons, but their division and occurrence are dependent upon the fixed date of Christmas and the movable date of Easter.

Since the early middle ages, it has been customary to divide the church year into six main seasons, the first two related to the date of Christmas, the other four to the date of Easter. The six seasons are: Advent, Christmastide, Septuagesima, Lent, Eastertide, and Trinity season. The year begins with the Advent season, which in turn begins on Advent Sunday, the Sunday closest to St. Andrew's Day, November 30. Advent is a season of four Sundays of preparation for the celebration of the birth of Christ. That event in turn ushers in Christmastide, with its well-known twelve days beginning December 25 and culminating in the visit of the Magi, the Feast of the Epiphany on January 6, but containing also the following period of two to six Sundays (depending on the date of Easter in any given year), which are reckoned as Sundays after Epiphany. The calendar then moves to the pre-lenten period of Septuagesima, Sexagesima, and Quinquagesima, three Sundays named in terms of the approximate number of days before Easter (seventy, sixty, and fifty, respectively).[11] The lenten season proper begins with the Wednesday after Quinquagesima, Ash Wednesday, forty days before Easter, and moves through six Sundays in Lent to Easter, some of these Sundays bearing their own special names, such as Passion Sunday and Palm Sunday, but all part of the lenten season. Easter is followed by five Sundays called Sundays after Easter, and then by Ascension Day, the Thursday falling forty days after Easter. The following Sunday is called the Sunday after Ascension Day. All of the period from Easter day through the Octave of the Ascension is Eastertide or Paschaltide. The next Sunday is Pentecost, or Whitsunday, fifty days after Easter, the day commemorating the founding of the visible Church. In the Roman Church (and increasingly today in the Anglican) all following Sundays up to Advent are reckoned as Sundays after Pentecost, but historically in the Church of England, following medieval Sarum use (that is, the pattern followed at Salisbury), the Sunday after Pentecost is known as Trinity Sunday and all Sundays following it up to Advent are reckoned as Sundays after Trinity. The maximum possible number of such Sundays after Trinity is twenty-six (twenty-seven if reckoned after Pentecost), but again the date of Easter will determine just how many such Sundays actually are observed in any given year. In Anglican use the final Sunday in Trinity (or Pentecost) season is called The Sunday next before Advent. Then the year begins anew.

The foregoing is the main outline of the church year, but there are also other special feasts and observances commemorated on particular, usually fixed, days in the church year. In the Church of England there are relatively more such days than in dissenting churches, but relatively fewer than in Roman or Orthodox churches; in all Christian churches some elements of the liturgical year are observed, at a minimum Christmas, Easter, and the division into weeks. It is an obvious rule of thumb that the "higher" the denomination, the more extensive and elaborated the liturgical year, not only in terms of specific seasons, saints' days, festivals, and other commemorations, but also in terms of the appropriate vestments, colors, and prescribed prayers and procedures for seasons and days within the liturgical year.

In Anglican usage the liturgical year finds its expression in the Book of Common Prayer. From its earliest form as the First Prayer Book of Edward VI in 1549, to the 1559 Elizabethan Prayer Book, through the 1662 revision that held sway to our own times, the Book of Common Prayer adhered more rather than less to the fully elaborated year. In addition to provision for all the main seasons and festivals cited above, the Prayer Book provides also for thirty-two other named saints' days, holy days, and festivals: such days as the feasts of St. Stephen, St. John, and the Holy Innocents, which fall in immediate three-day succession after Christmas day; or the days in Holy Week preceding Easter; and such long-established feasts as the Purification or Candlemas (February 2), the Annunciation or Ladyday (March 25), All Saints (November 1), and the like. In keeping with the historic practice of the Church, the Book of Common Prayer provides for each of these named Sundays, festivals, or saints' days specific readings, normally a collect, epistle, and gospel, to be read at the appointed place in the communion service on the Sunday or holy day in question. These are known as the proper prefaces, or propers, for the day, being the readings proper or appropriate to the particular named celebration. Also in keeping with the medieval missals, breviaries, and service books from which it was derived, the Book of Common Prayer provides forms of worship and orders of procedure for various other sacraments and aspects of Church life. For example, at the beginning, the Prayer Book offers forms for Morning and Evening Prayer (or Evensong), which are Anglican adaptations of medieval matins and vespers, with additions from the other canonical hours. Following the cycle of the Church year and of named feasts and saints' days, the Prayer Book provides forms and prayers for the sacraments of Baptism, Matrimony, Ordination, Burial of the Dead, and then some distinctively Anglican prayers, such as those for the deliverance from the Gunpowder Plot, the martyrdom of Charles I, the Restoration, and so on, for a total of sixteen such forms. Keble included poems for all special services and procedures in the Prayer Book, omitting only poems on purely utilitarian and undevotional Prayer Book inclusions like the Lectionary, the Thirty-nine Articles, and the Tables of Kindred.[12] The result is a series of poems that matches in exact order the sequence of worship in the Book of Common Prayer and that was designed to be read in the light of that book.

The liturgical pattern of the Prayer Book not only dictates the sequence of poems in *The Christian Year* but in fact gives the volume a coherence and purpose that it would otherwise lack. So overriding is the importance of this shaping element that one can understand why the volume is sometimes referred to as a single poem, though it is in fact a collection of 109 poems, for in one sense the collection is a single poem, a poem on the Book of Common Prayer. Much of the modern mis-understanding of what the volume is stems from the unwill-ingness or inability to approach it in relation to its model. It is as though the reader came to *Paradise Lost* without any awareness of its relation to the Bible, or to the *Divine Comedy* without an understanding of the concepts of Hell, Purgatory, and Heaven, though such parallels are inexact, for Dante and Milton draw on multiple sources and they structure their poems independently of any single source. *The Christian Year* not only refers to something outside itself; it exists and is shaped by virtue of the prior existence and form of that out-side work. Without it, *The Christian Year* would not be.

The dependence of *The Christian Year* on the form of the Prayer Book could be called slavish were it not for the fact that Keble aspired to no originality in the matter. "Don't be original," was a Keble watchword often quoted by the young Tractarians with something like approving awe. Yet that same avoidance of originality became in itself a kind of originality; by making it old, Keble made it new. The few an-ticipations of Keble's pattern that exist in seventeenth-century poetry or among the small number of eighteenth-century col-lections of hymns must be considered no more than suggestive to Keble, even allowing for the unlikely assumption that he knew of the hymn collections in the first place.[13] The idea of a collection of poems organized in exact sequence of the order of worship in the Prayer Book turns out to be a strikingly original concept in devotional poetry. But it was an idea whose time had come. Keble, perhaps without fully realizing it, catalyzed a latent sensibility. He was to do something of the same kind in 1833 with the Assize Sermon. Twentieth-century readers view the Assize Sermon with some perplexity, seeing in it the very modest expression of ideas put more vigorously by Newman and others. They are likely to do the same with *The Christian Year* and to puzzle over its enormous popularity and influence. In both cases the quiet activation of something just below the surface sparked the imagination of the Tractarians and eventually of the population at large. It was Keble's capacity for calling attention to those "long-neglected truths" of Leslie and Sikes that made his Assize Sermon electrifying, and his capacity for looking afresh at so familiar a document as the Prayer Book that made *The Christian Year* a new departure in poetry.

As has been noted, *The Christian Year* parallels the Book of Common Prayer throughout, from the opening poems "Morning" and "Evening" (corresponding to the offices for Morning and Evening Prayer at the beginning of the book), through the year and the holy days, to the special offices and provisions of the Prayer Book, and ending with the Ordination Service. This organization is vital to the character and effects of *The Christian Year* overall, but another formal element in *The Christian Year* that reflects the shaping influence of the Prayer Book is the structure of the poems themselves as prayers. Perhaps the most common, certainly the most memorable, phrase in the Prayer Book orders for worship is "Let us pray." Keble's frequent pattern in the poetry of *The Christian Year* follows this recurring Prayer Book injunction, and it would be possible to specify in the poems the various recognized types of prayer—petitionary, intercessory, prayers of thanksgiving and praise, and the like; Charlotte Mary Yonge has virtually done so in her study of *The Christian Year*.[14] The most characteristic form for a poem in the collection is a meditation or reflection on nature or daily life seen from a Christian perspective, or a retelling of a Christian story (normally one appointed for the day), both generally concluding with an explicit prayer. The final stanzas of "Morning" and "Evening" illustrate the practice in its simplest form:

> Only, O Lord, in Thy dear love
> Fit us for perfect Rest above;
> And help us, this and every day,
> To live more nearly as we pray.
>
> (Morning)

and

> Come near and bless us when we wake,
> Ere through the world our way we take;
> Till in the ocean of Thy love
> We lose ourselves in Heaven above.
>
> (Evening)

The frequency of prayers within and at the end of poems reinforces the Prayer Book identification of the volume and invites the reader to link his own prayerful reflections to the liturgical pattern provided by the Prayer Book.

The structural linkage of *The Christian Year* with the Book of Common Prayer had several obvious practical consequences. It made possible the use of the volume as a companion to the Book of Common Prayer. Countless Victorian families came to use it in that way, reading aloud the appropriate Keble poem along with family Bible verses throughout the year. These readings tended to reinforce each other, making *The Christian Year* a kind of extension of the Prayer Book and probably in many minds intermingling the two, transferring even some of the sanctity of the Book of Common Prayer onto Keble's volume. The organization of Keble's collection also served to renew attention to the Prayer Book itself and to the liturgical year, both of which became hallmarks of the Oxford Movement and eventually spread beyond the confines of the Movement. Thus while Keble may have been the recipient of some of the piety and devotion directed to the Prayer Book, he was also the cause of renewed interest in that book and therefore of renewed interest in an ordered, liturgical system of worship. *The Christian Year* also directed attention to the Church itself as a visible body, for it was the Church that was the source and keeper of the ecclesiastical year and of its observance through the Prayer Book. *The Christian Year* thus exercised a gentle polemic in favor of the visible Church and her formularies. One of the points on which the Tractarians insisted in all of their arguments and "innovations" was that they were doing nothing more than what was enjoined by the Prayer Book itself. By creating a mirror-effect of influence on and subordination to the Prayer Book, *The Christian Year* benefited from the authority of the Prayer Book while also reinforcing that authority.

Much has been made in earlier criticism of the fact that the poems in *The Christian Year* were not originally composed in the sequence they occupy in the volume and that many are not uniquely appropriate to the Sunday or holy day to which they are ostensibly directed. In truth, the period of composition of the poems ranged from 1819 to 1827, and later editions carrying the date of composition next to the poem (these did not appear in the first edition) show clearly how Keble rearranged a gathering of poems written over a long period to correspond to the Church year. Likewise, there are poems attached to a particular Sunday or holy day referring to some other season of the year than the one in which the day falls (an April poem in Epiphany season, for example[15]). But these aspects of Keble's arrangement only make the more clear his liturgical and devotional purpose when he collected his poems, and they have the same value (and no more) as the examination of the order (where it can be known) of Tennyson's stanzas in the poem some Victorians held to be a kind of secular *Christian*

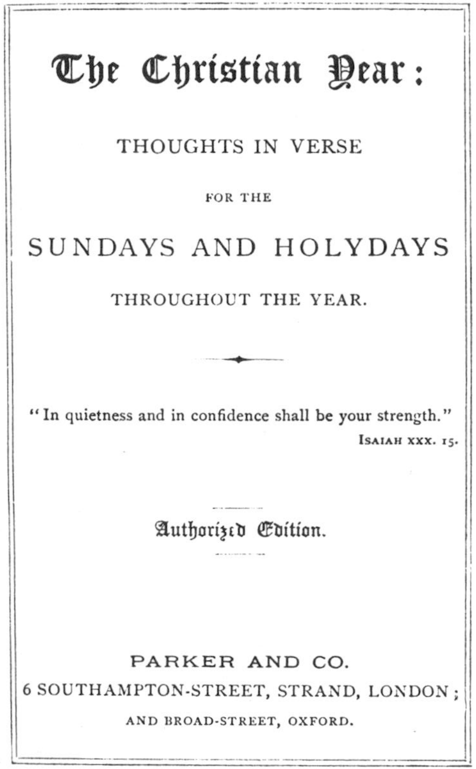

The Christian Year:

THOUGHTS IN VERSE

FOR THE

SUNDAYS AND HOLYDAYS

THROUGHOUT THE YEAR.

"In quietness and in confidence shall be your strength."
ISAIAH XXX. 15.

Authorized Edition.

PARKER AND CO.
6 SOUTHAMPTON-STREET, STRAND, LONDON;
AND BROAD-STREET, OXFORD.

Figure 3. *Title page of the first edition of* The Christian Year, *1827.*

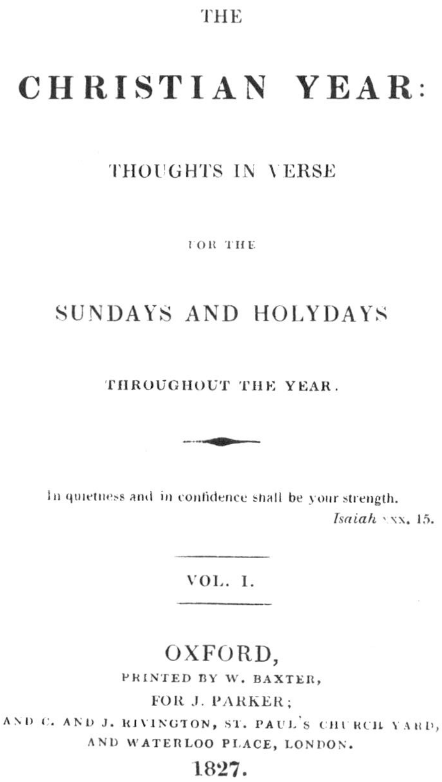

THE

CHRISTIAN YEAR:

THOUGHTS IN VERSE

FOR THE

SUNDAYS AND HOLYDAYS

THROUGHOUT THE YEAR.

In quietness and in confidence shall be your strength.
Isaiah xxx. 15.

VOL. I.

OXFORD,
PRINTED BY W. BAXTER,
FOR J. PARKER;
AND C. AND J. RIVINGTON, ST. PAUL'S CHURCH YARD,
AND WATERLOO PLACE, LONDON.
1827.

Figure 4. *Title page,* The Christian Year, *c. 1866.*

Figure 5. *Title page*, The Christian Year, *c. 1875.*

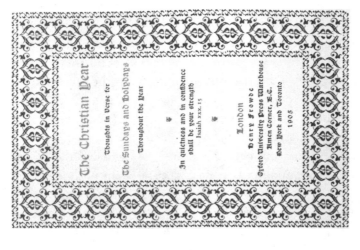

Figure 6. *Title page*, The Christian Year, *1905.*

Year—In Memoriam.[16] Keble's final arrangement of his poems shows that the idea informing *The Christian Year* grew on him throughout the 1820s, when he was composing the poems, much as *In Memoriam* grew on Tennyson. And the arrangement also shows that the final form in which he presented his poems to the public is one in which the sequence is a fundamental part of the presentation and that *The Christian Year* is what it is because of that sequence.

Yet a further link between Keble's volume and the Prayer Book comes through his prefacing each poem with a biblical epigraph, in most cases a passage from the proper readings for the day from the Prayer Book. Thus the poem for Christmas Day is preceded by the passage from Luke, "And suddenly there was with the Angel, a multitude of the heavenly host, praising God"; the poem for Whitsunday or Pentecost is preceded by the passage from Acts telling of the cloven tongues of fire. And so on. These passages of course appear in the readings for the day appointed in the Prayer Book. One can move from the Prayer Book readings to the corresponding day in *The Christian Year* with a sense of passing to an elaboration of or commentary on the reading in the Prayer Book.[17]

Largely as a consequence of his High Church background and his own clerical experience (Keble was serving as his father's curate during the time of the composition of most of these poems), Keble's mind moved naturally in terms of the Church year, and most of the poems, whenever composed, turn on events commemorated in the ecclesiastical year. Poem after poem in the collection offers reflections on (and therefore reinforcement of) the events of the Christian story and their liturgical commemoration.

With the sequence of the poems, the epigraphs from the propers, and the subjects of the poems themselves directing the reader ever and again to the Prayer Book and to the cycle of worship throughout the year, there would appear to be no further way to emphasize the Prayer Book affinities of *The Christian Year*. Yet it proved possible to make the Prayer Book connection and the devotional character of the volume even more evident in succeeding editions. The course of this development is extremely revealing of the way in which the collection was received and the way in which its potential was realized, even beyond the presentation of the first edition. It makes us realize how much *The Christian Year* developed in concert with the Oxford Movement. Margaret Oliphant gives us the flavor of these later editions in *Salem Chapel* (1863) when the dissenting minister Mr. Vincent ventures into the Anglican bookshop and bends over "the much-multiplied volume . . . poising in one hand a tiny miniature copy just made to slip within the pocket of an Anglican waistcoat, and in the other the big red-leaved and morocco-bound edition, as if weighing their respective merits." Shortly afterwards she refers to it as "the Anglican lyre." She has Lady Western order two gift copies. "I know they are all on the side table, and I shall go and look at them," says Lady Western. "Not the very smallest copy, Mr. Masters, and not that solemn one with the red edges; something pretty, with a little ornament and gilding: they are for two little *protégées* of mine. Oh, here is exactly what I want! another one like this please."[18]

What had happened in these succeeding editions of *The Christian Year* offers the ultimate proof of its symbiosis with the Prayer Book. It offers as well an illustration in miniature of the course of the Anglo-Catholic movement in the Church of England and of the way in which Keble and the Tractarians opened new avenues for religious expression. *The Christian Year* became in itself a kind of Prayer Book, an Anglican devotional manual complete in physical detail with the features characteristic of devotional publications.

Keble had early toyed with the idea of illustrations to accompany the collection but abandoned the notion before publication. Later editions, especially after the book went out of copyright, put the idea into practice, sometimes with a vengeance. Illustrations ranged from vague pastoral scenes of

Figure 7. *Illustration facing "Good Friday" from 1890 edition of* The Christian Year.

the sort the Victorians used for editions of Wordsworth, to the sentimental Sunday School style pictures of biblical events, to vivid and very Continental religious iconography of the Crucifixion, the Crown of Thorns, the Sacred Heart, and the like. That is, they range from Evangelical to Catholic. And while the illustrations were growing in frequency and intensity, the physical format of the volume was changing. Increasingly, later editions appeared with gilt edges in the manner of Prayer Books, Bibles, and missals. Colored streamer

---

Good Friday

He is despised and rejected of men.—ISAIAH liii. 3.

Is it not strange, the darkest hour
    That ever dawned on sinful earth
Should touch the heart with softer power
    For comfort, than an angel's mirth ?
That to the Cross the mourner's eye should turn
Sooner than where the stars of Christmas burn ?

Sooner than where the Easter sun
    Shines glorious on yon open grave,
And to and fro the tidings run,
    " Who died to heal, is risen to save "?
Sooner than where upon the Saviour's friends
The very Comforter in light and love descends ?

Yet so it is : for duly there
    The bitter herbs of earth are set,
Till tempered by the Saviour's prayer,
    And with the Saviour's life-blood wet.

Figure 8. *"Good Friday" from 1890 edition of* The Christian Year.

bookmarks were added; margins were marked in black or red ruled lines, frequently with religious devices at the corners or elsewhere on the page. Bindings went to soft white, red, or black stippled leather with gold crosses on them. The volume was issued, as Mrs. Oliphant makes clear, in a multitude of sizes, from the tiny vest-pocket size to large, almost lectern-sized editions. There even appeared individual editions of separate poems from the volume, normally the poems for Morning and Evening, the two from the collection that had the greatest currency as hymns. The great bulk of these decorated editions aimed at the market for religious gifts, and, like the Prayer Book itself, were probably thought of far more in religious than in literary terms.

It is almost impossible today to trace in detail the exact dates of the changes in format of these editions, but from an examination of many library and private copies, I find that the movement toward what we may call the "missalization" of *The Christian Year* began fairly early in the course of its publication history, was well established before Keble's death, and must therefore have had his approval. By the 1870s, when the volume could be freely reprinted, the decorated style had reached flood tide, rather like the Gothic Revival. Cause and effect cannot be disentangled here to say with confidence that either the Prayer Book or *The Christian Year* led the way. Both were subject to an increasingly Catholic visual presentation as the Tractarian Movement became more ritualistic. The increasing elaboration of the physical format of *The Christian Year* must be seen as the bibliographic counterpart to priestly vestments and altar decorations, which are the outward and visible signs of an inward and spiritual conviction about the nature of worship. The Book of Common Prayer itself appeared in more obviously religious formats throughout the age, in contrast to the publication style of eighteenth-century Prayer Books, which was indistinguishable from that of any

Figure 9. *"Easter Day" from 1875 edition of* The Christian Year.

other kind of book. That *The Christian Year* lent itself to ever more Catholic treatment illustrates one of the inherent characteristics of the Tractarian position. The volume was from the start an incitement to devotion; it was inevitable that this quality would find expression in the physical presentation of the book.

Yet all are One—together all,
In thoughts that awe but not appal,
Teach the adoring heart to fall.

Within these walls each fluttering guest
Is gently lured to one safe nest—
Without, 'tis moaning and unrest.

Figure 10. *Portion of poem for "Trinity Sunday" from 1870 edition of* The
Christian Year.

None of these developments appears to have dismayed the Tractarians. Nor could they have, given the aesthetic position the Tractarians held. Poetry was the handmaiden of religion, and religious handmaidens were rightly vested in garments suited to their office.

The Poetry of *The Christian Year*

Once we recognize that the form of *The Christian Year* is both its most distinctive feature and an exemplification of the Tractarian poetic, which construed literature as a mode of "seeking the Deity in prayer" — once, that is, we recognize the work as a devotional manual — we are able to take an equally Tractarian approach to the poetry in the volume. Such an approach reminds us that, however necessary it is for critical purposes to isolate a given poem or portion of it for examination, the poem still functions as part of the larger construct of a sequence of poetic devotions keyed to the Church year. The poem takes much of its coloration and force from its setting and from the devotional attitude of the rightly disposed reader. A Tractarian approach offers other pointers to the character of the poetry in *The Christian Year*, for like the structure of the volume, the poetry also grows out of Tractarian poetics. The poetry exemplifies the two leading Tractarian concepts of Analogy and Reserve; Analogy governs the subject matter of the poetry, Reserve the style.

We have seen that the doctrine of Analogy in Tractarian eyes is more than a kind of nature typology whereby certain objects in nature symbolize and point to truths of both natural and revealed religion, though it is of course at least that. At most, however, Analogy is the doctrine of the sacramental system. Newman put it well in speaking of *The Christian Year* as one of the main avenues by which he came to understand the meaning of that system:

yet I think I am not wrong in saying, that the two main intellectual truths which [*The Christian Year*] brought home to me,
were the same two, which I had learned from Butler, though
recast in the creative mind of my new master. The first of these
was what may be called, in a large sense of the word, the
Sacramental system; that is, the doctrine that material
phenomena are both the types and the instruments of real things
unseen, — a doctrine, which embraces, not only what Anglicans,
as well as Catholics, believe about Sacraments properly so called;
but also the article of "the Communion of Saints" in its fulness;
and likewise the Mysteries of the faith. (A, p. 29)[19]

It is the sacramental system, Tractarian Analogy, that comprehends the overall subject matter of the poems of *The Christian Year*. Walter Lock recognized this element in his edition
of the volume, though Lock did not specifically link it to
Tractarian Analogy. He wrote: "The most striking feature [of
The Christian Year] is its width of sympathy, its sense of the
consecration of all life" (CY, p. xii). And later he wrote of its
"large-hearted sympathy which includes all creation within its
embrace, and sees the consecration of God's presence on every
side" (CY, p. xiii).[20]

If the subject matter of the poetry of *The Christian Year*
generally is the sacramental system, specifically that system is
most often illustrated through external nature. Nature is the
single most visible topic of the poems and the one most likely
to be interpreted as a kind of defused Wordsworthianism. Accordingly, we must consider Keble's use of nature, the subject
of so many of his poems, in the light of both Wordsworth's
work and of Tractarian Analogy.

In 1832 Wordsworth wrote a poem called "Devotional Incitements" that reads almost like a poem from *The Christian
Year*.[21] One is tempted to speculate that it may have been an
instance of Wordsworth's improving upon or even answering
Keble. In the poem, Wordsworth urges man to aspire heaven-

ward just as all things in Nature do—the spirits of the flowers, fragrances, the songs of birds and brooks, and so on. He regrets that religious practices that also teach man to aspire—the use of hymns, incense, pictures—have decayed or been spurned. But Nature, he assures the reader, unchangingly teaches, providing in all seasons "divine monition" that we do not live by bread alone and that "Every day should leave some part / For a sabbath of the heart."

Keble would surely have agreed that nature regularly yields divine monition, and he would have agreed that church forms have been permitted in some quarters to "decay and languish" or to be spurned. But Keble, whose motto was "in medio Ecclesiae,"[22] would certainly not have accepted nature as sufficient substitute for the Church, as Wordsworth appears to do in "Devotional Incitements." It is precisely the willingness to accept nature as sole teacher that renders Wordsworth's poem not quite Tractarian and that points to the peculiar quality Keble brought to nature poetry in *The Christian Year.*

The locus classicus for Keble's view of nature lies in the poem for "Septuagesima Sunday," which begins:

> There is a Book, who runs may read,
>   Which heavenly Truth imparts,
> And all the lore its scholars need,
>   Pure eyes and Christian hearts.
>
> The works of God above, below,
>   Within us and around,
> Are pages in that Book to shew
>   How God Himself is found.

These first two stanzas are Wordsworthian and something more. Like Wordsworth, Keble is asserting that nature offers "divine monition," but Keble makes plain that the lessons of nature require "pure eyes and Christian hearts" for correct understanding. The rest of the poem provides a capsule version of Tractarian Analogy: the sky is like the love of the Maker, for it embraces all; the Church on earth is an analogue of the moon in heaven, for each borrows its radiance from its "sun," which is both the heavenly body and the Son of God; the saints in heaven are stars; the saints on earth are like trees, having for their root, flower, and fruits, the virtues of Faith, Hope, and Charity; dew that falls is like heavenly grace; storms and tempests are analogues of God's power; and the gentle breeze is like the activity of the Holy Spirit.[23]

All of this analogizing marks the poem as something more than Wordsworthian, as indeed distinctly Tractarian. And what is done so transparently in the poem for Septuagesima is done with greater or lesser explicitness in the treatment of nature (and other topics) throughout the volume, beginning even with the opening poems corresponding to Morning and Evening Prayer. In the latter, for example, Keble shows the way a Christian heart sees Analogy in nature:

> When round Thy wondrous works below
> My searching rapturous glance I throw,
> Tracing out Wisdom, Power, and Love,
> In earth or sky, in stream or grove.

And in the former he assures his readers that they will know the "bliss of souls serene" when they have sworn to see God in everything. Also very much to this point is the poem for the "Fourth Sunday after Advent," which begins with the assertion that it is not an idle "poet's dream" that we should see messages in nature, that we should hear

> In the low chant of wakeful birds,
> In the deep weltering flood,
> In whispering leaves, these solemn words—
> "God made us all for good."

All true, all faultless, all in tune,
    Creation's wondrous choir
Opened in mystic unison
    To last till time expire.

Numerous other poems in the volume give varied expression to Keble's conviction that "the low sweet tones of Nature's lyre" are meant to instruct us about God's works and ways. For all the love of nature readers discern in *The Christian Year,* they do not come away from Keble's volume with the same sense of nature as herself a deity that readers of Wordsworth can well take away from his poetry. They see nature rather as a system offering a series of correspondences with qualities of her creator.

Readers come away from Keble not only with a sense of nature offering correspondences but also with an awareness of the Tractarian sense of sin touching even nature. In the recital of the analogy of nature in the poem for Septuagesima, Keble concludes:

Two worlds are ours: 'tis only Sin
    Forbids us to descry
The mystic heaven and earth within,
    Plain as the sea and sky.

Thou who hast given me eyes to see
    And love this sight so fair,
Give me a heart to find out Thee,
    And read Thee everywhere,

In the poem for the "Fourth Sunday after Trinity," Keble dwells at greater length on the way sin beclouds perception of the two worlds:

Sin is with man at morning break,
    And through the live-long day
Deafens the ear that fain would wake
    To Nature's simple lay.

The solution he offers is twofold. First, it is Wordsworthian: to hear nature's lay one must remove oneself from the sound of man, from the din of human cities;

> When one by one each human sound
> Dies on the awful ear,
> Then Nature's voice no more is drowned,
> She speaks and we must hear.

But Keble does not stop there:

> Then pours she on the Christian heart
> That warning still and deep,
> At which high spirits of old would start
> E'en from their Pagan sleep.

The "warning" is that behind the appearances of nature stands the creator of nature: "Streaks of brightest heaven behind / Cloudless depths of light."

Keble's implied reader is thus always a Christian reader. It is not enough to be responsive to nature's beauties as things in themselves, or even as vague pointers to a higher power. One must have a Christian understanding of nature as an analogue of God and a Christian understanding of sin as an impediment to seeing God clearly through nature:

> Mine eye unworthy seems to read
> One page of Nature's beauteous book;
> It lies before me, fair outspread—
> I only cast a wishful look.
> (Fourth Sunday in Advent)[24]

The corrective to such a condition is Christian patience and humility:

> But patience! there may come a time
> When these dull ears shall scan aright
> Strains that outring Earth's drowsy chime,
> As Heaven outshines the taper's light.

These eyes, that dazzled now and weak,
　　At glancing motes in sunshine wink,
Shall see the King's full glory break,
　　Nor from the blissful vision shrink:

In fearless love and hope uncloyed
　　For ever on that ocean bright
Empowered to gaze; and undestroyed,
　　Deeper and deeper plunge in light.

(Fourth Sunday in Advent)

The insistent theological reminders of human sin and the imperfections of nature give a mournful cast to Keble's nature poetry, but at the same time they give it a peculiar tension quite different from the tension in Wordsworth's poetry, though Keble rarely knows how to exploit it for the best poetic effect. Where Wordsworth, even in a late poem like "Devotional Incitements," finds a pure delight in nature ("where birds and brooks from leafy dells. / Chime forth unwearied canticles"), Keble's joy in nature usually draws forth somber reflections on the imperfections of this world as a consequence of original sin:

Hence all thy groans and travail pains,
　　Hence, till thy God return,
In wisdom's ear thy blithest strains,
　　O Nature, seem to mourn.

This mournful element on the one hand harks back to the eighteenth-century graveyard school (though Cowper is an even more likely source) and on the other anticipates the sadder and more elegiac character of so much Victorian nature poetry as compared with Romantic. Keble's poetry may have been a contributing factor to the subtle but unmistakable difference between Victorian and Romantic response to nature; and in many an inward ear, when a Victorian contemplated nature, may have been sounding (as it did for Pendennis) the "solemn church music" of *The Christian Year*. One rather thinks it was in Arnold's ear when he wrote on the occasion of Wordsworth's death of Wordsworth's "healing power."

Even when Keble and Wordsworth agree in finding epiphanies in nature, they part company in attribution of the source. Wordsworth, especially in his early poetry, is far less specific than Keble in attributing the transcendent experiences of nature to the traditional Christian God. By not doing so Wordsworth lays himself open to charges of pantheism, but perhaps he also commends himself to less theologically inclined readers then and now. Keble insistently relates the glories of nature to a right understanding of Christian truth:

> Till thou art duly trained, and taught
> The concord sweet of Love divine:
> Then with that inward Music fraught,
> For ever rise, and sing, and shine.
>
> (Fourth Sunday in Advent)

Nature for Keble is sacramental in the sense that, like a sacrament, it is an "outward and visible sign of an inward and spiritual truth."[25] The key words in the poetry, however, are not "sacrament" or "sacramental" (neither of which appears in *The Christian Year;* nor does any form of the word "analogy"), but words like "dew," "divine," "light," "radiance," "rapture," "sweet," and above all "love" (this latter the most frequent word in the volume).[26] While he can be overly didactic about the function of nature in a poem like that for Septuagesima, the doctrine of Reserve prevents him from speaking as openly and directly of something as holy as a sacrament. Yet the atmosphere breathed by the volume is precisely that of "consecration of all life," as Lock put it, or the sacramental system, as Newman recognized. Nature occupies center stage in this system, but it is the system, not nature itself, that the poetry is designed to illuminate. Nature to the Tractarian

mind is, like poetry, a handmaiden to divine truth. No
wonder that the lines Newman found himself thinking his
own were Keble's:[27]

> Every leaf in every nook,
> Every wave in every brook,
> Chanting with a solemn voice
> Minds us of our better choice.
>
> (First Sunday after Epiphany)

Nature, like poetry, serves to reinforce Christian truth, not to
originate her own. Nature and the analogical system also reinforce the characteristic structure of the poems that moves from
contemplation to prayer, for nature leads the Christian mind
from observation of physical beauty to reflection on what lies
behind the appearances to worship of the creator of all things.

Thus the widespread belief that Keble's poetry is Wordsworth and water is really off the mark, as far as concerns its
intellectual content. Keble's nature poetry is rather Wordsworth *moralisé* or Wordsworth plus theology. If it is less effective than Wordsworth's nature poetry, this has more to do
with Keble's gifts as a poet than with the intellectual assumptions behind the poetry, for those same assumptions—nature
as God's creation and sign, nature as fallen with man and yet
redeemed through Christ—when exploited so brilliantly by
Hopkins, become a basis for transcending Wordsworth and
reinvigorating a faded Romantic nature, moving it to
something far more deeply interfused with a philosophy and a
theology.[28] Keble's strong sense of the sacramental system
must be counted a bridge between the two. In Keble's case the
theological dimension—nature as part of the analogy of creation—is always dominant.

It is mainly as a reflection of the sacramental or analogical
system that Keble approaches the other topics of his poetry in
The Christian Year. The treatment of nature can stand as a

paradigm for Keble's treatment of these other topics: daily life, the home, family relations, work, rural scenes, and, of course, biblical and Christian story in conjunction with saints' days and Church feasts. Like nature, all of these are regularly related to traditional moral and theological teaching, with perhaps an especially Tractarian stress on humility and self-denial:

> The trivial round, the common task,
> Would furnish all we ought to ask;
> Room to deny ourselves; a road
> To bring us daily, nearer God.
>
> (Morning)

Also especially Tractarian is the emphasis on the role of the Church, though this aspect is less pronounced in the poetry (as opposed to the organization) of *The Christian Year* than it would come to be in later Tractarian verse.[29] Perhaps this is why only the most severe dissenters found the volume too Catholic. The poem for the First Sunday in Lent links both Church and home as forms of God's blessings to humankind. "The Church, our Zoar,"[30] Keble calls it. In the poem for Whitsunday (Penetecost) he recalls the founding of the visible Church by the tongues of fire. For Tuesday in Whitsun-week he speaks of the function of the Church to remind one of God: "And yet of Thee from year to year / The Church's solemn chant we hear." Most arresting in this connection is his poem for Trinity Sunday in which he very modestly anticipates what will provide Isaac Williams with the subject of most of his devotional poetry—the physical structure of the Church as a means of teaching about God:

> Along the Church's central space
> The sacred weeks with unfelt pace
> Have borne us on from grace to grace.

From each carved nook and fretted bend
Cornice and gallery seem to send
Tones that with seraph hymns might blend.

Three solemn parts together twine
In harmony's mysterious line;
Three solemn aisles approach the shrine.[31]

The seven sacraments also appear, but chiefly in the poems
especially appointed for them in correspondence with the
Prayer Book. The sacramental element is thus conveyed as
much through references to nature, daily life, and Christian
story as through specific actions of the Church, striking that
balance between personal feeling and formal ritual that the
Tractarians tried to maintain.

Finally, among topics of poems in the volume, the reader
cannot but be struck by the intense Christology of Keble's
views. The words "Christ," "Jesus," and "Saviour" appear far
more often than the word "Church." Keble's Christ has not
the valor and act of a windhover, but neither is he exclusively
the gentle Jesus, meek and mild, of so much Evangelical hymnody. He is shown often in suffering and in triumph, while
the poems retrace the events in Christ's life that are commemorated throughout the year, and he is especially compared to light and radiance and glory in nature, and, with
almost medieval consistency, to the sun. Keble's "Sun of my
soul! Thou Saviour dear" from "Evening" is but the best
known example of a persistent imagery of light and dazzling
radiance associated with Christ in the poems. But Keble's
position is encompassing enough to allow for the subsequent
illustrations of the text that could be tailored to Protestant or
Catholic views.

There are some more or less polemic pieces in the volume,
but these are very much in the minority. Discussion of poems
like that for Gunpowder Treason, with its jibe at Rome and

its much agitated doctrinal change in its lines on the Eucharist,[32] should not be allowed to obscure the fact that, for the most part, the volume found favor for its absence of polemics and its capturing of the "soothing tendency" of the Prayer Book that Keble claimed was his purpose in the introduction. The real "polemic," as I have argued, is far subtler; it comes through the adaptation of the form of *The Christian Year* to the Prayer Book, providing continual reinforcement of the idea of formal worship through the visible Church. The cumulative effect of the poetry itself is to offer guidance and reassurance to the reader as he goes through the Church year that there is possible in the world about him holiness, devotion, and consecration of life—in other words, Tractarian Analogy made accessible to everyday experience. It is the atmosphere, the ethos, of Keble's own circle, of the so-called Bisley School, and of Tractarianism itself. As Keble remarked, "we are taught to make every scene in nature a topic of devotion."

The Style of *The Christian Year*

The Tractarian ethos shapes also those aspects of the poetry of *The Christian Year* that come under the general heading of style, by which I mean such technical matters as language, diction, imagery, and metrics, as well as such elusive qualities as verbal complexity, ingenuity, ambiguity, irony, and the like. Most modern critics place a higher value on these aspects of poetry than on any others, certainly a higher value than did Tractarian poetic theory, which is notably silent on technical questions. Accordingly, Keble does not fare well when attention is directed exclusively to stylistic issues. Using these criteria alone we cannot but find Keble's poetic achievement a rather modest one, and I have no intention of making extravagant claims for him on purely verbal grounds. But I do believe that even on purely verbal grounds much of what Keble does can be better understood if it is related to Tractarian poetic theory and to the personal ethos that in Keble so thoroughly complements it.

The meditative and contemplative character of the typical poem and pattern of poems in *The Christian Year* is a consequence of the shaping power of the Book of Common Prayer and a complement to the doctrine of Analogy. The meditative character is also a consequence of another aspect of Tractarian, and especially Kebelian, poetic theory. In the *Lectures on Poetry,* Keble distinguishes between poetry of action and poetry of comtemplation, clearly preferring the latter. Contemplative poetry, as Keble sees it, reminds us of our human limitations; in his view, such poetry nicely coincides with Tractarian ideas of humility and holiness: "The vein of poetry that seeks a life of quiet and tender feelings, that loves to hide in sheltered nooks, may stand as eternal proof how little mortal minds are self-sufficing, whether they betake themselves to worldly business or philosophic contemplation. It might reprove the folly of those who, when the certainties of heaven are offered them, prefer to cling to the uncertainties of earth" (LP, II, 280-281).

Keble's contemplative poetry lends itself to the use of nature as subject, which in turn means a preference for the country over the city, as in Wordsworth, a preference for Keble's own "trivial round, the common task." Nature inevitably involves the poet, especially the Christian poet, in Analogy and the Sacramental system. And the obverse of the Tractarian coin of Analogy is the concept of Reserve, for Nature both proclaims and conceals her message in something of the manner of Carlyle's Open Secret, that is, the secret of the goodness of the universe, hidden from the vulgar but visible to the poet. Just as Analogy prompts a certain kind of subject matter (and is itself prompted by that subject, hence the inadvertent virtues of pagan nature poetry), so Reserve inclines the poet to a certain kind of style, one that is subdued and humble, both as a means of showing reverence for the sacred truths with which he is dealing and as a discipline for denying the self. Reserve determines what, or how much, the poet will say and how he will say it. Reserve also inclines the poet to be a poet of contemplation rather than action. Once again we can see how remarkably self-consistent and self-contained the Tractarian position is, to say nothing of how much it is a codification of Keble's own methods as a poet and of Keble's own personal style, which by the late 1820s had been stamped on the other Tractarians-to-be.

Reserve, then, dictates that the poet will be guarded and gradual in revealing sacred truth, hence in writing verse at all. While poetry serves as a safety-valve for the expression of intense religious emotion, Analogy and Reserve see to it that the expression will be veiled, indirect, subdued, and self-effacing. Keble versified the concept of Reserve in his poem for the "Fourth Sunday in Lent," a poem titled "The Rosebud." In it he notes how one can never actually capture the exact moment when a flower opens:

> Fondly we seek the dawning bloom
>   On features wan and fair, —
> The gazing eye no change can trace,
> But look away a little space,
>   Then turn, and, lo! 'tis there.

The rose is a type of heavenly and human love; these things hide themselves from sight. And it is meet and right that they do:

> No — let the dainty rose a while
>   Her bashful fragrance hide —
> Rend not her silken veil too soon,
> But leave her, in her own soft noon,
>   To flourish and abide.

There can be no question that Reserve is the problematic element in Tractarian poetics, one that will later come to be mainly honored in the breach, but for Keble it was as firm a ruling principle as any in Tractarian poetics. His poetry accordingly is a poetry that hides itself in sheltered nooks, that has as its "chief purpose" to exhibit the "soothing tendency of the Prayer Book." By design it does not overpower the reader by force of language or compel him by the ingenuity of its technical devices. Rather it stands almost as an antitype to the poetry of the figure with whom Keble was most often compared in his own day, George Herbert.[33] Since it is the devotional poetry of Herbert and Donne that for modern readers provides the paradigm of what devotional poetry is supposed to be, Keble's poetry by comparison seems plain, flaccid, and sedate. One is reminded of the remark about the difference between a biblical angel and a Victorian one. The former strikes terror and appropriately says to the beholder, "Fear not"; the latter seems to say to the observer, "There, there."

Yet underneath its plain and modest vesture, Keble's poetry contains some elements of novelty and vigor that help explain its appeal and that give it more staying power than one would expect of poems governed by a principle like Tractarian Reserve, especially when Reserve is construed, as by Keble, to require extreme reticence. The chief element of novelty in the poetry is the surprising metrical and stanzaic variety of the verses, surprising because somehow this diversity does not stand out in the reading. Partly, it escapes notice because the stanzaic patterns are not reinforced by physical devices in the manner of emblem verse or by wordplay in the manner of metaphysical verse. Moreover, the metrical and stanzaically varied forms coexist with a good deal of quite conventional verse forms and throughout, use of language avoids calling attention to itself and hence to the form. Like the intellectual virtues of *The Christian Year*, the technical ones emerge only

107

after repeated and reflective reading, and they are oddly more effective for it, being like the discovery of new facets of something familiar and well known.

B. M. Lott has catalogued the technical data for the poems in *The Christian Year*.[34] Seen against a background of Reserve as a stylistic concept, the data are extremely revealing. On the one hand the most common metrical and stanzaic forms in *The Christian Year* are long meter and long meter doubled, and ballad or common meter, that is, forms best known through their use in hymns and ballads. On the other hand, these frequent forms, accounting for forty-one, or slightly over a third, of the poems in the collection, are more than balanced by thirty-eight other, different stanzaic patterns in the remaining two-thirds of the poems, for a final total of forty-two stanzaic patterns among the 109 poems in the collection. The thirty-eight other stanzaic forms do not derive from the hymn tradition, nor are they suitable for adaptation as hymns, being usually too complicated for such use. Some of Keble's forms come from the album verse popular in the period, that is, verse in miscellaneous literary collections, usually annuals (*The Keepsake* is a well-known example), designed especially for female readers. Other of Keble's forms are evidently his own creations. The result in any case is an abundance of stanzaic variety and experimentation, yet its effect is not haphazard because it is cemented by intermixture with hymn and ballad forms and by recurrence of the conventional metrical feet. Here Keble abides very largely with the usual iamb, his most notable departures being extra syllables at the beginnings and ends of lines, and these are not always happy additions. His consistent use of three-, four-, or five-beat iambic lines and of rhyme (there is only one unrhymed poem in the collection) makes his poetry seem immediately easy and familiar and lacking in surprises. The novelty comes only in the rhyme *scheme* and could pass unnoticed, especially when Keble relies, as he does excessively, on sight rhymes. Yet the variety of rhyme schemes has moved Lott to call Keble the chief stanzaic experimenter in the age until the appearance of Christina Rossetti.

Keble's poetic diction is also a function of Reserve and is as easily misunderstood as his metrics. His language is marked by conventional word choice, by traditional eighteenth-century poetic locutions—"fain," "vernal," "lo," " 'tis," "ere," and the like, and a heavy use of the biblical "ye" and the second-person familiar, with corresponding archaic verb endings. Such language is designed not to call attention to itself (if it does so today, it is by historical accident), but to blend on the one hand with conventional poetic language and on the other with the language of the Prayer Book and the Bible. This is not to say that Keble was a great lyric poet who denied himself his gifts, but it is to argue that he was not simply faltering or verbally inept and that he designed his language for particular effects. The Victorian concordance to *The Christian Year* is a substantial volume displaying a large vocabulary. What it contains little of is word coinages or verbal oddities, for these were consciously eschewed by a poet intent on exercising Reserve in his poetry.

To move beyond rhyme and diction to the texture of the poetry itself is to move into the atmosphere that these technical practices undergird. Apart from the novelty of the stanzaic variety and a tendency towards syntactic complexity that Keble's Victorian admirers felt obliged to apologize for because it diminishes his directness and clarity, the texture of the poetry itself is intentionally low-key and subdued. Keble does not aim for the tight expression, the compacted utterance, the surprising verbal turn. From time to time, of course, he attains these, but almost always he fails to stop, pressing on with yet a further elaboration of what seems a point fully made. His aim is not so much to make neat points as to dispose the reader to reflect on certain truths. Some of Keble's most telling lines are embedded within a poem. His sense of an ending is that of bringing the reader gently to a state of mind or condition of prayer that takes him outside of and beyond the limits of the poem. Sometimes, by virtue of his prayer structure, he does end with forceful expressions that are also pointers beyond: "To live more nearly as we pray," for example, or "For ever rise and sing, and shine," where each word seems to count, or his particularly telling conclusion to the idea of Nature as God's book: "Give me a heart to find out Thee, / And read Thee everywhere." But these occasions are outnumbered by those in which the language and sequence are designed to bring the reader to rest rather than to revelation.

None of the foregoing is to say that there are no poems of singular merit in the collection. More than one reader has fixed upon a particular poem as especially beautiful or memorable; Saintsbury on the "Third Sunday in Advent" and "Second Sunday in Lent," A. E. Housman on the "Second Sunday after Easter," David Cecil on the "Tuesday before Easter" and the "Twenty-third Sunday after Trinity" are some modern instances.[35] Victorian readers too had favorite poems, although more often they seem to have had favorite lines and passages.[36] But to join this process of singling out individual poems is to abandon the aid of the aesthetic by which *The Christian Year* was composed. It is not that here and there the volume throws up an individually good line or even entire poems; it is that the whole work breathes an atmosphere appropriate to its subject. The style of *The Christian Year* is always at the service of something other than itself. Keble's poetry is not meant to be but to mean, and not to mean in an original and arresting way but in an oddly translucent way. He would have considered his poetry to have performed its service if it succeeded in pointing the reader to something beyond itself; he would have considered it to have performed a disservice if it caused the reader (or the author) to think too much of style and method and too little of what it was designed to do.

In the poems for "Palm Sunday" and the "Sixth Sunday after Trinity" Keble considers the role of the poet in terms of the poet's mission, which is to open the hearts of his readers to eternal truth. Poets, whom he calls "Sovereign masters of all hearts," should be mindful of the source of their gifts, of who set them "God's own work to do on earth." And if they fail in their calling, or "in idol-hymns profane / The sacred soul-enthralling strain," the poet prays that God will show His power and mercy by infusing "noble breath" into these "vile things," until the poets give back His due to God.

> Childlike though the voices be,
>   And untunable the parts,
> Thou wilt own the minstrelsy,
>   If it flow from childlike hearts.
>
> (Palm Sunday)

In the poem for the "Sixth Sunday after Trinity" Keble admonished poets not to become so concerned with form as to remain poets only. The lines are based on David's repentance, hence the title of the poem "The Psalmist's Repenting," and the entire poem exhibits most of the characteristics of Keble's style—an eight-line stanza of alternating tetrameter and pentameter couplets with eye and slant rhymes, concluding with a prayerful request. Near the end he entreats those who have been moved to spiritual things by poetry to pray for the poet:

> If ever, floating from faint earthly lyre,
> Was wafted to your soul one high desire,
>   By all the trembling hope ye feel,
>   Think on the minstrel as ye kneel:

111

Keble is concerned above all that the singer may work his magic only on others and be himself indifferent to his own music:

> Think on the shame, that dreadful hour
>   When tears shall have no power,
> Should his own lay the accuser prove,
> Cold while he kindled others' love:
> And let your prayer for charity arise,
> That his own heart may hear his melodies,
>   And a true voice to him may cry,
>   "Thy God forgives—thou shalt not die."

The self-effacing style of Keble's verse is finally the appropriate complement to his organization and intention in *The Christian Year*. Like the landscape of Gloucester and the west country which is the source for most of the nature description, the poetry of *The Christian Year* is gentle and initially unremarkable. It grows on the reader by association with the Prayer Book and the Bible, by repetition and reflection; it induces in the reader the very contemplative cast of mind that produced the poetry in the first place. That it was astonishingly effective in touching Victorian readers is testified to by the reverence in which it was held in the age and by the way in which its peculiar music stole upon readers in Wordsworthian quiet or pensive moods. That a taste for such poetry has largely evanesced no one would deny, but something of that taste can be recaptured by an effort of historical imagination. As a historical phenomenon alone, the poetry deserves a permanent if modest place in literary history.

As always in matters relating to Tractarianism, Newman has the last word. His assessment, two decades after the first appearance of *The Christian Year*, fixes for posterity the high-water mark of that volume and can stand as its epitaph:

Much certainly came of the Christian Year: it was the most soothing, tranquilizing, subduing work of the day; if poems can be found to enliven in dejection, and to comfort in anxiety; to cool the over-sanguine, to refresh the weary, and to awe the worldly; to instil resignation into the impatient, and calmness into the fearful and agitated—they are these (N, *Essays*, I, 441).

IV

Newman and the
Lyra Apostolica

"You shall know the difference now that
I am back again."
— Epigraph, *Lyra Apostolica*

NOT QUITE TEN YEARS after the publication of *The Christian Year* there appeared in volume form the collection of verse that marks the other pole of Tractarian poetics and the Tractarian ethos—the *Lyra Apostolica*. If "Tractarian" is construed narrowly as the twelve years marked out by Newman, the *Lyra Apostolica* is the first (and one of the few) truly Tractarian volumes of verse.[1] As the word Tractarian in its earliest sense suggests the didactic and polemic tone of the *Tracts for the Times,* so this volume of verse is a consciously didactic and polemic product of the Oxford Movement. The *Lyra Apostolica* is the poetry of the Church militant; yet for all that, it is Tractarian devotional poetry as well.

The character of the *Lyra Apostolica* exhibits a number of parallels with that of *The Christian Year*, but just as surely, it exhibits contrasts that set it apart from Keble's pioneering volume. *The Christian Year* was the work of the solitary pre-Tractarian poet-priest seeking the deity in prayer and only later shyly and reluctantly sharing his private religious emotions with the public. By contrast, the *Lyra Apostolica* contains poems for the most part written and entirely arranged with the intention of reaching and influencing a reading public by poet-priests who conceived of themselves as charged with a mission. The difference is very much the difference between John Keble and John Henry Newman.

Although six poets contributed to the *Lyra Apostolica*, the dominant influence was that of Newman, who contributed the greatest number of poems to the volume (109 out of 179) and whose poems and plan gave the *Lyra* its distinctive tone. The other seventy poems were written by Keble (46), Isaac Williams (9), Hurrell Froude (8), John William Bowden (6), and Robert Isaac Wilberforce (1). Keble wrote nearly twice as many poems as Wilberforce, Bowden, Froude, and Williams combined; Newman, on the other hand, wrote more than twice as many as Keble. The volume is thus quantitatively more than two-thirds Newman; qualitatively, it is easily three-fourths Newman.

Tuning the Apostolic Lyre

Newman's influence in the *Lyra* is evident even in the prehistory of the volume. All of the poems[2] first appeared in the *British Magazine* between 1833 and 1836 under the editorship of Hugh James Rose, the sponsor of the famed Hadleigh conference that helped launch the Movement. That the publication of verses was Newman's idea is well documented. Before leaving on his Mediterranean trip with Hurrell Froude in December 1832, he had projected the plan, and the poems began appearing under the title "Lyra Apostolica" separately from other verse in the magazine, in June 1833. Presumably it was Newman who gave the title to this section of the magazine, although that is not absolutely clear; yet, as we shall see, one of the most enduring influences of the volume proved to be its name, an influence that only recently seems to have spent itself.

In projecting his plan, Newman sought poems from likely contributors, which means from Tractarians-to-be, and to Hurrell Froude's student Frederic Rogers he describes his aim for the proposed poetry section in the magazine as that of "making an effective quasi-political engine, without every contribution being of that character." He goes on to connect the writing of poetry to the circumstances of the times: "Do not stirring times bring out poets? Do they not give opportunity for the rhetoric of poetry and the persuasion? And may we not at least produce the shadows of high things, if not the high things themselves?"[3] In this keen declaration there is sufficient indication of the peculiarly Newman-like emphasis that will be stamped on the *Lyra*. Newman, who only four years before, in his essay on Aristotle, opposed poetry to rhetoric, is now actively enlisting, and himself intending to write, verse that will exhibit the "rhetoric" and "persuasion" of poetry. No doubt we can see a distinction between rhetoric as a classical mode of prose discourse and the "rhetoric of poetry," but it remains a distinction not an opposition. Both must involve argument, and this disposition toward argument points up the underlying conflict between Tractarian Reserve, construed as restraint, and the expression of intense feeling. It is wholly in character that Newman should be the first to chafe under the restrictive aspects of Reserve and to seek a way of modifying it for his own prosletyzing purposes. He does so by incorporating into poetry the concept of argument and persuasion, and hence of relevant social and political circumstances, while still retaining the fundamental Tractarian view of poetry as a religious undertaking, the expression of "high things" or at least "the shadows of high things." Newman's Kebelian views as expressed in the 1829 essay have not so much been abandoned as given social and political point, in addition to their obvious devotional point. In the *Lyra*, Newman is proposing that poetry will not be confined to private devotional impulses on the part of the poet, though these will not be wanting, but poetry will comprehend also the expression of intense feelings about the Church in her relations with society and the world. This is the first crack in the wall of Kebelian and Tractarian Reserve.

This intense, and what we should call ideological, attitude about poetry reflects Newman's growing sense of urgency about the state of the Church and his own religious convictions. It reflects as well the temperament of Hurrell Froude, his companion on the first part of the southern trip and the man generally recognized as the firebrand of the Oxford Movement. Froude contributed only eight poems to the final collection, for he was in ill health and only a few years away from his early death, but his mood is strongly evident in Newman's poems and therefore in the entire volume. It was Froude who in Rome seized upon the passage from the *Iliad* that Newman adopted as the bellicose motto for the *Lyra*. As Newman tells it, "The motto shows the feeling of both Froude and myself at the time; we borrowed from Mr. Bunsen[4] a [volume of] Homer, and Froude chose the words in which Achilles, on returning to the battle, says, 'You shall know the difference, now that I am back again'" (A, p. 42). As arresting as the Homeric epigraph itself is the phrase "on returning to the battle," for it describes Newman's own feelings in the Mediterranean and the mood of his *Lyra* poems, the overwhelming bulk of which were composed on the Mediterranean trip. What is perhaps most arresting of all, however, and generally overlooked, is that Newman's first inclination in expressing the sentiments of the Movement was toward verse. The *Tracts for the Times* and the "Church of the Fathers,"[5] the other two early vehicles of Tractarian polemic, were both conceived and executed after the *Lyra Apostolica*, though to be sure very shortly after: the "Lyra" poems had been appearing for several months before the first of the Tracts came out in September of 1833 and before the first of the "Church of the Fathers" began appearing, also in the *British Magazine*, in October. For Newman as well as for Keble, verse was the indicated vehicle for expressing intense emotion.

That even a great prose writer like Newman should have been moved to express what was to become Tractarianism in the form of verse shows how powerful was the Kebelian exaltation of poetry as the form-giving art. In thinking first of poetry as the proper mode for a "quasi-political engine" for "stirring times," Newman was on the one hand responding to the Tractarian poetic imperative and on the other adapting it to his own talents and concerns. That he wrote so little poetry after his burst of activity for the *Lyra* is perhaps a measure of his aesthetic maturity in recognizing where his greatest gifts lay. Isaac Williams, writing in 1851, attributes Newman's leaving off poetry to the harsh remarks made by Samuel Wilberforce in his review of the published *Lyra* volume.[6] Such an explanation seems to me insufficient for a man like Newman, who knew how to pursue his own course in spite of opposition. More to the point is the almost unconscious expression by Williams of the Tractarian aesthetic applied to Newman the poet:

> When Newman published the 'Lyra Apostolica,' he got Samuel Wilberforce—now the Bishop of Oxford—to review it, as one who would do it in a popular manner. Newman was then much annoyed with the reflections of the review on himself, and this was the cause, I consider, of his never writing a verse afterwards. Indeed I have heard Miss Keble [John Keble's sister] observe that it appeared to have stopped in Newman what Providence seemed to have designed as a *natural vent to ardent and strong feelings;* whereas had it not met with that untimely discouragement he would probably have continued to write poetry, as he had then begun, to the profit of himself and us all.[7]

118

Newman certainly thought of poetry as Williams did, as a "natural vent to ardent and strong feelings." In fact, Newman's two major lifetime outbursts of writing poetry both came at times of intense personal crisis for him, and both of these crises involved physical illness that led him to believe that death might be imminent. The first such period was the general crisis atmosphere and his specific Sicilian illness on his Mediterranean trip in 1833; the second was much later, in 1865, and provoked Newman to the writing of *The Dream of Gerontius*. But Newman's personal crises always became linked to public ones, became in effect the occasion for public crises. The process is quite clear in Newman's account of the Mediterranean illness in the *Apologia*. First, Newman affirms to Nicholas Wiseman in Rome that he has a work to do in England; then he feels this presentiment grow upon him in Sicily; and finally, after recovering from a three-week illness in Sicily and about to set out for Palermo, he breaks down in violent sobbing. "My servant, who had acted as my nurse, asked what ailed me. I could only answer him, 'I have a work to do in England'" (A, p. 43). The writing of the "Lyra" poetry that had been underway throughout the Mediterranean trip was then intensified, and most of the poems were written during Newman's journey home from Sicily, especially during the week when the ship lay becalmed in the Straits of Bonifacio, during which time he wrote "The Pillar of the Cloud."

In describing his illness and his "presentiment" of the work he had to do in England, Newman was clearly trying to trace the hand of destiny in his own life, to mark out the way in which he had been chosen to do the work that was to result in the Oxford Movement and his own further spiritual development. I am here not seeking to dispute this interpretation of Newman's motivation but only to note effects of this uniquely Newmanian linkage of the personal with the public on the course of Victorian devotional poetry. Newman was writing poetry as a natural vent to ardent and strong feelings in the received Tractarian manner, but the practical difference, and hence practical contribution to Tractarian poetics through the *Lyra,* was that Newman's ardent and strong feelings could not be detached from social and political circumstances of the day, especially as these touched on the Church. The result was Tractarian devotional poetry of a decidedly more argumentative cast than anything hitherto undertaken by Keble, even though dictated by the same poetic principles.

When Newman gathered the periodical "Lyra" poems together for publication in book form in 1836, he wrote a brief "Advertisement" very much in the manner of Keble's similarly titled "Advertisement" for *The Christian Year* but stressing the didactic character of the *Lyra* and containing nothing of the "soothing tendency" Keble talked of. The poems in the *Lyra,* he wrote, have been published "in the humble hope that they may be instrumental in recalling or recommending to the reader important Christian truths which are at this day in a way to be forgotten" (L, p. vii). He explained that in order to stress these truths, the publication "would, according to the original intention, have been strictly anonymous; but one of the writers [that is, Hurrell Froude] in whom the work originated, having been taken from his friends by death, it seemed desirable so far to depart from it, as to record what belonged to him, while it was possible to do so; and this has led to a general discrimination of the poems, by signatures at the end of each" (L, p. vii). The "signatures," however, are but lower-case Greek letters, with no key provided for linking them to any author and no list of authors anywhere. This is Reserve with a Newman touch, restraint that points ever so subtly to the intensity lying behind it.

In his new edition to 1879 Newman added a "Postscript" to the original "Advertisement" in which he identified all contributors[8] and placed the original conception of the *Lyra* in historical context:

> [The poems] were contemporaneous, on their first appearance in 1833, with the "Tracts for the Times," and the "Church of the Fathers," being contributions month by month, as were the papers called the "Church of the Fathers," to the "British Magazine." All three had one object, that of enforcing what the authors considered to be Apostolical or Primitive Christianity, at a time when its principles, doctrines, disciplines, usages, and spirit seemed, in the length and breadth of the Anglican Communion, to be well nigh forgotten. The "Lyra Apostolica," on the whole, took the ethical side of Christianity; the Tracts the theological and controversial; while the "Church of the Fathers" was mainly historical.[9]

It is interesting to see that with hindsight Newman used the expression "ethical" for the *Lyra* in distinction to the "theological and controversial" for the Tracts and "historical" for the "Church of the Fathers." In fact, all of these Tractarian productions were in some measure controversial and polemic, though admittedly the Tracts were the most explicitly so. The "Church of the Fathers," however, implied a polemic in stressing the undivided, apostolic Church over the later, divided body of Christendom, and the *Lyra* sought to "recall" or "recommend" those "important Christian truths which are at this day in a way to be forgotten"; and, as Newman says, all three sought to "enforce" apostolic Christianity. All of these productions were manifestations of the Tractarian concern with the "moral," a somewhat elastic term in Tractarian use and yet essential for understanding Tractarian attitudes. When Keble uses it in his disquisitions on poetics, he does so in the direction of worship; that is, "moral" becomes for Keble a synonym for "religious," and "morality" for "religion." When Newman uses the term in his 1829 essay, he also often means "religious," but he inclines at the same time toward a meaning close to "conduct" and "ethics." By 1879 Newman does not use the word "moral" but says that the poems of the *Lyra* were directed to the "ethical side" of Christianity. From religious to ethical, then, is the range of Tractarian "moral." It can thus encompass history and society as well as individual conduct and personal devotion. Each Tractarian was able to emphasize his own inclinations within the same terminological framework. Newman's inclinations were simply more contentious than Keble's. The poems of the *Lyra Apostolica* certainly bear this out.

Yet our frank awareness of the polemic character of the *Lyra* should not obscure for us the inclusion in it as well of the more traditional devotional element deriving from *The Christian Year* that was destined to be a permanent part of Victorian devotional poetry. At least one of Keble's poems, for example, had been composed as early as 1827, and one other, the celebrated "The Winter Thrush" (No. 89), is very much in the solitary nature-worshiping vein of his previous poetry. Though all of Newman's poems in the *Lyra* were composed under the spell of his sense of mission, many are also poems of the individual worshiper in communion with God. When Newman is at his most successful, as in the well-known "Pillar of the Cloud," he is able to link the voice of the private worshiper to the sense of urgency and purpose that implies, even when it does not state, a wider public relevance.

The very title of the collection tells the story of its Tractarian blend of religious and Romantic sensibilities—the Apostolic Lyre. The lyre calls to mind a common Romantic image, the poet as inspired singer. More, it suggests that supremely Romantic lyre, the Aeolian lyre or harp, as in the poem by Coleridge or in Shelley's impassioned plea in "Ode to the West Wind"—"Make me thy lyre." But there is an ambiguity in the Romantic lyre that has been removed from the Tractarian one. Coleridge had already sensed that ambiguity.

In "The Eolian Harp" he is not quite sure that he may go so far as to posit that all of "organic Nature" is but a group of lyres strummed by an "intellectual breeze" which is God; that is, he fears he may be speaking too familiarly and perhaps too pantheistically of the deity. There is always an element of the wayward and unpredictable in Romantic inspiration, especially as it is imaged through the lyre, that is uncongenial to the intensely religious sensibility. For the Tractarians, inspiration is not an errant breeze, or even whisperings of the muse, but rather the breath of the divine, and a very orthodox divine at that. Theirs is an *apostolic* lyre, one in harmony with the stirrings of the Apostolic Church, which is both Newman's Church of the Fathers and the Church that secured its perpetuity even to the present through the apostolic succession, a principle of enormous importance to the Tractarians and the source for their arguments on behalf of the authority of the visible Church and the validity of the Church of England as part of the Church Catholic.

To many modern readers, an apostolic lyre must seem almost an oxymoron, the linkage of an inherently poetic image, the lyre, with an inherently unpoetic and dogmatic one, apostolicity. But this only points up the distance between the modern cast of mind and the religious cast of mind of the Tractarians. To the Tractarians, the Church herself is poetry. An apostolic lyre would be the appropriate successor under the Christian dispensation to the inspired, but still imperfect, lyres of pagan antiquity, and perhaps even of the immediate Romantic past. The apostolic succession was not a purely technical device for maintaining the continuity of the Church, still less an empty formality, but a mystical and moral, hence poetical, instrument of God to perpetuate the Church and to preserve in it the poetry that comes from God. Thus in the words Lyra and Apostolica Newman contributes to the Tractarian theologizing of Romantic poetics and the Tractarian poeticizing of the Church. That the very title exercised an extraordinary appeal to the Victorian mind is the subject of an appendix to this study.

Several dozen poetry collections in the remainder of the century appear to have had their titles inspired by the *Lyra Apostolica,* and altogether, since 1836 some seventy titles descend directly or indirectly from it. The complete union of Tractarian motifs appears in those collections that use a *Lyra* title to present poems or hymns arranged for reading in terms of the Christian year. All of these later volumes, like later editions of the *Lyra Apostolica* itself, follow the pattern set by *The Christian Year* that came to mark almost all Victorian devotional poetry, that is, an increasingly visible devotional format. The first edition of the *Lyra Apostolica* of 1836 is, like the first edition of *The Christian Year,* a simple octavo volume. But at least as early as the fifth edition of 1842, ruled lines and religious emblems had appeared, and subsequent editions elaborated the procedure so that later *Lyra Apostolicas* like later *Christian Years* strikingly resemble missals or prayer books.

Newman had transferred copyright of the *Lyra* to Keble in 1845 or 1846, and after Keble's death in 1866 it was eventually returned to Newman. He issued a new edition in 1879, then transferred copyright to Keble College, Oxford, in 1881. Newman's new edition of 1879, the subsequent reprints of it, and editions by other hands are all very much in the prayer book mold. The 1879 edition has both red and black ruled lines — red to enclose the printing on the page, black at the top to under-line the section headings, which were now printed in black letter (gothic) type, a device that came into use with the poetry of Isaac Williams. There are also usually in later editions red and black streamers for bookmarks as in missals. The *Lyra Apostolica,* for all its polemic, was received as a volume of devotion.

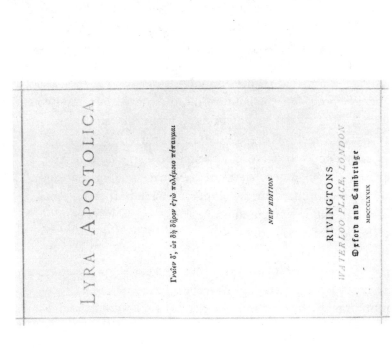

Figure 12. *Title page of late edition of Lyra Apostolica c. 1910.*

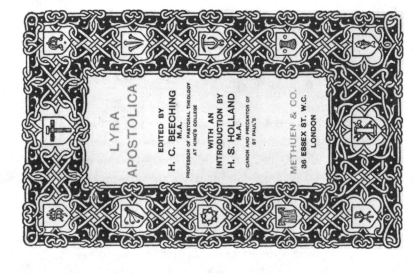

Figure 11. *Title page of Lyra Apostolica from Newman's new edition of 1879.*

The Poetry of the *Lyra Apostolica*

The "missalization" of the *Lyra Apostolica* follows the pattern
set by *The Christian Year,* and the pattern in turn reflects the
increasing ritualism of the Oxford Movement. While such a
treatment was invited by the very nature of *The Christian
Year*—one remembers that Keble himself had considered illustrations for first edition—neither is it out of place with the
Lyra. Newman, like Keble, put a good deal of stress on the
organization of the printed volume after the poems had appeared in groups in the *British Magazine.* The original sequence
of poems as they appeared in the magazine bears only a
tenuous relation to the sequence in the volume itself. Nor did
the original magazine appearances bear the section titles that
were devised for the volume: the poems simply appeared
month after month under the general title "Lyra Apostolica"
I, II, and so on. The *Lyra Apostolica,* as the collection we
know, was arranged for particular effects by its editor. These
are at once "ethical," in Newman's sense, and "moral" in a
Tractarian sense, that is, devotional.

The 179 poems of the collection are disposed in forty-five
separately titled sections, containing as few as one and as many
as nine poems each. There is no external pattern to these sections comparable to the organization of *The Christian Year.*
They represent mainly concerns of Newman as a Christian and
as a Tractarian, but then, his concerns were both traditional
and topical, and they focused on matters readers were coming
to care about. Sections like "Remorse," "Forgiveness," "Affliction," and "Holiness," deal with common issues of the
Christian life from an intensely felt Tractarian perspective.
More polemically Tractarian, however, are sections that focus
attention on the history and practices of the Church, such as
"Commune Doctorum," on the great teachers of the Church,
and "Religious States," which includes such a roster as

"Heathenism," "Superstition," "Liberalism," and even "Apostasy." The first of the forty-five sections is titled "Home," and the last "Waiting for Christ." It would be stretching matters to say that this represents some progression from the present to the hereafter, but it seems that the earliest sections are more concerned with general topics of faith, Church history, and Church practices, and the later sections (after section XXIV, "Commune Doctorum") more concerned with theological issues and with the state of the Church and the modern world. It is certainly true that particular poems take on a coloring from the section in which they are placed. Thus a section titled "Captivity" lends further force to the poems in it which contain attacks on contemporary ills like "Science" and "Protestantism" as examples of the modern bondage of the Church. And a section titled "The Rule of Faith" with its single poem by Isaac Williams titled "Always, Everywhere, and By All" (the translation of the classic phrasing of Catholic orthodoxy by Vincent of Lerins) proclaims its polemical intent, though this is evident enough in the poem itself in lines like "Romish, and Swiss, and Lutheran novelities."

Often the poems themselves give the section titles significance. Thus the section titled "Trade" is recognized as expressing Tractarian distaste after one reads the three poems in it, which are also something like a flyting among the three leading Tractarians. "Tyre," "England," and "United States" (Nos. 139-141) were written by Froude, Newman, and Keble respectively. "Tyre" tells of course of that once great center commerce now vanished from the earth. In the following poem, Newman indicts England as "Tyre of the West" and warns that England may follow the path of the first Tyre. Keble tops this in "United States," by beginning "Tyre of the *farther* West! be thou too warned." Such is the Tractarian judgment on commercial civilization.

In the main, however, the sections offer no trim unity to the *Lyra Apostolica* overall as they do to *The Christian Year*. In that respect they may betray something of the waywardness of the Romantic lyre after all, except that Newman has tuned the instrument to give a unity of theme to individual sections and a unity of tone to the volume overall. The individual sections contain groupings of related poems that can be isolated for devotional reading. More often than not, the sections are composed of poems by the same hand, chiefly the groups of Newman or Keble poems. One can imagine the red or black streamer being placed by a Victorian reader to mark a section like "The Lighting of Lamps," which contains five poems by Keble on aspects of the symbolic significance of light in Christian worship and theology. Or the streamer being placed by sections like "Home," "The Past and the Present," "Faith," or "Ancient Scenes," each composed entirely of poems by Newman from his Mediterranean journey, and each having its own unity of atmosphere and tone as well as of subject. Thus, while the sections do not lead from one to the other in a necessary progression, they each have an inner consistency that encourages reading by sections, and they are all infused with the tone that Newman imparted to the whole.

The unity of tone imparted by Newman is the most notable feature of the *Lyra Apostolica*. It is at once urgent, intense, confident, and purposeful; it is a tone of passion that strikes a new note in Tractarian verse. This is, of course, Newman's contribution, not only to his own poems, but to the poems he inspired from his contributors. Even Keble's poetry in the *Lyra* has a force and urgency rarely encountered in the verse of *The Christian Year*. H. Scott Holland recognized this quality of the *Lyra Apostolica* in his introduction to the Beeching edition and described it as going beyond even the severity of the tone and teaching of *The Christian Year* to add a "sense of alarm, anxiety, revolt, even scorn" (L, p. xx). Holland also noted the frequency of austerity and asceticism as themes in the poetry of the *Lyra* and the constant denunciation of Liberalism, as Newman defined it in the *Apologia*. Holland further identified three "notes" of the *Lyra*, using the term Newman favored, to describe the "ruling motives" of the collection—Authority, Discipline, and Mystery (L, pp. xl-xlii). These too can be found in *The Christian Year*, but there they are subordinated to the soothing tendency Keble prized in the Prayer Book. In the *Lyra*, the "notes" are imbued with the passion Newman brought to the volume and the Movement. Thus sections like Newman's "Religious States" (eight poems all by Newman) have direct attacks on topics like "Liberalism"—"Ye cannot halve the gospel of God's grace; / Men of presumptuous heart!"—and a section like "Let Us Depart Hence," containing five poems all by Keble, is almost equally resolute in denouncing the "ruffian band" of Reformers and modern light half-believers in casual creeds. The bracing tone of the *Lyra* helps give the volume a sense of immediacy even now, when many of the battles are no longer the same.

Because of the sense of urgency that informs the volume, the *Lyra* has overall much tauter verse and much more vigorous diction that *The Christian Year*, as suits its more polemic intent. Newman's verse, in any case, is not normally lulling or soothing.[10] Biblical and Prayer Book echoes abound, as they do in Keble's *The Christian Year*, but Newman's practice shows that the Bible and the Prayer Book have thunder in them as well as balm. Newman frequently uses both the iambic pentamenter and the common meter dear to Keble, but he is far less frequently guilty than Keble in *The Christian Year* of run-on lines, sight rhymes, contorted syntax, and outmoded eighteenth-century diction. There are certainly halting passages in the *Lyra* from Newman's hand as well as from others', but in the main the poetry has a directness and a simplicity that commend it to modern readers and, perhaps more important, that became after the *Lyra* an available mode in Tractarian practice.

Though the poems breathe the same spirit and to a large extent exhibit the same style, a few generalizations are still possible about the character of the poems from each of the contributors. Newman as the main contributor rightly comes first. His poetry runs from the conventional iambic and common measures already mentioned, to sonnets (not highly successful) and experiments in form inspired by Greek choric modes. These latter are stylistically the most arresting of Newman's poems, in part because they anticipate his practice of short choral sections by angels and demons in *The Dream of Gerontius*, but mainly because they are the most adventurous and memorable of the poems in the collection. These are poems either entirely in two and three-beat lines or poems in which such short, emphatic lines are interspersed in a recurrent pattern among pentamenter or hexameter lines. "Rest" (No. 51), "Knowledge" (No. 53), "The Elements" (No. 71), "Judaism" (No. 106), "Superstition" (No. 107), "Prospects of the Church" (No. 171), and "The Good Samaritan" (No. 174) are the best of this type. The poem variously titled "Light in Darkness" (No. 25) and "The Pillar of the Cloud," but still best known by its opening lines, "Lead, Kindly Light," is also cast in an untraditional mold and gains much of its force from the two-beat second and fourth lines of each stanza. Being in so uncommon a form, it never was ideally suited for hymn singing, but the appeal it exercised from its first appearance has made it a staple of hymnbooks, the only Newman poem, apart from an excerpt from "The Dream of Gerontius," that has passed into common usage.

It goes almost without saying that in all of Newman's poems in the *Lyra* the doctrinal edge is very keen. His denunciations of Rome—for the volume, though Catholic, was definitely anti-Roman — are as severe as his denunciations of liberalism and the current state of British churchmanship, though Roman denunciations are less frequent. At the same time, in a poem like "The Cruel Church" (No. 173) one can discern the yearning towards Rome that was to prove a permanent and almost fatal aspect of the Oxford Movement: "O Mother Church of Rome! why hast thy heart / Beat so untruly towards thy northern child?" Newman's poem on the Eucharist (No. 33), though it declines to define the nature of the Real Presence, allows no such ambiguity in interpretation as was to bedevil Keble's "Gunpowder Treason" poem in *The Christian Year.* "Enough," writes Newman, "I eat His Flesh and drink His Blood, / More is not told — to ask it is not good." But he seeks no middle ground in devotional practices that were coming in with the Tractarian revival. "The Cross of Christ" (No. 14), also known by the title "The Sign of the Cross," is at once a moving devotional expression and a poem that could easily give offence to low churchmen and dissenters, quite apart from its having a Latin epigraph from Tertullian; Newman writes:

> Whene'er across this sinful flesh mine
>   I draw the Holy sign
> All good thoughts stir within me, and collect
>   Their slumbering strength divine.
>
> (L, p. 12)

The poem is genuinely devotional, but by treating a "Romish" practice it becomes polemic as well. The same is true of Newman's "Awe" (No. 13), which begins with the assertion that the speaker bows his head at Jesus' name, a High Church practice during the service which was looked upon as akin to making the sign of the cross.

Intensity of feeling coupled with what H. C. Beeching called the "gnomic" character of Newman's verse — its brevity of form and sharpness of diction—is what makes Newman's poetry generally the best in the volume. The pervasive awareness of sin and guilt, the honest fear of death, and the sense of the embattled soul compassed round by trials are the elements that give Newman's *Lyra* poetry an appeal beyond the purely doctrinal. These qualities are most apparent in the early sections of the volume, which are almost entirely Newman's. Poems like "Shame" (No. 6), "Terror" (No. 8), "Confession" (No. 12), "Awe" (No. 13), "Obscurity" (No. 19) are, in addition to poems already cited, among the most effective of the large group of personal poems that have primarily a devotional appeal.

Newman does not for the most part turn to scenes of nature to draw the lessons of Analogy. In "Nothingness of Matter" (No. 43) he even declares that the lessons of the seasons spoke meaningfully only in childhood and that now all is "blent in one dusk hue," for this world is but a phantom. But Newman does show a fondness for signs, types, and invisible forms. Thus, in "The Cross of Christ" ("The Sign of the Cross") (No. 14) he speculates that the act of making the sign of the cross might discomfit "hateful spirits" and cause "some lonely Saint" to hail "the fresh odor, though / Its source he cannot know." Similar views of the significance of signs are expressed in "Tokens" (No. 27), "Guardian Angels" (No. 30), and "Warnings" (No. 31), this last subtitled "For Music" and cast in Newman's choric style:

> When Heaven sends sorrow,
>> Warnings go first,
>> Lest it should burst
>> With stunning sight
>> On souls too bright
>>> To fear the morrow.

(L, p. 29)

Newman's (and others') poems on biblical figures also avail themselves of aspects of traditional biblical typology.[11]

For all the virtues of his poetry, Newman is not another Herbert, but more than Keble, he recalls some of the seventeenth-century intensity of religious feeling in verse. The worshiper posited by Newman's poetry is not a figure passively receiving divine impulses from a vernal wood; he is rather someone who feels keenly the call and the challenge of a devout and holy life. The effect seems to be a function of Newman's adaptation of Tractarian Reserve. With Keble, Reserve means a drawing away, a quiet closing of the door; with Newman it appears to be rather a holding back against the tide of almost irrepressible emotion, letting out only a portion of the passion that lies beneath. As a technique, it is very much what Newman was able to do even more successfully in prose and that gave his sermons at St. Mary's their compelling attraction for Oxford undergraduates.[12] One senses that even more is being suppressed than expressed. Victorian devotional poetry needed the qualities of intensity, passion, fervor, and zeal found in Newman's poetry. In the hands of greater poets like Christina Rossetti and Hopkins they eventually come into their own.

Newman's contribution covers almost the entire range of the *Lyra Apostolica,* both in terms of style and in content. There would certainly be some loss to the volume were the seventy poems by other hands removed—it is to that extent a genuine blend—but the tone would remain much the same, for the contributions of the other poets to the collection vary the tone but do not substantially alter it.

Keble's forty-six poems for the *Lyra* are notable for their pungency, at least by comparison with *The Christian Year,* and for their general avoidance of the nature themes of his other verse. Only one poem in the collection is fully in the nature vein of *The Christian Year*, and that poem was not originally conceived for the "Lyra" sequences in the *British Magazine*. It appeared separately a few months before the "Lyra" began and was not included in the volume until the third edition. Yet it proved to be one of the most popular of the *Lyra* poems with Victorian readers, precisely because it was in the vein they had come to know from *The Christian Year*. For modern readers "The Winter Thrush" (No. 89) is likely to have the weaknesses they find in other Keble poetry, and its interest today may reside chiefly in the way in which it appears to have been intentionally reversed by Hardy in his mordant "Darkling Thrush" at the end of the century.[13] "The Winter Thrush" finds a typical Kebelian divine message in the song of the bird in midwinter:

> Are we not sworn to serve our King?
> He sworn with us to be?
> The birds that chant before the spring
> Are truer far than we.
>
> (L, p. 92)

More in the general mood of the *Lyra* while still retaining some of the gentler qualities of Keble's other verse are the poems in sections composed wholly of Keble's contributions— "Bereavement" (Nos. 49-50), with two poems dating back to 1827, provoked by the death of Keble's sister Mary Ann; "The Lighting of Lamps," already mentioned; a group of five Keble poems under the section title "Jeremiah" (Nos. 123-127); and two sections containing a total of eight poems under the title "Fire" (Nos. 151-158), on Biblical and early Church themes; and, very much in Keble's vein of organizing poems around an external pattern, the section titled "Commune Pontificum" (Nos. 161-165), composed of five poems each preceded by a biblical epigraph from New Testament accounts of Christ's life.

That Keble could speak fiercely even without Newman's prompting is evidenced by the sonnet grouping in "Let us Depart Hence" (Nos. 114-118), and by the poem "Suppression of the Irish Sees" (No. 134) in the section "Sacrilege." The sonnets were published in the *British Magazine* before the "Lyra" series commenced, and the "Suppression of the Irish Sees" was written in March 1833, also before the "Lyra" began. It was in fact Keble's first reaction to the problem of the Irish sees that later the same year formed the subject of his Assize Sermon, which Newman took as the beginning of the Oxford Movement. Keble's poem is another instance where the first Tractarian response to a matter affecting the Church came in verse.

The contributions of the other four poets require only brief mention. Some of Hurrell Froude's nine poems have the intensity of Newman's best in this collection and suggest, as does so much about Froude, a potential that might have been fruitfully developed had he lived. In "Weakness of Nature" (No. 36) Froude strikes with the directness he and Newman imparted to the volume:

> Lord, I have fasted, I have prayed,
>   And sackcloth has my girdle been,
> To purge my soul I have essayed
>   With hunger blank and vigil keen;
> O God of Mercy! why am I
> Still haunted by the self I fly?
>
> (L, p. 34)

This was the tone that found its way into Froude's *Remains*, which Newman and Keble published in 1838 to the widespread shock of non-Tractarians. Froude's poem "Old Self and New Self" (No. 79) is notable chiefly for the novelty of the dialogue form in this setting.[14] Froude's "Farewell to Feudalism" (No. 159) is testimony to the fact that, although he was the first champion among the Tractarians of the medieval Church, he was also here fully aware of the passing of the feudal system.

Isaac Williams' nine poems in the collection are mainly sonnets, with little hint of his productivity as a poet in the decade after the publication of the *Lyra*. He contributed four of the poems to the section "Commune Doctorum" (Nos. 90, 92, 93, 96), including sonnets on Clement, Origen, and Basil, this last being his strongest. Just as Keble in "Lights in the Church" provides an early instance of Tractarian translation of hymnody from the ancient Church, so Williams in "The New Jerusalem" (No. 179), the last poem in the volume, gives a translation of a poem from the Paris Breviary that begins a Tractarian flood of translations of breviaries and missals and a general Victorian resurrection of medieval and especially monastic Church texts. Both Newman and Williams published Breviary volumes.

J. W. Bowden (1798-1844), the only lay contributor to the *Lyra*, was Newman's close friend from undergraduate days at Trinity. He and Newman had collaborated on a long verse production in 1819, "St. Bartholomew's Eve."[15] Bowden's six *Lyra* poems are imitations of Newman's manner. Robert Isaac Wilberforce (1800-1857) contributed only one poem to the *Lyra* (No. 128), a somewhat forced parallel between Israel at the time of Samuel and contemporary England.

Even though the contributors to the *Lyra* were distinguished by lower-case Greek letters in the earliest editions and were eventually fully identified, there is a sense in which, as in *The Christian Year*, the impact of the volume is lost by dwelling overmuch on individual contributions. To be sure, such attention is more justified in the *Lyra* than in *The Christian Year*, but the important point of the volume is the total atmosphere it projects: religion and the Church as fit subjects for verse. The *Lyra* also makes explicit the unstated argument of *The Christian Year* that the Anglican Church is the vehicle of God's grace. On a practical poetic level the *Lyra* also provided a sharper focus and a faster pace to the emerging body of Tractarian poetry, while retaining at the same time the element of personal sanctity and devotion that Keble had popularized. That the devotional appeal of the volume was strong is clear from the continued issuance of later editions, for its popularity could not be justified on polemic grounds alone, certainly not as late as the turn of the century, when the last edition was published. The *Lyra Apostolica* showed Victorian readers that devotion included not only worship of God but also concern for the state of His Church in the world. Like all calls to renewal it drew on ancient sources. For the Tractarians there was no more authoritative source than the apostolic Church. They tuned their lyre to its song and in so doing helped to make the Victorian Church poetical.

V

Isaac Williams: Reserve, Nature, and the Gothic Revival

Nature withdraws from human sight
   The treasures of her light;
In earth's deep mines, or ocean's cells,
   Her secret glory dwells.

    — *The Cathedral,* "The Skreen: Disciplina Arcani"

EIGHTEEN THIRTY-EIGHT was something of an annus mirabilis for Isaac Williams, the third of the Tractarian poetic triumvirate. In that year he published his first two independent volumes of verse and the first of his two massive Tracts on Reserve. He was thirty-five years old at the time, a minor contributor to the *Lyra Apostolica,* and one of Newman's curates at the University Church of St. Mary the Virgin. Though well known to the Tractarians, his only public notice would have come from the *Lyra* poems, and these had of course appeared anonymously, or nearly so. From 1838 on, however, he became well known as a poet and religious writer, for over the next two decades and more he published a large quantity of verse and prose, all of it on religious subjects and most of it anticipated in the range of material in his three publications of 1838, *The Cathedral, Thoughts in Past Years,* and "On Reserve in Communicating Religious Knowledge." The Tracts on Reserve present Williams as a prose writer on religious and literary subjects, especially the elucidation of biblical and patristic teaching that would find its chief expression in his lengthy and popular *Devotional Commentaries on the Gospel Narrative* (1842-1849). *Thoughts in Past Years* reveals him as a nature poet and devotional poet in the manner of Keble, though with his own distinctive voice. *The Cathedral* shows Williams in his most original and arresting role as the Tractarian poet of the Gothic Revival.

Isaac Williams had been a Tractarian from the start. One of the circle of earnest High Churchmen Keble gathered round him in the 1820s, Williams was the product of the High Church tradition in Wales. Much that he professed as a Tractarian was the legacy of his upbringing as clarified and deepened by his association with the Keble brothers. In his early Oxford years, the dominant Keble was John; in his later years, and especially after he had left Oxford in 1842, the dominant Keble was John's brother Thomas, vicar of Bisley in Gloucestershire. In between, during the early and mid-Tractarian years, the dominant influence was Newman. Williams and Newman were closely associated in the 1830s in their joint work at St. Mary's and at Littlemore. Newman always said in later times that Isaac Williams was the one Tractarian who never forgot him or failed to maintain contact with him. Yet for all his devotion to Newman, Williams claimed always to have had reservations about the restlessness of Newman's intellect, and it is to Williams that much of the later speculation about Newman's skepticism can be traced. Williams was fond of noting that it was those who came to Tractarianism from Evangelical backgrounds who eventually went over to Rome; those from traditional High Church backgrounds stood firm for the Church of England.[1]

Williams' career was not, for the most part, outwardly eventful. Born in Cardiganshire but reared in London, the son of a barrister, he attended Trinity College, Oxford,

Newman's undergraduate college, of which he later became Fellow and tutor. Having gained Keble's favor with his 1823 Latin Prize poem *Ars Geologica*, Williams associated with the Keble set at Oriel and was one of the group that Keble took with him to Fairford for summer reading sessions. It was there that he imbibed the Kebelian principles of churchmanship, especially the principle and practice of Reserve with which his own name became so strongly identified. Later he served briefly in a curacy at Windrush near Fairford, and later still, after he had left Oxford for good, he served in two cures in Gloucestershire. In this way he became identified with the so-called Bisley School of Tractarianism, the name for the group around Thomas Keble and eventually a byword for the strictest and most severe segment of Tractarianism that looked on even John Keble as too indulgent with his friends, by which the Bisleyites meant Newman. Williams married in 1842, the year he left Oxford, and he died in 1865 at Stinchcombe.

Insofar as Isaac Williams is remembered today as a Tractarian, it is for two controversies which he, for the most part unintentionally, precipitated. Both touch on his poetry. The first was the controversy mentioned earlier over Williams' Tract 80, "On Reserve in Communicating Religious Knowledge" (1838). This was the Tract that Evangelicals took as an attack on their own religious style. In the history of the Movement, the attack is important as signaling the most sustained assault against Tractarianism except for the condemnation of Newman's Tract 90 three years later.[2] The Movement weathered the challenge, but the damage it did to Williams' reputation foreshadowed the second and more serious controversy of his Oxford years: the campaign for Williams to succeed Keble as the Oxford Professor of Poetry when Keble resigned the post in 1841. By this time the greater eruption over Newman's Tract 90 had taken place, and the

Tractarians were on the defensive. Given the dissatisfaction the Evangelical party felt about Williams from the Tract on Reserve and the growing concern most non-Tractarians felt about the Romeward direction of the Movement, opponents made the nomination of Williams a party matter. Williams was defeated in an advance test poll and withdrew his name from consideration.[3] Shortly thereafter, he left Oxford for good to take a living under Thomas Keble at Bisley, later removing to nearby Stinchcombe.

Although these two controversies of Williams' career are primarily matters involving the outward course of the Oxford Movement, they have their relevance for Williams as a poet, and they have certainly influenced later assessments of his poetry, which has been seen almost entirely in the light of these two Tractarian battles. Because of the first, Williams is remembered as the apostle of Reserve, and his poetry and his life are referred to almost exclusively in terms of that concept and that style reduced to a meaning akin to withdrawal and self-effacement. Because of the second, he is depicted as having been broken by the loss of the poetry professorship and as having retired to his rural living, where, in the words of R. W. Church, he "spent the remainder of his life devoting himself to the preparation of those devotional commentaries which are still so well known." Such a picture is false in emphasis and to some degree in fact. Although Williams was a conscious exponent of Reserve, he, like other Tractarians, understood it in his own way and knew how to adapt it for his own purposes. His is not, quoting Church again, merely poetry "in a lower and sadder key than *The Christian Year*."[4] Williams' "retirement" was in part the function of the poor health that plagued him all his life, and in part of the fact that he married in the year of his removal from Oxford and thus had to find a suitable occupation and residence for his new circumstances. In any case, his more than two decades in

141

Gloucestershire after he left Oxford did not see the end of his writing of poetry or exclusive concern with the *Devotional Commentaries*.[5] On the contrary, approximately half of Williams' poetic output, though arguably not the better half, appeared after he had left Oxford for the country. Therefore, his creative activities span the twelve years of Tractarianism proper and extend well into the 1850s, ten years after Newman's defection.

As theorist and poet of the Oxford Movement, Williams carved out his own niche. That he has been overshadowed by both Newman and Keble is largely justified in terms of his public role as a Tractarian but rather unjustified in terms of his distinctive contribution to Tractarian devotional poetry. His contribution has been neglected because of his public reticence and because of the general distaste for devotional poetry that distinguishes our age so sharply from the Victorian. In order to understand Isaac Williams as a devotional poet, we need to look at his work in the three areas outlined above: aesthetic theory, nature poetry, and poetry of the Gothic Revival.

Reserve, Analogy, Typology

As noted earlier, Williams' chief contribution to the development of Tractarian poetics was his treatise on Reserve. It occupied two of the longest *Tracts for the Times*, Nos. 80 and 87. Williams formulated his view of the doctrine of Reserve as a complement to the doctrine of Analogy. Modern commentators, taking the work "reserve" as their sole guide, have tended to reduce the doctrine to simply extreme reticence. Certainly there is much in Tractarian Reserve to support such a shorthand description, but, as I have argued, although Reserve as reticence did lay heavy, and eventually intolerable, restraints on the artist that were being subverted as early as the *Lyra Apostolica*, as a doctrine it does not mean only renunciation. Reverence is the better synonym, for Reserve as

Isaac Williams conceived it, and as it was understood by the Kebles, has as much to do with the mystery of religion as with its constraints. In addition to signifying a sense of dignity and limit to expression in order that it not become mere effusion, Reserve also denotes the indirection necessary in speaking of religious matters as a parallel to the indirection used by God Himself in conveying truths to humankind, for example, through the lessons of nature so beloved of Keble. For the Tractarians, Reserve does not exist apart from Analogy; the one implies the other: both bespeak reverence and mystery.

In his Tracts on Reserve and in other writings, Williams makes clear his acceptance of the general Tractarian position that art is the expression of intense religious emotion. We have seen him indicate as much in speaking of Newman's poetry. What Williams is especially concerned to do in treating poetic theory is to show that artistic emotion must be governed by the principle of Reserve and must therefore seek expression through indirect means, that is, through Analogy. As I have shown, Keble sought support for the analogical view in Bishop Butler and also in the "mysticism" of the early Fathers. Williams did likewise, with special attention to the patristic *Disciplina Arcani* and to patristic biblical exegesis.

In looking to the Fathers, Williams was pursuing a typically Tractarian line that subtly offended Protestants without being open to the charge of Romanizing, since it was an appeal to the "primitive" and undivided Church that all Christians professed to hold in honor. It was an appeal to the same apostolic Church that motivated the *Lyra*. In fact, patristic appeals are at least as much appeals to Eastern Orthodoxy as to anything, since all of the great theologians among the Fathers except Augustine wrote in Greek and all exhibit the characteristically mystical tendencies of the Orthodox Church. It is noteworthy, too, that when the Tractarians, including Williams, were moved to poetry on the subject of Church divines, they wrote poems to two categories of religious figures—Greek Fathers and the Anglican Caroline divines. Only later did they begin to include Western Catholic figures, and only later still did converts to Rome include distinctly Roman Catholic, that is, post-Reformation, figures, as for example Newman's poems from the 1850s on St. Philip Neri. The Low Church discomfort with patristic appeals betrays the extent to which Protestants in the age unconsciously thought of the Church as dating only from the Reformation.

Williams' particular favorite among the practices of the early Church was that of the *Disciplina Arcani*. Newman too had high praise for the "teaching of the secret" at least as early as his *The Arians of the Fourth Century* (1833), but, as Williams' modern biographer notes, Newman was concerned to argue for the existence of the practice from the first days of the Church, whereas Williams was content with evidence that could not date the practice before the second century, for he was interested in the principle more than in the unbroken continuity of the practice.[6] The principle, as I stated earlier, was that of withholding the deeper mysteries of the faith from catechumens until their minds and spirits were in a state fit to receive them. It was even held by Tractarians that the Creed was not initially revealed to beginning Christians, though the evidence for this is uncertain. For Williams, the valuable elements in the *Disciplina* was not only the holding back but also the gradual revelation. That is, he saw in the early practice the element of restraint but also the element of unveiling, a kind of analogy akin to that by which external things lead gradually to hidden things. Williams found the ecclesiastical embodiment of the idea of the *Disciplina* in the rood screen (or *skreen*, as the early Gothic revivalists usually called it) that separates the chancel and hence the altar from the congregation. It was only one of the points of correspondence he found between the physical Church and her teachings.

The preoccupation with the screen, in which Williams and the Tractarians preceded even A. W. N. Pugin, marks another point of contact with at least the spirit of Eastern Orthodoxy. Probably to Williams the screen served as a Western equivalent to the Orthodox iconostasis, which separates the choir from the altar. Modern researchers, however, argue that the Western screen arose mainly out of practical considerations in medieval Western collegiate churches and not in direct imitation of Orthodox practice.[7] The Western screen is also normally an openwork structure enabling the congregation to see through to the altar, and it stands farther forward than the Orthodox iconostasis, that is, it stands along the chancel between the nave and the sanctuary area. Nevertheless, chancel and rood screens came to have a somewhat similar effect to that of the iconostasis in that they separated laity from clergy and removed the awesome mystery of the consecration from direct view. Thus, to Williams, screens reinforced the concept of the *Disciplina Arcani* and linked medieval practice to that of the primitive Church.

Along with his desire to revive the spirit of the *Disciplina Arcani*, Williams laid stress on the early Church practice of biblical typology. Here too he was doing no more than Keble had done in advocating Analogy by appealing to the mysticism of the early Fathers. But, since typology in Victorian poetry and art also involves writers outside the Oxford Movement, it is necessary to make clear what it meant for the Tractarians. Typology, as literary criticism understands it, is defined by Earl Miner in a collection of essays on the subject:

Christian typology originated in the belief that Jesus Christ fulfilled certain Jewish prophecies, especially those of a Messiah. It therefore provided Christians from the beginning with a means of accommodating to Christian belief the Scriptures of the Jews. An "Old Testment" was related to a "New Testament" by virtue of "old" types, shadows, and figures that the Christian believer found fulfilled in Christ and other "new" elements in Christianity. Christians believed that the Jewish prophets had instructed the Jews in the Christian message, "informing them," as Milton said, "by types / And shadows."[8]

Typology flourished in early Christian writings and was adopted in secular writings in the Middle Ages and the Renaissance. Until recently it was assumed to have died out before the Victorian age, at least in secular literature, but the investigations of George Landow have shown that it enjoyed widespread use, especially among Evangelicals, throughout the nineteenth century.[9] Landow indeed credits the existence of typological and figural readings of Scripture and their employment in both religious and secular literature to the Evangelicals, even arguing that the High Church use of typology, which he recognizes and cites, may well stem from the prominence of former Evangelicals in the Oxford Movement. Sorting out lines of influence is notoriously difficult, and some Evangelical influence on High Churchmen may well lie behind specific typological allusions in Tractarian and other poetry. But it is by no means clear that the Evangelicals are really the source of Tractarian and High Church typology, especially because the most fervent Tractarian exponents of the practice, Williams and Keble, were not from the Evangelical background and had a strong distaste for anything that smacked of it. In fact, typology for Williams and Keble was attractive precisely because it was patristic, and the very Tracts in which Williams defended typology, those on Reserve, roused the ire of the "Peculiars," as the Tractarians dismissively called ardent Evangelicals, more strongly than anything before Tract 90, which suggests at the least that the Tractarian attitude to typology was uncongenial to Evangelicals if not typology itself.[10]

For the Tractarians, typology was a department of Analogy. At times they used the terms interchangeably. But typology narrowly construed would apply only to Scripture, specifically those characters, events, and prophecies of the Old Testament that are held to prefigure comparable elements in the New. Exactly which ones did and in what way has frequently been the subject of debate among students of the Bible. Like the distinction between High Church and Low in terms of elaborateness of the Christian year or of the liturgy, advocates of typology can be sorted out by the extent to which they are willing to read prefigurements in Scripture. Protestant-minded interpreters will hold to a fairly narrow typological reading that is concerned for the most part with finding prefigurements of Christ in the Old Testament. Catholic-minded, including Orthodox, interpreters will indulge in broader readings, finding also in the Scriptures types and shadows of Church practices. Not surprisingly, the Tractarians are in this second camp. Beyond that, the Tractarians held typology to be a warrant for various kinds of non-Scriptural symbolism, where it merges with Analogy. Analogy was held to apply so widely as to include all of the visible world, to be in general a mode of communicating religious knowledge. Thus Keble says in his Tract on mysticism: "There is every where a tendency to make the things we see represent the things we do not see, to invent or remark mutual associations between them, to call the one sort by the name of the other . . . In like manner, the Mystical, or Christian, or Theological use of [the material world] is the reducing to a particular set of symbols and associations, which we have reason to believe has, more or less, the authority of the GREAT CREATOR Himself" (T, Tract 89, p. 143). And Williams in the Tract on Reserve argues that, since the ancient Church interpreted Scripture as "being figured and shadowed out by an infinity of types," we may conclude that God "has hid this vastness of Analogy and types in His word and His works" (T, Tract 80, p. 46).

Williams' application of Analogy-typology is the most thoroughgoing undertaken by any Tractarian, for it provided for him the justification for the plans of three of his most ambitious volumes of verse, *The Cathedral, The Altar,* and *The Baptistery.* These books also exhibit Reserve as the counterpart to Analogy, and these two concepts, Reserve and Analogy, play their more purely Kebelian role in Williams' nature poetry as well.

Thoughts in Past Years

Williams' volume of nature poetry and miscellaneous verse, *Thoughts in Past Years,* appeared late in 1838. The "Advertisement" is dated "St. Luke's Day," which is October 18. *The Cathedral* and the first of the Tracts on Reserve had already appeared, but the poetry in *Thoughts in Past Years* had been written first. As Williams notes in the "Advertisement," the poetry had been composed over the previous twelve years, that is, from 1826 to 1838. He also observed in his *Autobiography* that he felt the poetry in this volume to be superior to that in *The Cathedral,* or, as he phrased it in typically Tractarian style, to have had "more poetry" in it. It was poetry, he said, written "rather to give vent to the passing feelings of [the writer's] own mind, than with any idea of publication."[11] All these remarks are indications that this was poetry written under the inspiration of the Kebles.

The little duodecimo volume of the third edition (1843) of *Thoughts in Past Years,* looking much like a miniature Prayer Book of the sort that Mrs. Oliphant described for *The Christian Year* in *Salem Chapel,* is divided into six separately titled sections. These correspond broadly to the time of composition and thus offer a picture of the growth of the poet's mind. That growth parallels the course of the Oxford Movement and of Victorian devotional poetry, for it moves from theologized Romantic nature poetry, to poems on Tractarian themes, to preoccupation with the Church as an institution and system of worship.

"The Golden Valley" is the first of the sections. It consists of a series of sixty-three sonnets, mostly on aspects of nature. There is a strong Kebelian influence in the attitude of the poems toward nature, at once symbolic, nurturing, and admonitory, but the poems are generally stronger in expression than Keble's own nature poetry. Hurrell Froude thought highly of these sonnets, which he read in manuscript, and it is possible even today to see evidence of poetic power in them. Unlike most Tractarian poetry written to plan and order, including especially Williams' own later work, in this collection there are single poems that can stand alone. Williams has a much more developed sense of an ending than Keble and at times is able to give the reader a genuine aesthetic experience. The conclusion of Sonnet 55 is a case in point. The speaker has sensed an unearthly radiance in nature and felt an obliteration of time and space, the source of which he cannot comprehend. He is in a trance-like state, a spot out of time which he makes into a sacramental moment:

> Where am I? Still I hear
> Deep to deep calling afar! O Thou
> That hast redeem'd me from the howling flood,
> What have I done? Thy garments are all blood!
>
> (p. 30)

At once, the radiance in nature of the earlier part of the poem is revealed as Christ's presence, and Analogy becomes an experience, not merely a system.

"The Country Pastor," the second section of *Thoughts in Past Years*, consists also of sonnets, forty-one of them. The title was inspired by Herbert's *Country Parson*. Here the subjects include not only nature but themes from the life and experience of the pastoral clergy as seen from William's Tractarian perspective. There are sonnets on traditional themes like friendship, mortality, self-deception, and many poems on Tractarian concerns like Reserve (three sonnets), fast days (six sonnets), and on controversial matters. In this latter category one poem stands out for its anticipation in fourteen lines of the entire theme of A.W.N. Pugin's *Contrasts*.[12] Though not the most accomplished of Williams' sonnets because of its convoluted syntax, "The Ancient and Modern Town" deserves reprinting for its historical interest and for its foreshadowing of Williams' own later preoccupation with ecclesiastical architecture:

> Where shall we find that widow's treasured mite,
> Saved for the temple's service, heavenly wise?
> Or where blest Mary's costlier sacrifice?
> As down Time's stream we sail, first rise to sight,
> The shrines of ancient faith; with ample might,
> 'Mid humbler homes of men, they pierce the skies.
> Then thick the domes of human pride arise,
> Rich-peopled hives, and numerous, large, and bright,
> But few, and far between, decay'd and old,
> While Avarice gathers up what Time impairs,
> Or mark'd with tasteless art and thrifty cares,
> Lest they o'er man's possessions stretch too bold,
> 'Mid growing flocks, which seek another fold,
> Stand houses of our God, while Mammon spares.
>
> (p. 53)

"The Mountain Home" section of the volume contains some of the earliest poems in the volume. The title refers to his native region of Cwmcynfelin in Cardiganshire, Wales. The first poem, "Reflections in an Illness in the Year 1826," is a blank verse meditation on life, death, and nature and contains some of Williams' most deeply felt poetry. Some passages simultaneously echo Romantic, especially Words-

worthian, nature poetry and anticipate Victorian religious
angst and sense of separation from God:

> I stood amid those mountain solitudes,
> On a rude plank that cross'd the torrent chasm,
> Roaring eternally, till on the eye
> Hung the cold tear unconscious, and I turn'd,
> Unworthy with those shadowy forms to blend,
> Nature's unsullied children: then came on
> Feelings of solemn loneliness and thought,
> Amid the silence of creation's works,
> Waking the echoes of the past; until
> The veil of things, and this mysterious being,
> And the dark world, and fall'n humanity,
> Hung like a weight upon the soul; then woke
> Stirrings of deep Divinity within,
> And, like the flickerings of a smouldering flame,
> Yearnings of an hereafter: Thou it was,
> When the world's din and Passion's voice was still,
> Calling Thy wanderer home.
>
> (p. 71)

"The River's Bank," section IV, takes its title from the
river Windrush in Gloucestershire where Williams served as
curate in the 1820s. The nature poetry here is characteristic of
the Fairford-Bisley school with its depictions of a gentler landscape than the wilder Welsh scenery of "The Mountain
Home." Other poems in this section treat specific Tractarian
topics, such as the poem "The Analogy," inspired by Butler.
Here too will be found proof of Williams' genuine pastoral
care, including what is sometimes said not to have been an interest of the Tractarians, a concern for the poor. In "Heavenly
Signs," for example, Williams points not only to the familiar
Tractarian evidences of God in Nature but also to the image of
Christ in the faces of the poor. He wants to show that God is
everywhere in Nature, including human nature.

One can see in these poems a Tractarian and Victorian fondness for the simpler aspects of domestic nature. In "A
November Scene" the poet speculates for a moment in
eighteenth-century style about parleying "with the dread
sublime," but draws back at once:

> It must not be: such thoughts but tempt the soul
> To dizzy crags that look on vacancy,
> And tamper with the infinite, Controul
> Dropping the reign of her blest mastery.
>
> But rather let me look where yonder breaks
> The fragment of a rainbow; o'er yon hill
> Eastward, 'mid the wild troop of shadows, flakes
> Of glory in the darkness, bright and still.
>
> (p. 131)

Williams seems to strike his own note in many of the
poems. He often renders nature sacramentalism more tellingly
than Keble and with some of the economy of Newman. His
short poem on "Holy Communion" is a representative
example:

> O Saviour from Thy bleeding fount of woes,
> Thy cup of love o'erflows; —
> Not to me only these Thy dews,
> Which life and health diffuse,
> But unto mine in distance found,
> May this blest tide abound,
> Which creeps to roots of desert flowers half-dead,
> Woke by the touch they live, and bow the thankful head.
>
> (p. 167)

Section V, "The Sacred City," strikes a more polemic and
Tractarian note. These are poems of Williams' Oxford experience and his closer association with Newman. The title
poem reminds us of how deeply the Tractarians felt about Ox-

ford: "Be ours to hold to thy parental hand, / And venerate and love thine ancient ways!" (p. 175). Other poems in this section include devotional nature poems—"The Hymns of Nature," "The Nightingale by the Bridge"—and verse on specifically ecclesiastical subjects—"The Church in England," "The Days of the Royal Martyr." There is also an unusual poem titled "The Natural and Spiritual Man, or Classical Complaints and Scriptural Remedies." Here Williams presents brief citations from classical and even biblical sources and replies to them with two common-measure stanzas for each. The poetry here is labored; it is the idea of structuring poetry in terms of challenge and response, using poetry to elucidate doctrine, that is arresting. This poem can be recognized as the germ for Williams' later volume of verse *The Christian Scholar* (1849) in which, following Keble's lead in the *Praelectiones*, he undertakes to submit the study of the classics to Christianity. At the end of "The Sacred City" section, Williams prints his 1823 Latin Prize poem, "Ars Geologica," the poem that brought him into contact with John Keble.

The final section of the volume bears the Tractarian title "Lyra Ecclesiastica," which is almost certainly the first use of this form of title after the *Lyra Apostolica*. The section consists entirely of facing-page translations of early Latin Church hymns, including the "Dies Irae," a long hymn on the rites of the dead by Prudentius, hymns by St. Ambrose, and translations without facing-page originals of five Greek hymns by Synesius, Bishop of Ptolemais. Hymns and translations are beyond the scope of the present study, but it is important to note that the Tractarian poetic impulse stands behind the enormous surge of interest in early Church hymnody that marks the rest of the century. Williams was among the Tractarians who waxed enthusiastic over the Parisian Breviary from which Newman, among others, was to make numerous translations.[13] Keble turned his hand to a metrical translation of the Psalter and to translations from many early Church hymns. This kind of interest inevitably also contributed to the rise of ritualism, for it drew attention to various services, offices, and formularies from the rich store of pre-Reformation Catholicism, as Newman noted in his 1836 *Hymni Ecclesiae*. For Williams, the interest demonstrated by the "Lyra Ecclesiastica" poems led to his preoccupation with the forms of worship and forms of ecclesiastical buildings suited to that worship that would bear fruit in his later poetry.

In all, the poetry of *Thoughts in Past Years* shows a development from Kebelian nature poetry to a poetry increasingly concerned with questions of Church history and the idea of the Church as a mystical body. By a curiously Tractarian paradox, the best poetry as poetry is that in which Williams experiences nature and transcendence directly, as a single fused religious experience, not merely as Keble's book of nature to be read as a text. Yet the direction of Williams' future writing was away from nature and toward the Church itself as the supreme poem.

Williams and the Gothic Revival

The nature poetry of *Thoughts in Past Years* reflects the influence on Williams of the Keble brothers and *The Christian Year*. It reflects a sensibility developed in the Anglican Church of the seventeenth century and preserved through the eighteenth, chiefly in rural High Church parishes through the tradition of the Nonjurors. The poetry of the "Lyra Ecclesiastica" section of the volume shows the influence of Newman's conception of the Church as a stream continuing from apostolic times. These two emphases—the Anglican Church of the Caroline divines and the apostolic Church—became a permanent part of the Oxford Movement. It was left to Williams to give poetic expression to the third strain in the sensibility of the Oxford Movement and the one that, at least in matters external, was to dominate the post-Newman course of the Movement. This was the medievalizing tendency that links the Oxford Movement to the Gothic Revival.

Modern researchers of the Gothic Revival in the nineteenth century, beginning with Kenneth Clark, have documented stirrings of the Gothic as early as the second half of the eighteenth century in the gentleman's fancies of Walpole, Beckford, and other proto-Romantics.[14] Scholars have traced its growth through Romanticism in all artistic forms in the first quarter of the nineteenth century. They have found evidence of a Gothic architectural style in many of the churches built as a result of the Church Building Act of 1818. This important measure inaugurated a century-long effort by the government to respond to population shifts into urban areas as a consequence of the industrial revolution. Some of the early results of the increase in church building are referred to as "carpenter's Gothic," the work often of unknown or obscure architects. By mid-century there were many distinguished architects working in the style now known as Victorian Gothic or neo-Gothic. Even Ruskin, who was once viewed as the voice of the Gothic Revival, has long since been displaced as a pioneer of Victorian Gothic, at least in scholarly assessments, in favor of such innovators as A. W. N. Pugin and the Cambridge Camden Society, both independently active in the 1830s. So thoroughly has the Gothic Revival been examined that it would seem there is no single contributor to it left to discover. Yet there is one in Isaac Williams.

On the Eve of the Feast of the Annunciation, that is, on March 24 in 1838, Williams completed the introductory remarks for his first published volume of verse. He titled these remarks with the obligatory heading "Advertisement" and dated them by reference to the appropriate feast day on the Church calendar, as had come to be the Tractarian practice.[15]

The volume itself was titled *The Cathedral, or the Catholic and Apostolic Church in England.* The work went through numerous editions in the nineteenth century, as did the two subsequent volumes of verse and meditations that complement it, *The Baptistery* (1842) and *The Altar* (1847). The three works constitute the most sustained Tractarian poetic homage to the principles of Church architecture that captured the Victorian imagination in the Gothic Revival.

Like many Tractarian works, Isaac Williams' three volumes of ecclesiological poetry are more interesting as instances of the sensibility of the Movement and as illustrations of its poetic theory than as poetry in their own right. Few today would have the dedication to read through even one of the lengthy volumes, filled as each is with verse subordinated to another purpose and written according to an external plan. Yet perversely, as with *The Christian Year*, Williams' verse in these volumes cannot be successfully detached to isolate individual pieces of merit: the whole is distinctly greater than any of its parts. The point of the three volumes lies in their linkage of verse to religious principles and to the physical expression of those principles in architecture.

The Cathedral remains the most interesting of the three volumes, perhaps because of the general familiarity of readers with the principles of Gothic architecture. Even without such knowledge the reader cannot help but find his way, for Williams has made abundantly clear the plan of his volume. He has undertaken to do nothing less than write poems for all of the features of a vast Gothic cathedral, taking the reader through four main aspects of the structure, the exterior, the nave, the choir, and finally the pillars and windows. He has provided a ground plan of such a building that identifies each part of the structure in terms of what it symbolizes, and he has included engravings of the appropriate portions of various existing cathedrals, English and French, to face each section.

The Cathedral,

OR THE

CATHOLIC AND APOSTOLIC CHURCH

IN

ENGLAND.

"The House of God, which is the Church of the living God, the pillar
and ground of the Truth." 1 *Tim.* iii. 15.

Third Edition.

OXFORD:

JOHN HENRY PARKER;

J. G. F. AND J. RIVINGTON, LONDON.

MDCCCXLI.

Figure 13. *Title page of third edition of* The Cathedral, *1841.*

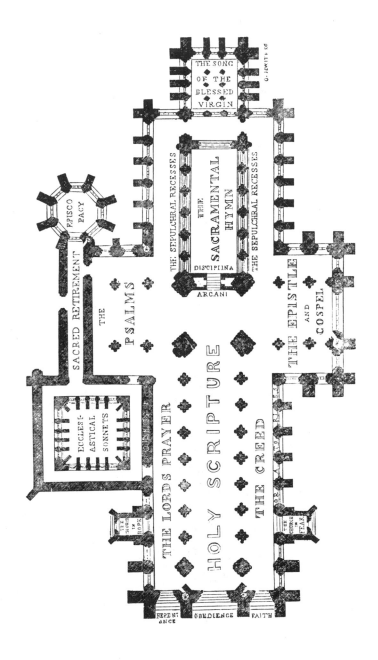

Figure 14. *The plan of a cathedral coordinated with the subjects of Williams' poetry. From 1841 edition of* The Cathedral.

Thus, the section on the Chapter House (which symbolizes episcopacy) is accompanied by an illustration of the chapter house from Wells Cathedral, the section on the cloisters (the sacramental hymn) from the cathedral at Beauvais, and so on. The frontispiece is an engraving of the facade of Lichfield Cathedral.

Nor is this all. Each section of Williams' church is so divided and subdivided in terms of its symbolic significances that he is able to extract an almost endless variety of religious topics from the intricacies of the plan. Within the great nave, for example, he finds "sepulchral recesses" that enable him to write poems on Anglican worthies like William Laud, Thomas Ken, and Charles I, "oratories" that provoke poems on the Doxology, the Athanasian Creed, fast days and festival days; among the pillars and windows he finds objects that generate poems on Old Testament patriarchs and prophets, the Apostles, and Fathers of the Church, for a total of forty-eight poems on historical figures in this section alone, in addition to poems on the nativity scene in the west window and the crucifixion scene in the east window, and so on. In short, Isaac Williams is teaching the nineteenth century how to "read" a cathedral, much as he and Keble had tried to teach it how to read the book of nature. To make assurance doubly sure, he adds four pages of notes at the end explaining the structure and symbolism he has been elucidating throughout. His aim calls to mind the twentieth-century efforts of such scholars as Emile Mâle, except that Williams' does not limit itself to providing information.

With the abundance of illustrations, the numerous epigraphs from biblical and poetic sources (especially Herbert and Wordsworth), the religious motifs and decorations at the beginning and end of each section, Williams has created a work that is sui generis. It is on the one hand poetry, but it is also a devotional manual, a guide to faith and doctrine, a cicerone for him who would know the symbolic intricacies of a Gothic cathedral. Nothing quite like this had been done before, though Williams is at pains to relate his undertaking to two revered predecessors, Herbert and Wordsworth, to give it poetic validity, and to biblical Analogy and typology to give it religious sanction.

Williams explains in the "Advertisement" that the idea is perfectly in accordance with the spirit and principle of the ancient Church and that there were "hints of the kind" in Herbert's *Temple* where Herbert attaches moral and sacred lessons to the "Church Windows" and "Church Floor." He also quotes Wordsworth's preface to the *Excursion* to the effect that Wordsworth's own poems "might be considered as capable of being arranged as the parts of a Gothic church, of which the minor Pieces might be 'likened to the little cells, oratories, and sepulchral recesses' " (C, p. v). What Herbert did sporadically and what Wordsworth suggested as a loose description of the quality of his long poem, Williams has done fully, literally, even excessively.

The religious sanction Williams calls upon, in addition to according with the spirit of the ancient Church, is the Tractarian standby, Analogy. He explains his use of Analogy thus:

> The principle indeed of sacred associations of this nature comes to us with the very highest authority, by the constant use of it throughout the whole of Scripture, from the Tabernacle in the Wilderness, which served for an "example and shadow of heavenly things," to the fuller application and extensive unfoldings of the same symbolical figures in the Book of Revelation. And, indeed, the practice is hallowed to us by the use of our Lord Himself, Who from the pouring out of water on the great day of the Feast of Tabernacles, took occasion to speak to the Holy Ghost, and likened a door (presented to their eyes as is supposed in the precincts of the Temple) to Himself; and made bread, and the water of the well, significative emblems of things heavenly and divine. And indeed, if we may say it with

reverence, it was the very characteristic of our Lord's teaching to draw moral and religious instruction from visible objects. (C, p. vi)

The poetry in *The Cathedral* displays some passages of power, and even eloquence, but it is so strictly subordinated to the structural plan that its real impact is as an illustration of the appropriate style and attitude of worship in a Gothic church. The dominant themes of such worship are mystery, awe, and adoration. Williams does have several controversial poems, including one that calls attention to the sad disuse into which the cathedral has fallen in modern times and one that, somewhat perversely in this context, tries to justify the relative simplicity of Anglican worship against more colorful Continental styles. To do so, Williams fixes, of all things, upon the subject of "Foreign Breviaries," the very books that he himself did so much to recover for English use. As in Newman's *Lyra* attacks on Rome, one senses as much yearning here as disapproval. The poem is noteworthy also in light of Keble's "Winter Thrush" and Hardy's later poem:

> Dear Church, our island's sacred sojourner,
>> A richer dress thy Southern sisters own,
>> And some would deem too bright their flowing zone
> For sacred walls. I love thee, nor would stir
> Thy simple note, severe in character,
>> By use made lovelier, for the lofty tone
>> Of hymn, response, and touching antiphone,
> Lest we lose homelier truth. The chorister
> That sings the summer nights, so soft and strong,
>> To music modulating his sweet throat,
>> Labours with richness of his varied note,
> Yet lifts not unto Heaven a holier song,
>> Than our home bird that, on some leafless thorn,
>> Hymns his plain chaunt each wintry eve and morn.
>
> (C, p. 21)

More characteristic of the volume as a whole, and yet equally Tractarian with its image of the lyre, is the first of Williams' group of poems on the Chapter House:

> Mysterious harp of heaven-born harmony!
>   Touch'd by th'all-hallowing Spirit from above,
>   Thou fill'st the Church, else dead, with duteous love,
> Obedience, such as holds the hosts on high,
> And pure heaven-soothing order. Mortal eye
>   Beholds not, nor can mortal hearing prove
>   The musical soul which on thy chords doth move,
> Tempering to holiest union; but the sky
>   May catch the echo of the unearthly sound,
> For Christ himself, and His appointed few,
>   Moulded the frame, and in the silvery bound
> Set all the glowing wires. Then potent grew
>   (Like that pale starry lyre 'twixt sea and cloud
>   Seen fitfully in Heaven when winds are loud)
> The treasury of sweet sounds; deep aisle and fane
> Prolong, from age to age, the harmonious strain.
>
> (C, pp. 43-44)

The poem that most completely captures Williams' ideas of worship, and hence the reasons for his dedication to the Gothic style, is the poem "The Skreen," the first half of the first stanza of which prefaces this chapter. It is the feeling of simultaneous concealment and revelation that the screen conveys so compellingly to Williams. Only in a Gothic structure can such screens be meaningfully deployed. That Pugin and the other Gothic Revival architects lavished extraordinary attention on the rood screen is an indication of how much they too responded to its mystery, to its unique combination of the principles of Analogy and Reserve. Following are the remaining two stanzas of the poem:

> When out of Sion God appear'd
>   For perfect beauty fear'd,

The darkness was His chariot,
　　And clouds were all about.
Hiding His dread sublimity,
　　When Jesus walked nigh,
He threw around His works of good
　　A holier solitude;
Ris'n from the grave appear'd to view
　　But to a faithful few.

Alone e'en now, as then of old,
　　The pure of heart behold
The soul-restoring miracles
　　Wherein His mercy dwells;
New marvels unto them reveal'd,
　　But from the world conceal'd,
Then pause, and fear, — when thus allow'd
　　We enter the dark cloud,
Lord, keep our hearts, that soul and eye
　　Unharm'd may Thee descry.

(C, pp. 210-211)

Williams' adaptation of analogy typology as the rationale for his versification of the structure of a cathedral also serves for his subsequent treatments of the baptistery and the altar. In the works devoted to these two ecclesiastical structures, Williams has let his love of symbolism carry him even beyond the novelties of *The Cathedral,* for each of the two subsequent volumes is a mélange of verse, prose, and illustrations that has no parallel among previous Tractarian writing, not even Williams'. They resemble earlier works like *The Christian Year* and Williams' own *Cathedral* in that there is an external form around which the poems are constructed, but they also depend heavily on illustrations from earlier works of Catholic piety, and both contain prose material as well that amplifies the point of the illustrations and the poems. They are thus quite as

Figure 15. *Illustration from Isaac Williams'* The Baptistery, *1842.*

original as anything done by the Tractarians, even while they are justified by Williams on the basis of ancient practice.

According to O. W. Jones, Williams' modern biographer, *The Baptistery* proved to be the most popular of Williams' volume of verse. It contains a series of thirty-two "images" with accompanying prose explanations of the multiple sym-

IMAGE THE TWENTY-SIXTH.

𝕬ttend to t𝔥e benefits 𝔴𝔥𝔦𝔠𝔥 𝕲od confers upon t𝔥ee, b𝔶 𝔴𝔥𝔦𝔠𝔥 t𝔥ou art stimulated to 𝔥oliness.

Consider the blessings with which God invites thee to virtue; that of Creation [A], that of our Lord's Incarnation [B], that of Redemption [C], those of Sacraments and Graces [D]. For it is God that feeds thee and clothes thee [E], delivers thee from many evils and miseries [F], and by His Angels sendeth His gifts [G], as He did of old upon the Israelites [H]. It is God Who giveth thee showers [I], and sunshine [K], and increase of fruits for thy use and delight [L]; and these He bestoweth upon thee in order that thou mayest follow Virtue [M]. And since God doeth all these things out of His very great Charity [N], wilt thou not also in thy turn be melted with love? Surely although Virtue be of itself lovely, and vice detestable, yet independently of these considerations it were but reasonable that we should embrace Virtue from the love of God and our Lord, and on account of those blessings with which He hath prevented us.

Figure 16. *Text accompanying illustration shown in Figure 15.*

bolic elements in the illustrations. The allegorical drawings were the work of the Flemish artist Boethius a Bolswert (1590-1634) and were taken by Williams from Sucquet's (1574-1626) *Via Vitae Aeternae,* providing Williams with his subtitle "The Way of Eternal Life." The drawings are construed as illustrations on the walls of a baptistery, and each provokes a verse meditation from Williams. The subjects cover a wide range of themes in the Christian life, which allows Williams to rove from biblical typology to Tractarian polemics on the state of the Church, as well as permitting him to dwell on the symbolic structure of a building consecrated to that sacrament so dear to the Tractarians—Baptism.

Despite a strong anti-Roman element in the poetry for which Williams was reproved by Newman, it is clear that

Williams has moved into a kind of ecclesiolatry that Victorians in general would associate with Romanism. He was well aware that Roman imputations would be made about his volume, and he sought to deflect this sort of criticism while defending his heavy use of symbolism in a dialogue poem titled "Prefatory Thoughts." There, "A" and "B" exchange comments about the present undertaking. "A" explains the source of inspiration:

> The portraitures in these old cloistral books
> Have bodied forth to meet the eye of sense
> Stories of divinest wisdom: these might range
> To aid our new conception, and thus wed
> Painting with poesy . . . [16]

The dialogue proceeds with "B" warning against the danger of incorporating "emblems of Roman worship," and "A" (obviously Williams himself) expressing straight Tractarian poetic theory:

> The Church, 'tis thought, is wakening through the land,
> And seeking vent for the o'erloaded hearts
> Which she has kindled, — pours her forth anew, —
> Breathes life in ancient worship, — from their graves
> Summons the slumbering Arts to wait on her,
> Music and Architecture, varied forms
> Of Painting, Sculpture, and of Poetry.

(p. x)

It is an extraordinary performance, almost unreadable today as poetry, yet fascinating as an exhibition of a highly developed religious sensibility at work and as a pointer to some of the more extreme forms of devotional poetry to come later in the age.

Five years after he versified the baptistery, Williams turned to the altar. But here he overreached himself, for the volume contained illustrations thought to be too Roman by Thomas

Keble and others. They were dropped from subsequent editions. Williams had tried to anticipate such objections in the "Advertisement" and to disarm them by his customary appeal to Analogy:

> But with regard to the particular parts of the symbolical representation; — there are some persons who seem naturally incapable of entering into such analogies; and even among those who are disposed to appreciate them, some may think, there is sometimes but little grounds of correspondence, on which to found the connexion. But it must be considered that where the adaptation is continuous and successively sustained both in the history of the Passion above and in the Divine Office below, it must necessarily be the case that in some points the application should be less appropriate, and even, it may be, sometimes appear forced and constrained. But the analogy upon the whole, and correspondence to our own Service, is sustained almost, if not quite, as well as it is in the work from which it is taken; and, indeed, the adaptation is in many instances the same. If, again, any should doubt the propriety of at all altering the original work by a new adaptation, and thus appropriating to ourselves what was intended for another Communion Service, it must be observed, that although the principle of a symbolical application is generally received in the Church from which it is taken, yet the particular points thus applied, and the mystical sense thus given them, does not appear to be always the same in their own publications; and therefore it may be considered as in some degree arbitrary . . . It appears a part of dutiful piety to make the best of what it has pleased God to afford us, and the reverential improvement of which seems the most dutiful way of obtaining our lost privileges, and of strengthening the things that remain; while we hold fast the better part, or pray for its restoration and lament its loss.[17]

What Williams ventured here was soon to come to pass in the ritualist movement, but the Bisley Tractarians were not yet ready for it; Williams was a dutiful member of the Bisley School, so the illustrations were sacrificed.

The poetry of *The Altar,* however, continued to be published. It is a series of over two hundred sonnets on all aspects of "the Great Christian Sacrifice," as the subtitle of the volume puts it, beginning with Gethsemane and ending with the descent of the Holy Spirit on Pentecost, in other words, the events from Holy Week to Whitsunday as reflected in the Mass. Many of the sonnets work on nature and typological themes, but there is also an increasingly fervid—some might say morbid—concern with the physical suffering of Christ. Methodist hymnody has often been reproached for its preoccupation with the blood of Christ, but Williams' inspiration appears to be Continental Catholic piety. A sufficient example is his sonnet "The Cross Dropping Blood":

Blood from His Hands is falling, drop by drop,
    And from his Temples; now in streams they roll—
    Haste downward to the earth as to their goal;
Now hang on His pale Body, and there stop,
Or on the wood below; till from the top
    Unto the base the blood-stains mark the whole.
    Such is the value of each human soul,
Which doth outweigh the world; and such the crop
    Of thorns which Adam sowed in Paradise.
What marvel, then, at sight of such deep woe,
    If penitential love should hide her eyes
From all the pleasant things which are below,
    In cloistral cells of prayer; nor seek relief
    But in each sternest discipline of grief?

(p. 85)

In addition to the interest in the sensual images of blood and suffering and the moral lessons that can be drawn from them, Williams shares and continues the Tractarian revival of interest in holy places, sacred wells, and veneration of saints,

THE PRAYER.

O Lord Jesu Christ, Who, although judged to be innocent by Pilate the Governor, yet didst willingly hear the multitude crying out against Thee, grant unto me Thy suppliant to have my conversation in so great innocency of life, that the mouths of those who speak evil against me may be stopped.

AMEN.

S⸆ IRENÆUS.   S⸆ CYPRIAN.

O God, Who art the invisible strength of those that contend for Thee, be favorable, we pray Thee to our supplications, that as we on this day commemorate the glorious triumph of Thy sacred martyrs Irenæus and his companions, we may also be fortified by Thy aid against spiritual wickedness; through our Lord.

We praise Thee, O Lord, for giving to Thy Church this example and the prayers of the blessed Cyprian, who hath become renowned both for his Priestly zeal, and for the triumph of his glorious passion, through our Lord Jesus Christ. &c.

Figure 17. *Illustrated prayer from Isaac Williams'* The Altar, *1847.*

though the Tractarians preferred to speak of the latter as simply the Communion of Saints. All of these topics can be found in the pages of *The Altar*.

Individually, the sonnets in *The Altar* leave much to be desired. Though Williams had enjoyed some success with the sonnet form in "The Golden Valley" section of *Thoughts in*

Past Years, his poetic muse is unequal to such a sustained performance as required by the task he set himself in *The Altar.*
But in this, as in so much Tractarian poetry written to
enhance devotion, the point is the total impact, not the individual poem. That total impact is one of a more intense
churchly devotion than conveyed by either *The Christian Year*
or the *Lyra Apostolica.* The focus is no longer purely
theological or doctrinal; it has been localized within the
physical structure of the church. Williams insistently places
religious experience within the confines of a properly disposed
ecclesiastical structure (or, at the very least, by an acknowledged holy spot), and he adjusts that experience to the
rhythms of formal worship, to the Mass, though that word
was still shunned by Tractarians.

The Cathedral makes unmistakably clear the connection between a Gothic church and devotional feeling. While *The Baptistery* and *The Altar* are less intimately tied to the Gothic, they
too reinforce the growing Gothic inclinations of serious-
minded churchmen. Together the two later volumes glorify
the two dominical sacraments especially favored by the Tractarians, Baptism and the Eucharist, the two that most clearly
require specific physical arrangements for their celebration. It
has long been a commonplace of writing on the Gothic
Revival that the typical Tractarian church gives special prominence to the altar and the baptismal font, in contrast to the
centrality of the pulpit that dominated eighteenth-century
congregational worship.[18] Williams' poetry is, of course, not
the cause of this emphasis, but it is the fullest expression of it
outside the pages of *The Ecclesiologist.* Had there not been a
disposition to see the Gothic style of architecture as uniquely
suited to worship, the efforts of *The Ecclesiologist* would have
been in vain. That disposition was nurtured not so much by
the scholarly investigations of the Camden societies as by the
appeal of the Tractarian devotional poetry of Isaac Williams.

Of the three major Tractarian poets, Isaac Williams may well have had the greatest natural bent for poetry. Keble had no ear for music; Newman wrote too little poetry to develop his gifts, and these were perhaps too analytical in any case; Williams, however, had the capacity to carry nature poetry much farther than Keble had done, and he had a richness of symbolic imagination that outstripped all the other Tractarians. But Williams was hampered not so much by the Reserve that later commentators see as hobbling his verse as by a determination to apply his poetry too programmatically. The increasing Tractarian emphasis on the forms of worship caught Williams' imagination and led him to the overambitious efforts of his later volumes. In his own age his early poetry lay permanently in the shadow of Keble (he was once called "Keble's moon"), and today it has been entirely forgotten. His later poetry realized its objective of poeticizing the Church, but at the expense of the poetry itself. Once Williams' perception of the poetry of worship became generally accessible, others were able to exploit it to greater effect and to realize in practice the color and pageantry of the illustrations to *The Altar* that Williams submitted to having suppressed.

Though Williams will doubtless remain a minor figure, something of what he contributed to both the religious and the poetic sensibilities of the age should now be credited to him. This is, above all, a great range of sympathy in poetry and religion. If virtually all of his topics and his premier mode of treating them—that is, in conjunction with an external devotional model—were anticipated to some degree by Keble, Williams pursued the implications of Tractarian poetics and methods farther than any of his contemporaries. Nature sacramentalism, intense Incarnationalism, mark his poems in *Thoughts in Past Years,* and a perception of the mystery and grandeur of religion and worship mark his works of ecclesiological poetry. Williams was the poetic force in the creation of the Tractarian admiration for the Gothic and for things medieval. He was as ardent an admirer of the early Church as Newman and was one who grasped the possibilities for renewed devotional intensity in the hymns and forms of the pre-Reformation Church and the devotional riches of Eastern Orthodoxy. For one who is called retiring, severe, and narrow, all this is an achievement that is imaginative in conception, vigorous in execution, and catholic in breadth of sympathy.

VI

Tractarian Postlude

Thy desecrated shrines once more
   Shall their true God receive;
And kneeling Englishmen adore,
   Where now they disbelieve.
    —Edward Caswall, "England's Future Conversion"

BY THE MID-1840s, the Tractarian phase of the Oxford Movement was coming to a close. Newman's departure in 1845 is customarily taken as the decisive closing date, but from the vantage point of Tractarian poetry, the end of the first phase is best signaled by the publication in 1844 of Keble's *Praelectiones Academicae,* fixing and codifying the poetics that had been developing since his essay on Copleston in 1814. The time between these works spans just over one generation, and in Keble's life, the years from age twenty-two to fifty-one. In the creation of Tractarian poetry itself, as opposed to the adumbration of theory, the time span for the publication of the formative volumes is shorter still. It runs from *The Christian Year* in 1827 to Williams' *Cathedral* and *Thoughts in Past Years* in 1838. Within those eleven years, the forms, themes, and techniques of Tractarian poetry were set forth in the key volumes of poetry by Keble, Newman, and Williams. In the 1840s, Tractarian poets published works that tended to consolidate, or even belabor, rather than to advance, their position: for Keble the *Lyra Innocentium* in 1846, for Williams, *The Altar* in 1847. In the following year, Newman moved his poetic impulse into prose fiction with the publication of *Loss and Gain,* which did not inaugurate, but certainly stimulated, the flow of Tractarian and anti-Tractarian novels that would for the next several decades occupy the energies of religious-minded writers who in the early years would probably have turned to verse.[1]

This is not to say that verse ceased to be a vehicle of religious expression. On the contrary, the Tractarians had won the battle on behalf of poetry as a fit form for the expression of religious emotion, and had established it across the religious spectrum as the prime literary form. But the addition of prose fiction marks a widening of the range of possible expression, and ultimately a vulgarizing of it, that left many aspects of Tractarian Reserve behind.[2] Religious poetry itself spread out from the Tractarian base, moving into hymnody of all shades of religious conviction and into personal expression no longer governed by the strict Tractarian code. Converts to Rome even used a Tractarian style of verse to denounce the Church of England and the Catholic pretensions of the Oxford Movement. The varied outpourings from Protestant, Anglican, and Catholic poets and hymnodists eventually made the poetry of the Tractarian years seem old-fashioned.

Short of another volume, it would be impossible to trace the course of later Tractarian-inspired devotional poetry, let alone the influences exerted by the Tractarian mode on hymnody. But some of the direction of Tractarian influence can be seen in Keble's *Lyra Innocentium* and in the work of some lesser transitional Tractarians and quasi-Tractarians, that is, those affected in some degree by Tractarian concerns but not themselves members of the Oxford party. All these look both before and after in the history of Victorian devotional poetry.

Lyra Innocentium

The *Lyra Innocentium* is both the last volume of Tractarian verse and the first of the post-Tractarian wave of mid-century.[3] The very title calls attention to the fact that it is Tractarian poetry. Isaac Williams had initiated the practice of imitating Tractarian titles with the "Lyra Ecclesiastica" section of *Thoughts in Past Years,* but the separately titled *Lyra Innocentium,* associated with the revered name of John Keble, probably gave the real impetus to the flood of *Lyra* titles after 1846. While the title draws on one established Tractarian association, the subtitle of the volume draws on another: "Thoughts in Verse on Christian Children, Their Ways, and Their Privileges," which calls to mind "Thoughts in Verse," the subtitle of Keble's *Christian Year;* as the "Advertisement" to the *Lyra Innocentium* makes clear, Keble had that volume very much in mind:

According to the first idea of this little work, it would have proved a sort of Christian Year for Teachers and Nurses, and others who are much employed about Children. By degrees it has taken a different shape: but it was thought advisable in the Table of Contents, to mention in many instances, with the subjects of the Poem, the Day to which it was meant to be adapted. (p. iii)

The volume thus partakes of aspects of both the *Lyra Apostolica* and *The Christian Year.* The poems all treat a general subject, in this case children, and individual poems are grouped according to particular aspects of the subject: "Holy Baptism," "Cradle Songs," "Children's Troubles," and "Children's Sports." Approximately half of the poems are also linked to particular Sundays and saints' days throughout the Church year, not, however, in sequence, as in *The Christian Year.* By selecting from the table of contents, one could read the volume in either the manner of the *Lyra Apostolica*—

groups of poems on particular themes—or in terms of *The Christian Year*—poems in connection with the Church calendar.

There are other Tractarian notes in Keble's *Lyra.* The theme of children is Wordsworthian,[4] and Keble emphasizes this by printing a stanza from Wordsworth as an epigraph. One section of poems is titled "Lessons of Nature," and in the simplified forms of most of the poetry in this collection, the section offers applied Tractarian Analogy for children. The poem "The Gleaners," for example, begins "The Church is one wide harvest field," and proceeds in ways that are by now familiar. Also in the older Tractarian vein, we find a section titled "Early Warnings," which is composed of poems of admonition regarding children's behavior. The poem titles tell the story: "Effect of Example," "Danger of Praise," "Envy," "Mistrust of Elders," "Irreverence in Church," and so on. The section "Lessons of Grace" contains poems based on biblical themes complete with typological readings and moral lessons to apply to the Christian life.

But there are later Tractarian elements as well, for the volume is more consciously doctrinally Catholic than *The Christian Year*, a measure of what had come to pass since Keble composed his earlier collection in the 1820s. The largest section in the book is the one titled "Holy Places and Things." It contains such modest pre-Tractarian homely and domestic "village-style" poetry as "Preparing for Sunday Services," "Walk to Church," and "The Lich-Gate," but it also contains poems on "Relics and Memorials," "Carved Angels," and even two extraordinary performances lamenting first the "Disuse of Excommunication" and then the "Disuse of Infant Communion." In the "Early Encouragements" section, Keble offers poems on confession and absolution, and in the final section, poems on "Holy Seasons and Days," including what must be the only poem ever written on the theme of "Octaves of Festivals" ("For each and all, the eighth mysterious morn / Doth of the first tell o'er the perfect tale"). Such efforts put to the test the Tractarian conviction that everything about the Church is poetical. Finally, the *Lyra Innocentium,* even in its first edition, was prepared with devotional use in mind. The section titles are given in gothic type, and the volume was equipped with a streamer bookmark; the corners of the outside front and back covers have intaglio floral decorations, and in the center of both is a kneeling child.

The tone of the poetry of the volume shows Keble in a lighter and more joyous mood than the poetry of *The Christian Year,* but the quality of the verse has all the faults of Keble's earlier volume and will not bear close scrutiny as poetry. Its chief interest resides in the extent to which it recapitulates Tractarian methods and points the way to their adaptation in volumes by others, written later, when the poetic impact of Tractarianism had moved outward.

Tractarian Epigones

Other Tractarian and quasi-Tractarian hands were already active by the 1840s, and a glance at a few representative poets will show how the Tractarian mode was being adapted to a wider range of purpose, and to some extent even being diluted. My aim here is not to assess the achievement of the poets cited but to point in each case to aspects of Tractarian poetry that were adopted and carried onward by their poetry, that therefore extended Tractarian attitudes into religious and other kinds of poetry in the age. I have chosen five poets who first began publishing devotional poetry around the 1840s, by which time the Tractarian mode had been established.[5] Three were Oxford men, though one of them was not a Tractarian; two were Cambridge-trained but influenced by the Church revival. Two were born in the first decade of the century and were thus contemporary with the major Tractarians; three

were born in the teens and were thus university students when
the Movement was in its first flower.

The eldest of the group was Robert Stephen Hawker
(1802–1878), a poet who has attracted a good deal of attention
in his own right, chiefly for his *Quest of Sangraal* (1864).[6]
Although an Oxonian, Hawker did not become a Tractarian,
having left the University in 1829. In 1834 he became Vicar of
Morwenstow in Cornwall, where he remained until his death
in 1878. His name became so identified with the place that he
is regularly billed as "R. S. Hawker, Vicar of Morwenstow."
Shortly before his death he was received into the Roman communion.

Hawker would appear to be an example of the general
religious revival that was taking place along with Tractarianism. But what is interesting about Hawker is that he
does not emerge as a devotional poet until 1840, and then in a
volume tellingly titled *Ecclesia.* He had published poetry as
early as the 1820s, and he had shown an antiquarian bent even
then, especially in regard to the antiquities of his native Cornwall. But it is not until Tractarian poetry had become
established that we find Hawker connecting his religious inclinations to his antiquarian and folkloristic ones. From *Ecclesia* on-
wards, Hawker writes poetry imbued with a sense of the
Church as a mystical body and preoccupied with an awareness
of specific places as repositories of sanctity. I cannot document
a direct, conscious Tractarian influence, but I note that the
first idea is a fundamental Tractarian given as part of the
medieval inheritance; the second is one that the Tractarians
greatly fostered. They sought to revive the feelings of
reverence and sanctity in connection with holy places, shrines,
and relics, but in their poetry the actual places often remain
vague; they honor some holy well, some roadside shrine. Isaac
Williams went farthest toward identifying particular places in
Thoughts in Past Years, and Keble in his later poetry moved in

this direction with poems about such things as the well at Ampfield near Hursley.[7] But it is Hawker who gives this Tractarian practice a specific local habitation and a name from British antiquity. Hawker's poetry seizes upon a Tractarian devotional idea and finds it operative in the daily life of rural people. He is able to link the living present with the medieval past through the Church, gathering together themes from Keble, Newman, and Williams. His many poems on Morwenstow (the place of St. Morwenna) capture these strains best. The final stanza of "Morwennae Statio" is sufficient to indicate these Tractarian elements that Hawker carried into mid-century:

> Still points the tower, and pleads the bell;
>   The solemn arches breathe in stone;
> Window and wall have lips to tell
>   The mighty faith of days unknown.
> Yea! flood, and breeze, and battle-shock
>   Shall beat upon this church in vain:
> She stands, a daughter of the rock,
>   The changeless God's eternal fane.[8]

Richard Chenevix Trench (1807–1884) was a Cantabrigian who became, successively, Professor at King's College London, Dean of Westminster, and Archbishop of Dublin.[9] He is well known for his philological research and his role in the founding of the movement that culminated in the publication of the *Oxford English Dictionary*. His ecclesiastical career, including a close friendship with F. D. Maurice, the eminent Victorian Broad Church theologian and advocate of Christian Socialism, bespeaks moderate High Churchmanship rather than Tractarianism,[10] and yet there is about Trench's poetry an element of the devotional impulse that points to the appeal Tractarian poetry had for those not directly involved with the Movement. As early as 1835, Trench published *The Story of*

Justin Martyr, a poem rather in the tradition of sacred poetry of Robert and James Montgomery than in the Tractarian vein, except that the very choice of a martyr and apologist of the second century may imply a turning toward the apostolic Church instead of the more conventional biblical story. Many other poems by Trench are also generally pious rather than Tractarian, and many are not religious at all, for Trench wrote poems on secular themes and on observations from his travels. But in the 1838 collection *Sabbation, Honor Neale, and Other Poems* and in two volumes from 1842, *Poems from Eastern Sources,* and *Genoveva,* there is a distinctly more Catholic element, as there certainly is in his edition of *Sacred Latin Poetry* of 1849. There are poems on the cross, the Eucharist, and similar themes, but the most arresting of all of Trench's early poems is a work in ten Spenserian stanzas titled "To Poetry."

"To Poetry" is not itself a devotional poem as that term has been used here, but it could well be described as a versification of Tractarian poetic theory as adapted to Broad Church purposes. In it Trench relates an early enthusiasm for poetry that turned eventually to distaste, because poetry could not answer the deeper questions of life. He found the answer "from another shrine, / A holier oracle, a temple more divine." Having found the answer to his questions in the Church, he found also that his love for poetry had returned in a form "wiser and more true," and he came to understand what poetry is capable of doing: it can "put new robes of glory" on nature; it can "give back the sacred gift of tears." The poet therefore has "one only worthy aim," which is to use poetry to make men feel the presence of "an eternal loveliness." The two concluding stanzas show both the devotional intensity Trench brings to the subject of poetry and his avoidance of charged Tractarian words that would suggest too strongly the visible Church and her rites and privileges:

And what though loftiest fancies are not mine,
Nor words of chiefest power, yet unto me
Some voices reach out of the inner shrine,
Heard in mine heart of hearts, and I can see
At times some glimpses of the majesty,
Some prints and footsteps of the glory trace,
Which have been left on earth, that we might be
By them led forward to the secret place,
Where we perchance might see that glory face to face.

If in this quest, O power of sacred song,
Thou canst assist, — oh, never take thy flight!
If thou canst make us gladder or more strong,
If thou canst fling glimpses of glorious light
Upon life's deepest depth and highest height,
Or pour upon its low and level plain
A gleam of mellower gladness, if this might
Thou hast — (and it is thine) — then not in vain
Are we henceforth prepared to follow in the train.[11]

Frederic W. Faber (1814–1863) was an out-and-out Tractarian, one of that generation of young Oxonians of Evangelical background who was caught up in, rather than an originator of, the Movement.[12] He has been the subject of considerable scholarly study in his own right, partly as a hymnodist and partly as Newman's great rival (though as a Tractarian, his disciple) among the converts who joined the Oratory of St. Philip Neri, for he enjoyed the worldly success at the London Oratory that was for so long denied Newman in Birmingham. Faber was one of the very few (Newman was another) who was active in verse both as a Tractarian and afterwards as a Roman Catholic, and the difference between his work before and after his conversion in 1845 is instructive in surprising ways.

As a Tractarian, Faber published no fewer than five volumes of verse before "going over to Rome." These exhibit both the nature vein of Kebelian verse and the more highly wrought Catholic vein of later Tractarian poetry. The best known today is his *Cherwell Water-Lily* (1840), a volume of nature poetry in the Wordsworth-Keble manner. But it is noteworthy that he also wrote a volume on a medieval theme, *Sir Lancelot* (1844) and, immediately before his conversion, a volume titled *The Rosary* (1845) and one titled *Lives of the Saints* (1845). If *The Rosary* is more Catholic than the Tractarians were yet disposed to go, the *Lives of the Saints* is nothing more than the versification of an undertaking that Newman inaugurated with full Tractarian approval. It would seem, then, that Faber was destined to carry the Tractarian devotional impulse all the way to Rome before Newman. Instead, as a Roman Catholic, Faber abandoned devotional verse and turned his literary energies entirely to hymns. By his own admission, his models were the *Olney Hymns* and the hymns of the Wesleys. This is not to say that Faber's hymns could always be mistaken for the work of a Methodist, for the content is at times forthrightly Roman, as the title of his earliest collection, *Jesus and Mary* (1849), suggests. But, while the hymns to the Virgin and the Sacred Heart and the like have been confined to Roman use, many of Faber's other hymns have passed into common use among Protestants as well, including his best known, "My God! how wonderful Thou art!" It is as though in converting to Rome, Faber succeeded in converting also to Evangelicalism. The ultimate and ironic proof of this assertion is that Faber's "Faith of Our Fathers," written for Irish Catholics, has been appropriated by the most zealously nonconformist sects as a Protestant hymn![13]

With respect to Victorian devotional poetry, our chief interest in Faber must reside in a negative: his abandonment of devotional poetry in favor of hymnody. It is likely that in so doing he was suppressing his own inclinations toward the more literary and private devotional style in order to render what he thought would be a greater service to his new communion. He explains his intention in the preface to his first collection of hymns:

> It was natural then that an English son of St. Philip Neri should feel the want of a collection of English Catholic hymns fitted for singing. The few in the *Garden of the Soul* were all that were at hand, and of course they were not numerous enough to furnish the requisite variety. As to translation they do not express Saxon thoughts and feelings, and consequently the poor do not seem to take to them.[14]

If I may read between his lines in terms of devotional poetry, I would suggest that Faber was asserting that hymnody was a more necessary service to the Church than the self-indulgence of devotional verse, and that such hymnody must be contemporary, rather than the sort that Tractarians had fostered in encouraging translations of hymns of the early Church.

Wordsworth is said to have remarked to Faber, when told of the latter's intention to enter holy orders in 1839, that "England loses a poet."[15] But the Tractarian ethos did not operate to stifle poetry, and Faber was a very active poet for the next five years. When he entered Roman holy orders, however, Wordsworth's prophecy came true, and England lost a poet to gain a hymnodist. In a positive way, we could say that Faber bridges the distance between the Catholic leanings of Tractarians, ill disposed toward hymns, and the increasingly popular hymnody of the Evangelical movement. Though he submitted his hymnody to the standards laid down by Methodism, he brought to it as well some of the sensibility cultivated as a Tractarian devotional poet.

It was left to Edward Caswall (1814–1878) to move in the

direction that one would have expected from Faber, though Caswall did so only after first venturing into hymnody, although a hymnody different from Faber's.[16] Caswall was Faber's exact contemporary and fellow youthful Tractarian. He did not become a Roman Catholic until 1850, when he joined Newman at the Oratory, but his publication in 1849 of *Lyra Catholica* was certainly a signal. The title goes just barely beyond the purely Tractarian, though by 1849 such a title could have been accommodated by the more "advanced" members of the Movement. Like almost all of the later *Lyra* volumes, this is a collection of poems by divers hands from earlier sources, in this case almost two hundred translations from the Roman Breviary, Missal, and similar publications. But the translations are Caswall's and well done, surpassed only by the work of John Mason Neale. Though the material here is hymnody, it is the kind of hymnody that Tractarianism had favored. Caswall is merely claiming the field for Rome.

Less than a decade after the *Lyra Catholica,* Caswall published his *Masque of Mary and Other Poems* (1858). This, along with later volumes like *A May Pageant* and *A Tale of Tintern* (1865), carries the Tractarian style into Roman Catholic poetry. Other poets, like Aubrey De Vere the younger, and Coventry Patmore, would add to the chorus, but Caswall is the only one who had, though narrowly, published both as a Tractarian and as a Roman Catholic devotional poet.

The Masque of Mary contains not only the lengthy "Masque of Angels before Our Lady in the Temple," an extraordinary mating of Milton and Roman triumphalism, but also numerous devotional poems and translations indistinguishable from what might have come from a Tractarian pen, as well as many poems that are specifically anti-Anglican and anti-Tractarian.[17] Thus there are odes and miscellaneous poems on nature that are purely Tractarian ("Nature's Mysteries" could have been written by Keble or Williams) and yet others of a polemic character like "Belief of Anglicans in the Real Presence Tested," or "The Catholic Church the Bond of the World," "Catholic Ruins," and "England's Future Conversion" (from which the epigraph to the present chapter was taken), that treat Tractarians as they were wont to treat Evangelicals. Caswall thus serves to show how many Tractarian attitudes were adaptable to Roman purposes and perceptions. As the poet who carries Tractarian devotional poetry to Rome before Newman, by the default of Faber, Caswall would repay investigation for his own sake. It would not be surprising to find that he also forms a link between Tractarian devotional poetry and the poetry of Hopkins.

John Mason Neale (1818–1866) is the last of the group of poets I consider who carry Tractarian concerns into mid-century. Neale is known to students of the Victorian age both as a hymnodist and as one of the founders of the Cambridge Camden Society,[18] itself in some measure the result of Tractarianism and of Tractarian poetry, as I argued in discussing Isaac Williams. The other side of Neale's work, his mammoth achievement in hymnody, was also a consequence of an interest first evoked by Tractarian devotional poetry, and was a counterpart to Neale's ecclesiology. For Neale did for hymnody what Faber might have done and what Caswall started to do with the *Lyra Catholica*. Faber, however, turned for stylistic guidance to Evangelicalism, and Caswall, though he did other translations than those in the *Lyra Catholica,* never threw himself into hymns with the zeal or the learning of Neale.

Neale's achievement was to make available the vast treasury of hymns and devotional verse of the early Church. He also wrote some devotional poems and many original hymns on his own, but the bulk of his energies—and they were prodigious—went into translations and adaptations. Renderings of Latin, Greek, and medieval hymns and sequences poured from Neale's pen. He especially cultivated the Eastern Church, a Tractarian favorite, and wrote extensively on it. Although his skill in translation was unsurpassed ("Jerusalem the Golden" is the best known), the relevant point is that the first stirrings of interest in what was to become Neale's lifetime literary activity are to be found in Tractarianism, and specifically among the Tractarian poets with their discovery of the Breviary and their translations of Eastern hymns. The line between devotional poetry as I have defined it and hymns is never absolutely fixed, and the Tractarian poets would have made little distinction between an original poem and a translated hymn, if both conduced to worship, devotion, and sound doctrine. Neale's translations certainly did. Still, we cannot pursue Neale's achievement any more than Faber's without leaving behind the field of devotional poetry proper. It is enough to note that Neale dedicated his last volume of verse, *Sequences and Hymns and Other Ecclesiastical Verse* (1866), containing poems on Church seasons and especially the minor festivals, to the "dear memory of John Keble who departed on Maundy Thursday 1866." Neale himself followed Keble only five months later.

Hawker, Trench, Faber, Caswall, and Neale are by no means an interacting group as were the Tractarian poets proper, and they would doubtless choose to align themselves otherwise than I have done, if they could be called upon to set forth their ideas of poetic affinity. But it is not as a group in relation to each other that I have chosen them, rather as individuals each having a relation to the Tractarian poets. Though each merits attention separately as a literary figure, what matters here is the way in which they all perpetuated such features of Tractarian devotional poetry as a concern for nature as a system of signs and a source of sacramental grace, a preference for rural persons and places over urban, a passion for holy places and holy structures, a sense of the Church as a mystical body and as an enduring institution in human history, an inclination toward verse related to an external religious plan or source like the Church year, and a love for early Church hymnody and devotional works. The Tractarians invented perhaps none of these things, but they brought them together and made them available to the Victorian age.

The Tractarian Achievement

The *Lyra Innocentium* and the transitional work of those I have dubbed Tractarian Epigones recapitulate the themes and techniques of the poetry that grew out of the Oxford Movement. Even what seem to be new tones will be found on examination to be simply the stronger sounding of notes already struck by Tractarians, in principle or in practice, in the period before 1840. It would require the talents of greater poets and poets less immediately in the ambience of the Tractarian ethos to develop new possibilities in devotional poetry and to give it renewed vigor—poets like Patmore, Christina Rossetti, and Hopkins. But that is another and later story that can only be touched on in a postscript.

I hope by now the themes and techniques of Victorian devotional poetry in the Tractarian mode are clear and require no summary, but some other issues do need summation and assessment. What, for example, did the Tractarians accomplish in their poetry as poetry? Certainly it could not be argued that they left any single work of great poetry or even a single great short poem. A case can be made here and there, and I hope I have made it, for the merits of some full-length Tractarian works as poetry alone. And certainly there are some good, though not great, single poems. The total impact of *The Christian Year* is far from negligible. It is as a "single

Lyra Anglicana

Hymns and Sacred Songs

Collected and Arranged

by the

Rev. R. H. Baynes, M.A.

OF ST. EDMUND HALL, OXFORD.

LONDON

Noulston & Sons

65, PATERNOSTER ROW.

Figure 19. *Title page of Lyra Anglicana, 1870.*

Lyra Sacra:

BEING A COLLECTION OF

HYMNS

ANCIENT AND MODERN,

ODES

AND

FRAGMENTS OF SACRED POETRY

COMPILED AND EDITED, WITH A PREFACE, BY THE

REV. BOURCHIER WREY SAVILE, M.A.

Curate of Tattingstone and Chaplain to the Rt. Hon. Earl Fortescue, K.G. &c.
Author of 'The First and Second Advent'
'The Introduction of Christianity into Britain' &c.

" *Sing us one of the Songs of Zion.*"—Psalm cxxxvii. 3

LONDON:

LONGMAN, GREEN, LONGMAN, AND ROBERTS.
1861.

Figure 18. *Title page of Lyra Sacra, 1861.*

Lyra Christiana

A TREASURY OF
SACRED POETRY

EDITED BY H. L. L.

THOMAS NELSON AND SONS

London, Edinburgh, and New York

1888

Figure 20. *Title page of* Lyra Christiana, *1888.*

The Cloud of Witness

A DAILY SEQUENCE

OF

Great Thoughts from Many Minds

FOLLOWING THE CHRISTIAN SEASONS

BY THE

HON. MRS. LYTTELTON GELL

"Certain even of your own poets have said, For we are also His offspring."
"Every good gift and every perfect gift is from above, and cometh down from the Father of lights."

London
HENRY FROWDE
OXFORD UNIVERSITY PRESS WAREHOUSE
AMEN CORNER, E.C.

Figure 21. *Title page of* The Cloud of Witness, *1891.*

poem" that it succeeds in its aim of complementing the soothing tendency of the Prayer Book. Likewise, the *Lyra Apostolica* conveys its sense of urgency in ways that not even the *Tracts for the Times* succeeds in doing, and those ways depend on the poetry of the *Lyra*. Isaac Williams intensifies Keble's theologized Wordsworthianism to a degree that makes some of Williams' individual poems more worthy of being anthologized than, say, the almost unreadable dialect effusions of William Barnes or, for that matter, some of R. S. Hawker, both of whom are regularly included in large anthologies. Williams also comes close to bringing off as tours de force his grandly planned volumes on the cathedral and the two chief sacraments. These are all accomplishments as poetry, to say nothing of their literary-historical and religious significance. But most readers of poetry want more than a soothing tendency, or a sense of urgency, or nobly ambitious attempts at large-scale poetic structures. Readers who cannot bring to the reading of poetry a sympathy with the ideas the Tractarians were at pains to advance will probably not be won over by the power of the poetry alone, as readers may be won over by Milton or Spenser or Dante whether they accept their beliefs or not. Readers who do bring a religious sympathy to their reading of the Tractarians will almost certainly find them worth the reading, for that sympathy will bridge the gap between Tractarian poetic aspiration and achievement, just as sympathy with the theology of Milton or Dante intensifies the pleasure of reading them.

All of the foregoing is to say that Tractarian poetry as poetry will remain minor and specialized poetry. But I hope it will be seen as not quite so very minor as current neglect would suggest, and not minor because it is religious and devotional. Indeed, the Tractarians themselves are least successful in their attempts at purely secular poetry. Their muse was a devotional one or no muse at all. Tractarian poetry is minor in ways that much eighteenth-century poetry is minor, as James Thomson or Cowper are minor. It is minor because the poetic talents of its practitioners were minor, which is what finally determines whether any poetry is minor or major. But Tractarian devotional poetry paved the way for some poetry of high intensity that would not have appeared or would have appeared in quite different form if the Tractarians had not written. And if Tractarian poetry is minor as poetry, it is major as an indicator of a sensibility and an ethos that help define the Victorian age.

What of the larger Tractarian enterprise that includes the theory as well as the poetry? This undertaking represents a Victorian adaptation of a dimension of Romanticism that was itself fundamentally religious; the Tractarians did not so much impose a religious perception on the Romantic world view as to isolate and refine one that was already there, and then to elevate it to first place in all their thinking about literature. This resulted less in a subordination of literature to religion, as is often claimed, than in a recognition that religion and literature were kindred undertakings. In an age as aggressively secular as our own, such a view may seem misplaced, distorted, perverse, but to minds that were as imbued with religious feelings as those of the Tractarians, it seemed only natural.

The establishment, or what the Tractarians would have felt was the re-establishment, of the intimate link between religion and literature remains their most distinctive contribution and ultimately looms larger than the poetry they themselves were able to produce. For, although the idea may at first seem merely quaint, it is one that any serious student of the nature of literature must contend with. If literature is anything more than neurosis, or stimulus-response, or a toying with the painted surface of the universe, what exactly is it? Does it have anything to do with the deepest spiritual needs of humankind, and if so, are not those needs as much involved with religion as with literature? Further, if there is an involvement between the two, what is its nature? Why have the two enterprises been intertwined since earliest times? Can one stand without the other? Can one subsume the other? At the very least, Tractarian poetic theory raised these questions for the age and continues to raise them for later times. That alone is a notable accomplishment.

As for the Tractarian response to the questions about the relation of literature and religion, that too deserves respectful attention. The response is not a simple equation of literature with religion, though it runs that risk; such a caricature would apply only fitfully to some of the more extreme members of the Bisley School. Nor is the response the absorption of one by the other, though it runs that risk as well. Such a step was left to the secular critics who came after, and they sought to absorb religion into literature rather than the other way around. As Lawrence Starzyk has pointed out: "Once the validity and necessity of the Church . . . is denied, then the only remaining sanction is the internal one. In which case, imagination and faith can be regarded as synonymous, and poetry can be considered as the only suitable replacement for the dead and bankrupt religion of Christianity."[19] Of course the Tractarians would never see Christianity as dead and bankrupt, even though they recognized it to be in need of reinvigoration. Moreover, the Tractarians retained, whether they were fully aware of it or not, enough of the Germano-Coleridgean concept of *Bildung* to want to preserve both religion and literature, to revitalize the former and ennoble the latter. At its best, Tractarian thinking about literature and religion tries to distinguish without dividing, to respond to the polarity of religion and literature. They would have agreed with T. S. Eliot that "literary criticism needs to be completed by criticism from a definite ethical and theological standpoint,"[20] though they probably would have framed their perception in more fervent terms. In fact, Keble did: "Poetry lends Religion her wealth of symbols and similes: Religion restores these again to Poetry, clothed with so splendid a radiance that they appear to be no longer merely symbols, but to partake . . . of the nature of sacraments" (LP, II, 481).

Apart from the poetry and the poetic theory that the Tractarians offered, there is increasing evidence that their work had a much greater impact in the age than was once assumed. Wordsworth's authority alone did not secure for nature that reverence the Victorians paid it, and none but the Tractarians can be credited with many specifically religious concerns that inform Victorian life and literature. As has been noted, they unintentionally contributed to the later transference, or attempted transference, of spiritual authority to literature by helping to formulate questions about the relationship of the two. The Tractarians themselves would have found the Arnoldian and later Aesthetic exaltations of literature over religion distasteful, just as they would find the contemporary critic-as-high-priest of the literary mysteries a case of parading in borrowed robes. But a knowledge of their position aids us in understanding what came after them and perhaps offers a perspective from which to assess later developments. As for particular influence and points of contact with other Victorian writers and other fields of artistic endeavor in the age, I have tried to indicate some of these in passing; the reader familiar with the age will doubtless have discerned others that went unremarked or escaped my notice. The subject is large enough for a study of its own. But there is one consequence of Tractarian poetry and poetic theory that must be separately stressed: in however much else they failed, they succeeded in the one thing that mattered to them — their impact on the Church itself.

Knowledge of ecclesiastical history is even rarer today than sympathy with a religious outlook, so most of us are unaware of the character of worship in churches of every denomination in the English-speaking world before the Oxford Movement. At the risk of overgeneralization, one can say simply that such worship was prosaic. This applies to a great extent even to worship in the Roman Catholic Church in England, and it certainly applies to Anglican and dissenting Churches. As a consequence of the Oxford Movement all this changed. The story has been told more than once. What is not so widely recognized is that the changes came about more through the theory and the poetry of Tractarian and post-Tractarian devotionalism than through any other source. As might be expected, the Victorian observer who perceived this most clearly was John Henry Newman. Even he did not see as far as we can with hindsight, for he spoke of the transformation of only the Church of England and credited it only to John Keble, but I think we should read his remarks in the light of what has been shown about Victorian devotional poetry and be ready to extend them to other churches, including Newman's own, and to credit other poets along with Keble, including Newman himself.

It was in his 1846 essay on Keble that Newman was moved to launch into that sublime encomium on the Catholic Church as poetry that may be seen as the final resting place of Tractarian theory:

Poetry is the refuge of those who have not the Catholic Church to flee to and repose upon, for the Church herself is the most sacred and august of poets. Poetry, as Mr. Keble lays it down in his University Lectures on the subject, is a method of relieving the over-burdened mind; it is a channel through which emotion finds expression, and that a safe, regulated expression. Now what is the Catholic Church, viewed in her human aspect, but a discipline of the affections and passions? What are her ordinances and practices but the regulated expression of keen, or deep, or turbid feeling, and thus a "cleansing," as Aristotle would word it, of the sick soul? She is the poet of her children; full of music to soothe the sad and control the way-ward, — wonderful in story for the imagination of the roman-tic; rich in symbol and imagery, so that gentle and delicate feelings, which will not bear words, may in silence intimate their presence or commune with themselves. Her very being is poetry; every psalm, every petition, every collect, every versicle, the cross, the mitre, the thurible, is a fulfilment of some dream of childhood, or aspiration of youth. Such poets as are born under her shadow, she takes into her service; she sets them to write hymns, or to compose chants, or to embellish shrines, or to determine ceremonies, or to marshal processions; nay, she can even make schoolmen of them, as she made St. Thomas, till logic becomes poetical. (N, *Essays,* I, 442–443)

Newman follows this immediately with a denunciation of the pre-Tractarian Church of England that documents my generalization about the prosaic character of pre-Tractarian worship as only Newman, who had lived through it, could:

Now the author of the Christian Year found the Anglican system all but destitute of this divine element, which is an essen-tial property of Catholicism; — a ritual dashed upon the ground, trodden on, and broken piece-meal; — prayers, clipped, pieced, torn, shuffled about at pleasure, until the meaning of the com-position perished, and offices which had been poetry were no longer even good prose; — antiphons, hymns, benedictions, in-vocations, shovelled away; — Scripture lessons turned into chapters; — heaviness, feebleness, unwieldiness, where the Catholic rites had had the lightness and airiness of a spirit; — vestments chucked off, lights quenched, jewels stolen, the pomp and circumstances of worship annihilated; a dreariness which could be felt, and which seemed the token of an incipient Socinianism, forcing itself upon the eye, the ear, the nostrils of the worshipper; a smell of dust and damp, not of incense; a sound of ministers preaching Catholic prayers, and parish clerks droning out Catholic canticles; the royal arms for the crucifix; huge ugly boxes of wood, sacred to preachers, frowning on the congregation in the place of the mysterious altar; and long cathedral aisles unused, railed off, like the tombs (as they were,) of what had been and was not; and for orthodoxy, a frigid, unelastic, inconsistent, dull, helpless dogmatic, which could give no just account of itself, yet was intolerant of all teaching which contained a doctrine more or a doctrine less, and resented every attempt to give it a meaning, — such was the religion of which this gifted author was, — not the judge and denouncer, (a deep spirit of reverence hindered it,) — but the renovator, as far as it has been renovated. (N, *Essays,* I, 443–444)

The passage is alive with the themes and images and even the language of Tractarian poetry, as Newman implies what worship should be. The renovation he attributes to Keble came through Keble's poetry: "His happy magic made the Anglican Church seem what Catholicism was and is. The established system found to its surprise that it had been all its life talking not prose, but poetry." Remembering the weight borne in Tractarian thinking by the words "poetry" and "poetical," we can recognize the supreme tribute intended by Newman to Keble in the previous remark and in this one from the same essay: "He did for the Church of England what none but a poet could do: he made it poetical."

That is, finally, the achievement of Victorian devotional poetry in the Tractarian mode: it made the Church poetical.

VII

Postscript: Christina Rossetti and Gerard Manley Hopkins

IN CONTRAST TO Victorian adulation of Keble and genuine Victorian affection and respect for the poetry of Newman and Williams, the modern response to Tractarian poetry, where there has been a response, has been mainly negative. Hoxie Neale Fairchild dismissed the work of the younger Aubrey De Vere, for example, by describing it as a vain attempt "to sprinkle the moribund Wordsworth's nature poetry with holy water."[1] Such was largely Fairchild's estimate of the poetry of all the writers considered in this book, and Fairchild's is but a characteristically dismissive expression of a generally held contemporary view. Modern anthologies would seem to bear out such an assessment. Newman and Keble have been very sparingly anthologized, and then only in the largest modern collections of Victorian poetry; Isaac Williams has been overlooked entirely. In the matter of Victorian religious poetry, contemporary favor has fallen not on the Tractarians but on a few other, later poets. These are, in descending order of contemporary esteem, Gerard Manley Hopkins, Christina Rossetti, Coventry Patmore, and Francis Thompson.

Hopkins, of course, stands in the modern estimate head and shoulders above the rest, and most moderns would accord only Hopkins, among the names cited, something like major status. Serious status would be accorded Christina Rossetti, with opinion probably equally divided as to whether she is a poet of the first or second rank. Patmore and Thompson would be regarded as interesting but distinctly minor voices. The Tractarians, of course, would trail off after even these. How is it that the poets involved with the most ambitious religious movement in the nineteenth century and the poets who developed the most extensive system of poetics should have turned out to be for modern taste so entirely negligible, while the few religious poets who have endured into our time seem to have been working apart from the Tractarian impulse? The purpose of this brief postscript is to point to an answer to that question, or perhaps simply to underline a dawning awareness that the question must now be regarded as misdirected.

In his fine treatment of Christina Rossetti in the chapter titled "Uphill all the Way,"[2] Raymond Chapman has made the long-overdue case for seeing Christina Rossetti as directly and fully a product of the Oxford Movement. I not only second this view but offer the further claim that Christina Rossetti is the true inheritor of the Tractarian devotional mode in poetry. Most of what the Tractarians advocated in theory and sought to put into practice came to fruition in the poetry of Christina Rossetti. Certainly the evidence for her Tractarianism has always existed, and even in some degree been acknowledged by biographers and critics — in the recorded religious practices of the Rossetti women, in the involvement of Christina and her sister with Anglican sisterhoods, and of course in certain undeniably devotional poems. But the insistently biographical bias of most of Christina Rossetti's critics has focused attention instead on her real or imagined life crises, and consequently on poems that cast light or can be made to cast light on her life. Nor has the linkage of Christina Rossetti with the Pre-Raphaelites helped to clarify her affinities with Tractarian poetry, though the problem of emphasis and interpretation in respect to the religious element in pre-Raphaelitism is yet more complex than merely her relation to the group. What is needed is a new look, which Chapman has so helpfully initiated, at Christina Rossetti as a devotional poet, one that takes account of the preceding generation of Tractarian poetry as a seedfield for much of her own verse.

In the William Michael Rossetti edition of Christina's poetry,[3] the poems are somewhat confusingly organized into six main divisions: The Longer Poems, Juvenilia, Devotional Poems, General Poems, Poems for Children and Minor Verse, and Italian Poems. The largest single category is that of the Devotional Poems (almost two hundred of the nearly five hundred pages of poetry), and even the next largest category, General Poems, contains many poems that could as easily be called devotional as general, to say nothing of the numerous nature poems in this category that bear heavy religious overtones. To observe that Christina Rossetti is primarily a devotional poet is not new, but the observation deserves stressing, in light of the biographical emphasis of criticism and the tendency of anthologies to underrepresent the devotional component of her whole output. It is also necessary to consider what we mean by devotional poetry in the case of Christina Rossetti.

Christina Rossetti is a devotional poet in the strict sense in which I have used the term in this study, a sense that is meaningful in the nineteenth century only as a consequence of the Tractarian experience. Hers is a poetry that grows out of the act of worship, poetry that is frequently tied to established forms of worship and liturgical observance. This sort of poetry was what the Tractarians made accessible again to English literature after more than a century of dominance of religious poetry by hymns and sacred verse. Except for an occasional Christopher Smart or an occasional ordering of a few hymns along lines of the Church year, devotional poetry as the Tractarians understood it had not been seen in England since the seventeenth century. When one comes upon Christina Rossetti without awareness of the intervention of the Tractarians, one is inclined to think she has sprung full-grown from the brow of George Herbert; yet when one comes upon her poetry from an encounter with the Tractarians, one can see that her genesis is of a more conventional kind.

Consider, for example, the prominence in Christina Rossetti's poetry of poems on the Church year. "Some Feasts and Fasts"[4] contains no fewer than sixty-eight poems organized on the Kebelian pattern from Advent Sunday through the Church year by major feast days and saints' days. Although she does not provide poems for every Sunday, she does follow the ordering in the Book of Common Prayer (and therefore in *The Christian Year*) in assembling the poems for major Sundays and feasts first, followed by the named saints' days. She takes greater liberties than Keble, offering, for example, three poems on Good Friday ("Good Friday Morning," "Good Friday," and "Good Friday Evening"), and certain other feast days inspire her to more than a single poem (Whitsunday, the Presentation, and the Annunciation). The inescapable Tractarian and devotional element lies in the fact that it is possible to assemble a kind of *Christian Year* from her many devotional poems, so frequently do they turn on the annual sequence of worship.

Her devotional poetry is marked by other typical Tractarian concerns as well as by the preoccupation with the

Church year. There are many poems in groups, like "Songs for Strangers and Pilgrims" inspired by the act of prayer ("Praying Always"), biblical passages and citations ("Balm in Gilead"), holy places ("God's Acre"), and parts of the worship service ("Sursum Corda"). One of her devotional categories, "Christ Our All in All," reflects the intense Incarnationalism that the Tractarians cultivated, especially Keble and Isaac Williams. Both the Keblian kind of Christology and the later, more passionate Isaac Williams sort are there: "Lord, hast Thou so loved us, and will not we / Love Thee with heart and mind and strength and soul" (p. 225) could almost have come from *The Christian Year*, while

> Lord Jesu, Thou art sweetness to my soul:
>> I to myself am bitterness:
> Regard my fainting struggle toward the goal,
>> Regard my manifold distress,
>>> O Sweet Jesu.
>
> (p. 224)

could have been the work of Isaac Williams, or indeed, of Newman. And when she begins a poem: "Have I not striven, my God and watched and prayed? / Have I not wrestled in mine agony?" (p.228), one hears the echo of Hurrell Froude in "Weakness of Nature" from the *Lyra*.

Indeed, one could illustrate almost every Tractarian topic and interest cited in the main part of this book with poems from the pen of Christina Rossetti. Exceptions would be doctrinally polemic poems and poems written as hymns, for Christina Rossetti was neither a theological controversialist nor a hymnodist. Some of her poems, to be sure, have found their way into hymnals, but only one, the hauntingly beautiful "In the Bleak Midwinter," can be said to be fully established as a hymn.

The same Tractarian tendencies are at work in her so-called

prose works, which are in many instances more like the hybrid forms of Isaac Williams than like conventional prose writings. Among these we have *Annus Domini, A Prayer for Each Day of the Year, Founded on a Text of Holy Scripture* (1874); *Called to Be Saints: The Minor Festivals Devotionally Studied* (1881); *Time Flies: A Reading Diary* (1885); and *The Face of the Deep: A Devotional Commentary on the Apocalypse* (1892). These are normally interspersed with poems, and editions of these works as well as of her *Verses* are pure Tractarian bibliographic undertakings, with missal-like ruled lines and gothic typefaces that had been established as early as the 1830s for Tractarian devotional poetry.

Stylistically, Christina Rossetti is a far finer poet than her Tractarian predecessors, and certainly the seventeenth-century example was more profitably studied by her than by Keble. But even in matters of style there are distinct affinities with the Tractarians. Like Keble, Christina Rossetti was stanzaically experimental and inventive. Like Newman, however, she preferred the brief line and the concentrated utterance. Like all Tractarians, she was receptive to nature as a vehicle of divine grace, and especially like Isaac Williams, she was willing to bring an intense personal response to nature as a religious experience. It is probably not accidental that she appeared to have had no special fondness for Keble's verse but a genuine liking for that of Isaac Williams,[5] and of course a deep admiration for Newman as a human being, as attested to by her well-known poem on Newman's death in 1890.

But finally, Christina Rossetti's most Tractarian element is her very approach to poetry itself as a way of seeking the Deity. Keble's bedrock principle that poetry is the expression of intense religious longing finds no more complete exemplification than in the poetry of Christina Rossetti. The biographical approach to her poetry, the strange, modern view that all longing must be sexual, especially if it is the longing of an unmarried Victorian woman, has obscured the extent to which Christina Rossetti's poetry illustrates not Freud's theory of art but Keble's. Much has been made of Christina Rossetti's yearnings in psychological terms, but not enough has been made of them in religious terms. Put in the context of Tractarian poetics, however, her yearnings are the material from which poetry and art proceed.

In the lead poem of her section "New Jerusalem and Its Citizens" in *Verses* Christina Rossetti strikes all the Tractarian notes: typology, nature, art, liturgical forms, and above all, the yearning for oneness with God. The final stanza expresses her view, and the Tractarian view, of the end and aim of art and all earthly striving:

> Jerusalem, where song nor gem
>   Nor fruit nor waters cease,
> God bring us to Jerusalem,
>   God bring us home in peace;
> The strong who stand, the weak who fall,
> The first and last, the great and small,
> Home one by one, home one and all.
>
> (p. 206)

If the problem of seeing Christina Rossetti as a devotional poet in the Tractarian mode arises from a lack of familiarity with Tractarian poetry and from a curiously sexist approach (not least of all by women) to her poetry, the problem of seeing Gerard Manley Hopkins' connection with Tractarian poetry arises from a misperception of his relation to the age, that is, the view that sees Hopkins as standing entirely apart from the times in which he lived. For those who hold such an ahistorical view of Hopkins, the enterprise of linking him to the unregarded poetry of the early part of the age would seem to be an exercise in reductionist frivolity. Yet even Hopkins has some affinities with the Tractarian mode that cast light on his practices as a poet.

Figure 22. *Christina Rossetti and mother, by D. G. Rossetti, 1877.*

Thanks to the work of Wendell Stacy Johnson and Allison Sulloway, we can now take it as established that Hopkins is, among other things, a Victorian poet.[6] And thanks especially to Sulloway, we can now take it as established that Hopkins was both a Tractarian and a Tractarian poet. Her study provides the necessary intellectual background to Hopkins' early development as man and poet — the late Tractarian wars at Oxford in the 1860s, Hopkins' own full-blown Tractarianism under the tutelage of E. B. Pusey and Henry Parry Liddon, the parallels between Hopkins and that other late Tractarian boy-poet, Digby Mackworth Dolben (who was also preserved for posterity through the offices of Robert Bridges),[7] and Hopkins' own submission to Rome through Newman. To read Sulloway's account awakens echoes of the early course of

Figure 23. *Gerard Manley Hopkins at 15, by Anne Hopkins, 1859.*

Tractarianism at Oxford and expecially of Newman's development in the Tractarian years. The important difference is that
Hopkins came to his maturity long after the Tractarian mode
in poetry had been established and well after other developments in Victorian life and literature had taken place, developments that had no parallels in the experience of the early Tractarians. Thus Sulloway pays due attention not only to the
Tractarianism of Oxford of the sixties, but also to influences

like Pater and Ruskin. Hopkins is the product of religious and aesthetic influences that encompass Tractarianism and much more. Sulloway's treatment makes clear that the influences on Hopkins very much include Tractarianism.

We may take the biographical case for Hopkins as a Tractarian as demonstrated. We can also take the case for many elements of Tractarianism in Hopkins' poetry as demonstrated, for Sulloway has noted a number of similarities between Hopkins' poetry and Tractarian concerns, though not Tractarian poetry as such. She notes Hopkins' intense love of Oxford as a typically Oxonian and Tractarian attitude, his early interest in nature as a subject for poetry, his concern as a post-Romantic for the problems involved in approaching nature, and even his awakening at Oxford to the merits of Gothic architecture. These Tractarian concerns are also tied to Tractarian poetry.

With Hopkins, as with Christina Rossetti, one ought to begin rather than to end with the observation that his poetics, much as they owe to non-Tractarian sources,[8] have affinities with the Tractarian linkage of poetry and prayer. There is, morevoer, in Hopkins' approach to poetry, a good deal of the Tractarian yearning after an object out of reach, an object that Hopkins, like the Tractarians, would equate with God. In Hopkins there is also a firm conviction that poetry should serve religion, though this conviction was clearly won at greater expense for Hopkins than it was for the Tractarians, who perceived no conflict between the two. Finally, Hopkins exhibits an even more powerful sense than Keble of the overburdened spirit characteristic of the poet. One suspects that much of this attitude toward poetry was imbibed rather than reasoned out by Hopkins when he was a young Oxford Tractarian. Sulloway mentions the Oxford climate of "moral intensity" characteristic of Hopkins and of the Tractarianism of his poetry: "The accounts of moral crises in so much of

Hopkins' poetry—the little vignettes of almost helpless humans held at bay by the forces of evil and protected only feebly by the thin strand of Christ's love—correspond exactly to the atmosphere of imminent catastrophe that he endured all during his residence at Oxford" (pp. 26-27). It would be possible, I think, to make a strong case for the extent to which Hopkins' ideas about poetry descend not only from his personal experiences at Oxford but also from the poetics that the Tractarians had worked out by the time of Hopkins' birth.

But the points at which Hopkins and Tractarian poetry most strikingly come together are nature, sacramentalism, and incarnationalism, three of the most often remarked features of Hopkins' poetry. Hopkins himself once observed that "the Lake School expires in Keble and Faber and Cardinal Newman."[9] The Lake School perhaps, but certainly not nature poetry, and certainly not nature sacramentalism. The difference between Hopkins and the Tractarians is that Hopkins can no longer accept as a given the Kebelian book of nature or the Butlerian analogy of religion, as the poem "Nondum" from the year of his conversion shows. At the same time, what he seeks to do in his nature poetry is to take by force of language the very analogies that the Tractarians thought were readily at hand in received biblical and patristic typology and analogy. Even an original and individual poem like "The Windhover" is based on the principle of analogy, albeit analogy freshly perceived by an observer next to whose tumultuous vision the nature views of Keble and Faber appear myopic. Even more specific by way of drawing analogies is his "The Blessed Virgin Compared to the Air We Breathe," in which the Caswall-like veneration of the Virgin finds expression in a freshly experienced comparison:

> I say that we are wound
> With mercy round and round

As if with air: the same
Is Mary, more by name.
She, wild web, wondrous robe,
Mantles the guilty globe,
Since God has let dispense
Her prayers his providence:
Nay more than almoner,
The sweet alms' self is her
And men are meant to share
Her life as life does air.[10]

The way that Hopkins perceives God's superintending design, His love, and His infinite variety in nature is a kind of Analogy rediscovered and made new. In the three Hopkins sonnets (a favored Romantic and Tractarian form), "God's Grandeur," "The Starlight Night," and "Spring," are there not echoes of Isaac Williams on nature expressed in "The Skreen: Disciplina Arcani," "In earth's deep mines or ocean's cells, / Her secret glory dwells"? Is not nature's secret glory "the dearest freshness deep down things" of "God's Grandeur"? In "The Starlight Night" one is exhorted to look in hidden places for nature's glory: "Down in dim woods the diamond delves! the elves'-eyes!" And in "Spring," Hopkins tells us that "all this juice and all this joy" of nature are "A strain of the earth's sweet being in the beginning / In Eden garden," which is a new way of saying that nature still contains signs of the Maker, that she still teaches by analogy.

Perhaps Hopkins would have come upon all this without the benefit of Tractarian devotional poetry. Certainly his is no servile imitation, unlike so much that followed in Keble's wake, but given the Tractarian background of Hopkins' own religious experience, Hopkins' attitude toward nature and analogy seem to be Tractarianism reborn, forged anew in a Heraclitean fire.

Once one thinks of Hopkins' poetry in the light of Tractarian devotional poetry, many other points of correspondence come into focus. For example, Hopkins has left a fragment on that old typological standby, the rainbow, some fragments relating to St. Winefred and her well (which Hopkins visited several times) that call to mind the Tractarian love of sacred places, and several poems on the city of Oxford that mix Keble's and Williams' Tractarian reverence with Newman's post-Tractarian sense of loss. Though Hopkins is in the main no controversialist in poetry, "The Wreck of the Deutschland" contains more than a hint of the confessional partisanship initiated by the Tractarians and later deployed against them by converts to Rome. "Our king back, Oh, upon English souls!" is a vast improvement upon Caswall, but it carries a similar meaning.

All that is missing from Hopkins' work seems to be that Tractarian fondness for poems on the liturgical calendar, or poems written to order, illustrating some Church principle or form. In this respect, Hopkins is far less oriented toward the visible Church than the Tractarians and their immediate successors, or than Christina Rossetti. One looks in vain in Hopkins for any appreciable number of poems on feast and fast days, or even on religious practices. The one exception is Hopkins' special fondness for poems on the Eucharist, as in "The Bugler's First Communion" or "Morning, Midday, and Evening Sacrifice." His youthful poems "Easter Communion" and "Easter" show that his devotion to the Eucharist had been longstanding. These are also interesting poems that bridge the gap between the standard Tractarian mode and the style of the mature Hopkins. "Easter" indeed reads almost as though it were written by Keble and revised for greater impact by Christina Rossetti, especially the final stanza:

> Seek God's house in happy throng;
> Crowded let His table be;
> Mingle praises, prayer and song,

> Singing to the Trinity.
> Henceforth let your souls alway
> Make each morn an Easter Day.

Even so, for all the talk by critics of sacramentalism, Hopkins is less concerned with the sacraments per se than the Tractarians, and more concerned with sacramental elements in nature. Perhaps the novelty of venerating the sacraments had already worn off. By Hopkins' time a high degree of elaborated worship and conscious sacramentalism could be taken for granted within the Anglican Church itself. Hopkins as an undergraduate made his regular confession to Dr. Pusey, whereas in earlier times, Keble and Pusey had served each other as confessors, and Pusey's encouragement of the sacrament of penance, especially among women, was looked upon as daring, if not diabolical.

Hopkins' celebrated Incarnationalism is another central feature of his poetry linking him to Tractarianism. The similarity between Hopkins and the Tractarians on the Incarnation is not so evident as some other similarities because Hopkins is no longer restrained by a notion of Reserve as reticence, or at least not in the same way as the Tractarians. Thus, in Hopkin's poetry, Christ emerges as a creature of brute beauty, valor, and act. On the other hand, Reserve as indirection, as a veiled mode of speaking, is still operative in Hopkins. The whole impact of "The Windhover" turns on the indirection created by the absence of explicit reference to Christ and by the implication of the analogy through the dedicatory subtitle. In other poems where Christ is explicitly mentioned, it is almost always in terms of some perceived likeness between Christ and nature or a quality in nature, and only after the initial depiction of that quality does Hopkins draw the parallel with Christ. The effect in Hopkins' nature poems of the delayed introduction of Christ by which the preceding lines are then illuminated is the effect of going at last beyond the screen, taking the reader to the teaching of the secret. Even Isaac Williams would have felt that Hopkins managed it with due reverence and appropriate sense of awe and wonder.

Hopkins, then, so long viewed as an isolated and inexplicable phenomenon among Victorian poets, was in many respects a successor to the Tractarian mode in devotional poetry. That he transcended the achievements of his predecessors is not to be denied. But to see him steadily and whole is to recognize that he also fulfilled the hopes for poetry advanced so fervently by the Tractarians of an earlier generation.

Neither Christina Rossetti nor Gerard Manley Hopkins, nor indeed the other mid- and late-Victorian devotional poets mentioned in passing, can be entirely encompassed by the principles of Tractarian devotional poetry. But these poets can be illuminated by these principles, as I hope this study has shown. What is more, the later poets can in turn illuminate the Tractarian poetic impulse itself. The later poets show that the currents set in motion by poets like Keble, Newman, and Williams did not cease to flow at the close of the Tractarian phase of the Oxford Movement, nor even long after. On the contrary, much of what Tractarian devotional poetry offered became a permanent part of the Victorian religious and poetic experience, a living tradition for the rest of the age. The work of the later poets shows also that the Tractarian poets, whatever their shortcomings as poets, were not tilling alien soil. Poetry and religion could flourish in the same field, even in an age assailed by doubt. The Tractarians themselves employed their talents chiefly for the purpose of making the Church once again poetical. The later Victorian devotional poets employed theirs for the purpose of making poetry once again religious.

Works, Persons, Events in Tractarian Devotional Poetry to 1850

1792	Birth of John Keble (d. 1866)
1798	Birth of J. W. Bowden (d. 1844)
1800	Birth of E. B. Pusey (d. 1882)
	Birth of R. I. Wilberforce (d. 1857)
1801	Birth of John Henry Newman (d. 1890)
1802	Birth of Isaac Williams (d. 1867)
	Birth of R. S. Hawker (d. 1878)
1814	"Copleston's *Praelectiones Academicae*" (Keble)
	Birth of F. W. Faber (d. 1863)
	Birth of Edward Caswall (d. 1878)
1818	Birth of John Mason Neale (d. 1866)
1823	Birth of Coventry Patmore (d. 1896)
1825	"Sacred Poetry" (Keble)
1827	*The Christian Year* (Keble)
1829	"Poetry with Reference to Aristotle's Poetics" (Newman)
1830	Birth of Christina Rossetti (d. 1894)
1832	*Origines Liturgicae* (W. Palmer)
1832-1833	Newman's and Froude's Mediterranean trip
1832-1841	Keble serves as Professor of Poetry at Oxford
1833	The Assize Sermon, "National Apostasy" (Keble)

	Birth of R. W. Dixon (d. 1900)
1833-1836	"Lyra Apostolica" in *British Magazine*
1833-1841	*Tracts for the Times*
1836	*Lyra Apostolica* (book publication)
	Hymni Ecclesiae (Newman)
	Death of Hurrell Froude
1838	*The Cathedral* (Williams)
	"On Reserve in Communicating Religious Knowledge," Tract 80 (Williams)
	Thoughts in Past Years (Williams)
	"Life of Sir Walter Scott" (Keble)
	Sabbation, Honor Neale (Trench)
	Hymns from the Parisian Breviary (Williams)
	Founding of the Cambridge Camden Society, later the Ecclesiological Society
1838-1839	*Remains* (R. H. Froude)
1840	"On Reserve in Communicating Religious Knowledge," Tract 87 (Williams)
	"On the Mysticism of the Early Fathers," Tract 89 (Keble)
	Ecclesia (Hawker)
	The Cherwell Water-lily (Faber)
1841	Tract 90 (Newman) — cessation of Tracts
1842	*The Baptistery* (Williams)
1843	*Symbolism of Churches and Church Ornaments* (Neale)
1844	*Praelectiones Academicae* (Keble)
	Sir Lancelot (Faber)
	Birth of Gerard Manley Hopkins (d. 1889)
1845	*The Rosary* (Faber)
	Newman and Faber join Roman Catholic Church
1846	*Lyra Innocentium* (Keble)
	"John Keble" (Newman)
1847	*The Altar* (Williams)
1849	*Lyra Catholica* (Caswall)
	Sacred Latin Poetry (Trench)
	Jesus and Mary (Faber)
1850	*The Seven Days* (Williams)
	Caswall joins Roman Catholic Church

Appendix B

Antecedents of
The Christian Year

DESPITE THE PERMEATION of British religious life by the language and forms of the Book of Common Prayer, no previous collection of verse or independent work of literature had been modelled so conspicuously on the Prayer Book as *The Christian Year*. Still, it was common in the Victorian age to allude to possible models for Keble's plan, and Keble's own avoidance of originality may seem to imply that he must have been following some predecessor in organizing his poems as he did. Because I have stressed the importance of the originality of Keble's method in *The Christian Year* for subsequent devotional poetry in the age, it seems advisable to direct some attention to antecedent works that share some of his organizing principles, if only to make clear the extent to which Keble's volume goes beyond them in its single-minded adherence to a pre-existing literary form.

The earliest possible antecedent work is the collection of hymns by Venantius Fortunatus (c. 530-609) *Hymns for All the Festivals of the Christian Year*. But the work itself is lost and only the title survives. Fortunatus could well have been known to Keble, for he was almost certainly the author of the well-known "Vexilla Regis," most of the other poems claimed for him being of disputed authorship. His work appears in Trench's *Sacred Latin Poetry* and of course hymns attributed to him were translated by John Mason Neale. But even if known to Keble, Fortunatus' cycle of hymns would have been a model in name only.

The earliest English-language collection that could have offered inspiration to Keble is not mentioned by Victorian commentators, but it offers a closer parallel than all but one other collection before Keble. It is George Wither's *Hymns and Songs of the Church* (1623). This work falls into two parts, the first being hymns based on the Bible, the second part anticipating Keble, called "Spirtual Songs appropriate to those times, in which are commemorated the principle Mysteries of the Christian Religion." This part totals thirty-five such spiritual songs keyed to the Church year and is followed by a group of songs for "other solemnities"; and to "praise God for public benefits." The first sixteen of the liturgically keyed songs are related to the major festivals (but not every Sunday) between Advent and Trinity Sunday; these are followed by nineteen songs for named saints' days. Though a total of thirty-five songs is a far cry from Keble's 109 poems, the order of the songs according to part of the liturgical calendar is strikingly similar. However, there is no evidence that Keble knew this work.

Commonly in the Victorian age *The Christian Year* was assumed to have been inspired by George Herbert's *The Temple* (1633); there is no question that Keble knew and revered Herbert's poetry. In *The Temple* there are poems for many of the feasts and fasts provided for in the Book of Common Prayer, poems about such days as Christmas, Good Friday, Easter, and Whitsunday, as well as about certain sacraments, such as Baptism, Communion, and Confession. (There are also poems on the physical aspects of a church, like those on church monuments and windows and the church porch. These may have been suggestive to Isaac Williams.) But *The Temple* contains much more, contains in fact Herbert's poetical works, including the often anthologized poems "Jordan," "The Elixir," "Affliction," and "The Pulley," that bear no relation to an overall external pattern in the ecclesiastical year or in ecclesiastical architecture. Even the poems on Church festivals and practices do not appear in a single unbroken sequence. It may well be, as T. S. Eliot finally decided, that *The Temple* has a unity of tone and spirit that makes it a single work, or as Stanley Fish has recently argued, a unity in terms of established procedures of catechizing, rendering the catechumen a "living temple" (*The Living Temple* [Berkeley, 1978]; however, its unity is not that of being a companion to the Book of Common Prayer. Given the Tractarian reverence for Herbert and the seventeenth-century Church, it is very possible that *The Temple* gave Keble the idea for the *The Christian Year*, because of its poems that do relate specifically to the Prayer Book and because of the devotional nature of its poetry in general, but it cannot be called a model.

Considerably closer to Keble—and closer yet to Isaac Williams—is the little known work of Christopher Harvey (1597-1663) titled "The Synagogue" (1640), which up to now has not been noted as a possible forerunner of Keble's volume. I discovered it as an appendix to a Victorian edition of *Herbert's Poetical Works* edited by the Scottish clergyman George Gilfillan (Edinburgh, 1853). "The Synagogue" was frankly inspired by Herbert's *Temple*. It is more rigorous in visible organization than *The Temple* (though of course much inferior as poetry) and is therefore of greater formal interest in terms of *The Christian Year*. It is also so little known as to require more explication.

Like *The Temple*, "The Synagogue" begins with an organization based on the physical structure of a church, starting, in fact, in the churchyard and moving in successive poems somewhat doggedly past the churchstile, the churchgate, the churchwalls, into the church itself. Once inside, the poet continues with poems on physical features of a church like the "Church-utensils," "The Font," "The Reading-Pew," and the like. Then there begins a sequence on the officers of the church: the sexton, clerk, overseer of the poor, churchwarden, deacon, priest, and bishop. Then, and most interesting for the student of *The Christian Year*, Harvey offers a poem called "Church Festivals," which is in turn followed by a sequence of ten poems on important liturgical feasts: The Sabbath, the Annunciation, the Nativity, the Circumcision, the Epiphany, the Passion, the Resurrection, the Ascension, Whitsunday, and Trinity Sunday. The remaining fifteen poems in the volume have no correspondence to any external pattern, either architectural or liturgical, but are, like the poems in *The Temple*, miscellaneous devotional poems, with titles like "Invitation," "Confusion," "A Paradox," "The Curb," "The Loss," and so on. Harvey's indebtedness to Herbert, revealed by the titles, is even more evident in the style and substance of these poems.

Harvey's sequential arrangement of poems (at first architectural and then liturgical) is carried out with somewhat greater consistency than Herbert's, but it still falls far short of the more rigorous organization of Keble's later collection. Harvey's volume is instructive for an understanding of Keble's work, however, in that it reveals even more clearly than Herbert's a tendency to seek an external model as a means of heightening and disciplining devotion. It also exhibits some of the problems inherent in writing poems to fit such a model, problems very like those encountered by a writer of occasional verse when the occasion does not always inspire. There is, for example, a poem in the church appointments sequence on the Book of Common Prayer. It comes immediately after the poem on the reading-pew, for the Prayer Book would be the object first encountered by the worshiper seated in his pew. That Keble alone occasionally falters when confronted with the task of writing a poem to order for a particular part of his plan is a notion that can be dispelled by the first stanza of Harvey's poem on the Book of Common Prayer:

> What! Prayer by the book? and Common?
>   Yes. Why not?
>   The spirit of grace,
>   And supplication,
>   Is not left free alone
>   For time and place;
> But manner too. To read, or speak by rote
>   Is all alike to him that prays
>   With's heart, that with his mouth he says.

Apart from the contorted syntax, one is struck in this and in other of Harvey's poems in "The Synagogue" by an aggressive tone that indicates the extent to which his collection is a polemic to defend High Anglicanism against Presbyterianism, for in many other poems he also begins with a challenge: "The Font, I say. Why not? And why not near / To the Church door? Why not of stone?," or "The Bishop? Yes, why not? What doth that name / Import that is unlawful, or unfit?" Keble, whose poems were directed more against indifference and the lethargy of custom, rarely strikes such a contenious note in *The Christian Year*. That note was reserved for the *Lyra Apostolica*.

In both Herbert's and Harvey's verse one should note too the prevalence of physically patterned verse like that especially associated with Francis Quarles and the seventeenth-century emblematists, best known from Herbert's "Easter Wings." In Harvey's case, there is rarely any readily discernible pattern that his poem mimics. The lineation of the poem on the Prayer Book, for example, appears merely arbitrary. Although Keble did not attempt such pattern verse, the use of it in seventeenth-century poetry may have contributed to his general receptivity to the idea of subordinating poetry to an exterior model. It is more probable, however, that if Keble received any impulses from the seventeenth-century poets of the High-Church tradition, they are to be found in the glancing hints at organization by the liturgical year in Herbert, Harvey, and Wither, assuming Keble knew of the last two.

The use of illustrations in seventeenth-century emblem verse may also have stimulated Keble's thinking about the presentation of his own volume, for at one time he considered publishing *The Christian Year* with a series of illustrations that he had even chosen. It was, of course, Isaac Williams who made the most extensive use of illustrations in conjunction with devotional verse, and one cannot discount the possibility that Williams found inspiration in the practice of seventeenth-century devotional poets. Perhaps "inspiration" is the most suitable word for the impact of seventeenth-century verse on Keble and the Tractarians. There is certainly no specific formal model on which Keble could have based his plan, but there is a shared devotional sensibility that looked to the established forms of the religious life as natural incitements to and patterns for poetry.

After Harvey, there is a gathering of "Festival Hymns, According the Manner of the Ancient Church" by Jeremy Taylor, appended to his *Golden Grove* (1655). Taylor, like Wither, organizes his thirteen poems in sequence of the main festivals between Advent and Whitsunday, but once again the relatively small number and the concentration n major festivals rather than on the Sundays of the ecclesiastical calendar make Taylor's collection, like all those of the seventeenth-century writers, seem very incomplete beside Keble's thoroughgoing companion to the Prayer Book. Keble certainly knew of Taylor, at least as a prose writer, just as he certainly knew of Herbert as a poet, for both represent the tradition in Anglicanism that Keble shared. It is plausible, but no more than that, that these partial seventeenth-century groupings of poems or hymns to accompany major festivals suggested to Keble the idea of a fuller and more rigorous compilation.

Between the seventeenth century and Keble's own day there occur a few other sequences of poems that precede in greater or lesser degree Keble's adoption of an external model as his organizing principle. For the most part these are related to the rise of hymnody, which in turn is normally considered an aspect of the Methodist and Evangelical revival and therefore not a notable factor in the staunchly High Church background from which Keble springs. But works that suggest the later pattern of *The Christian Year* show a curious intermingling of High Church and Evangelical impulses that in turn foreshadows what scholars have found in the Oxford Movement itself. The High Church tradition provides the form and order, the Evangelical tradition the passion and the zeal.

Hymnody as such cannot be counted as a dominant factor in Keble's religious experience. Anglican practice, continuing well into the nineteenth century, relied for church music almost exclusively on the metrical versions of the psalms, initially in the sixteenth-century forms of Thomas

Sternhold and John Hopkins and, from the eighteenth century on, in the forms devised by Nahum Tate and Nicholas Brady. Hymns were almost unknown and, in traditional Anglican churches, were frowned on as Methodist innovations. Keble himself, as late as 1839, undertook to translate the Psalter into a form he thought more suitable for chanting in the spirit of the original Hebrew, presumably in the expectation that chanting would continue to dominate congregational music. Yet even as he was doing so, hymns were displacing psalm-singing throughout the Church of England, and the organization of hymnals was reflecting the emphasis on the Church year that had received its greatest boost from Keble's own *Christian Year*. It is another instance of the way in which Keble quietly sired transformations of which he himself was only partially aware.

Although Keble may have been indebted to hymnody in some of his metrical forms, it is in the organization of hymnals according to the eccesiastical calendar that we find the clearest forerunner of Keble's plan in *The Christian Year*. Such organization is common today, but the indebtedness is almost certainly to Keble, not to the earlier compilations. Before the appearance of *The Christian Year* there were only a few instances of hymnals assembled on the plan of the Church year, but these few are nevertheless instructive because they show before Keble's time the union of the liturgically oriented High Church position with the more Evangelically inspired use of hymns.

The earliest gathering of hymns on a pattern following the Church year is Bishop Ken's *Hymns for all the Festivals of the Year*, posthumously published in 1721. I have found no direct evidence of Keble's acquaintance with this volume, but there is abundant evidence that he knew the life and works of Thomas Ken (1637-1711). Ken was a Nonjuror Bishop, which therefore aligned him with the High Church tradition, and specifically with that aspect of it that took an uncompromising view of the independence of the Church from secular authority. Such a view was congenial to the Tractarians, and they have often been mentioned as inheritors of the Nonjurors, a few of whom were still living into the nineteenth century. Ken was, moreover, the author of the "Morning Hymn" and the "Evening Hymn," two of the best known of all English hymns, and frequently cited as progenitors of Keble's own "Morning" and "Evening" from *The Christian Year*. Ken's two hymns were first printed in his *Manual of Prayers for the Use of Scholars at Winchester College* (1695) and they were later widely reprinted. The "Morning Hymn" concludes with the Doxology ("Praise God from whom all blessings flow"), which has become perhaps the most widely sung verse in all English hymnody. Although the specific texts of Ken's two hymns have no particular resemblance to Keble's "Morning" and "Evening" poems, they offer broad parallels in that they also complement the order of worship in the Book of Common Prayer.

As far as I know, the 1721 collection of Ken's hymns for the festivals of the Church year was not reprinted after its initial appearance until 1868, when it was reissued as *Bishop Ken's Christian Year, or Hymns and Poems for the Holy Days and Festivals of the Church,* a title reflecting the popularity of Keble's own volume. Had Keble known Bishop Ken's 1721 collection, he would certainly have found it congenial because of its organization and its consequent reinforcement of the Anglican liturgical emphasis. It is not, however, an entirely original collection of verses, but rather a compendium of hymns and paraphrases of ancient religious verse. Still, it appears to be the earliest collection of verse distinctly ordered to parallel the sequence of worship in the Book of Common Prayer.

Bishop Ken was firmly in the High Church tradition, where one could expect an emphasis on liturgical form and Prayer Book order. Such was not the case with the great dissenting hymnodists of the eighteenth century, yet they, too, frequently wrote hymns inspired by particular feasts of the Christian year. Isaac Watts and the Wesleys left many such hymns, but in the eighteenth century the hymns were not collected and organized in a pattern that clearly forecasts Keble's in *The Christian Year.* There was a hymnal published in 1748 in Portsmouth, *Hymns for the Festivals and other Solemn Occasions,* containing about a dozen hymns from previous writers on major festivals. I have not seen a copy, and it is unlikely that Keble would have known it. Keble probably knew the poetry of John Byrom (1692-1763), a disciple of William Law and an admirer of Ken; Byrom wrote a few poems on the cycle of the Christian year, and his sympathies were decidedly High Church. Byrom's poetry would have reinforced Ken's and encouraged Keble's tendency to look to the Church year as a guide to devotion.

It is very unlikely that Keble knew Christopher Smart's collection titled *Hymns and Spiritual Songs for the Fasts and Festivals of the Church of England,* which appeared with his *Psalms* (1765), for notice of it escaped the wide nets of both Julian in his *Dictionary of Hymnology* and Fairchild in *Religious Trends in English Poetry.* The collection is known to twentieth-century students of Smart, but they point out that the poems passed almost unnoticed in Smart's own day and remained unnoticed by Smart's late nineteenth-century admirers. (See Robert Brittain, ed., *Poems by Christopher Smart* [Princeton, 1950] and Moira Dearnley, *The Poetry of Christopher Smart* [London, 1968].) Along with Wither's collection, Smart's offers the closest antecedent parallel to Keble's. Again, the parallel lies in its general plan of organization by major festivals rather than in a Sunday-by-Sunday provision according to the Prayer Book. Smart's title is closer to Keble's and the Prayer Book idea than any previous collection. It was bound, however, into a volume with Smart's *Translation of the Psalms* and the second edition of *A Song to David,* which meant that the title itself would have gone unremarked unless one held the actual book. There is no evidence that Keble did, nor was Smart as likely to attract Keble's attention as Herbert and Taylor, though some of Smart's other poems like *Jubilate Agno,* display affinities with the High Church and Tractarian devotional impulse.

Smart's collection contains thirty-five poems, and his biographers and editors have speculated that he may even have written some or all of the poems on the very days to which they are directed. The relatively small number of Smart's hymns, in contrast to Keble's poems, reflects the same concentration on major festivals and saints' days as in Wither and the seventeenth-century poets. Smart does, however, venture hymns on those uniquely Prayer Book commemorations, The Martyrdom of Charles I, The Restoration, and The Gunpowder Plot, all of which provide him with occasion to excoriate Papists. Apart from these peculiarly Anglican provisions, Smart's collection shows no greater adherence to the sequence in the Prayer Book than Wither's.

Even less likely than Smart's *Hymns* to have come to Keble's attention is the appendix to the Dublin edition of Smart's *Hymns for the Amusement of Children* (1772), which contains, among others, a brief series of poems on four major festivals of the Church year by other authors than Smart. The John Newton-William Cowper collaboration that resulted in the *Olney Hymns* (1779) was probably known to Keble, as surely as was Cowper's other poetry, and the organization of the *Olney Hymns* into three books on different themes (scripture, occasional subjects, and the spiritual life) may have contributed to Keble's decision to arrange his poems other than miscellaneously.

Eighteenth-century hymnody, then, with its frequent hymns and songs on important Christian feasts and with its general movement in the direction finally carried through by Reginald Heber, is an area with many broad parallels to Keble's method, and although Keble professed disdain for hymn singing, the eighteenth-century examples of printed hymns and songs on aspects of the Christian year may have reinforced his own natural leanings toward seeing life in terms of the annual liturgical cycle.

Contemporary with Keble's writing and publishing of *The Christian*

Year there occurs yet another parallel from the Evangelical movement, Reginald Heber's *Hymns Written and Adapted to the Weekly Church Service of the Year* (1827). Though published in the same year as *The Christian Year*, Heber's collection had actually been assembled in England in the decades before he became Bishop of Calcutta in 1823. But he had been unsuccessful in gaining permission from the Bishop of London to publish the collection because of the continuing Anglican distrust of hymns. It was published posthumously, and along with *The Christian Year*, it exercised an influence in the shaping of hymnals throughout the rest of the century and has gained much attention from students of hymnody.

Heber's collection, like Ken's, is not a gathering of original poems written for the express purpose of accompanying the Book of Common Prayer. Rather, it contains hymns from several sources, including many of Heber's own (he is best known as the author of "From Greenland's Icy Mountains"), arranged according to their suitability for illustrating the themes of the unfolding liturgical year. Once again, the pattern marks the point of greatest similarity.

From hymnody, then, but hymnody of a decidedly Anglican, and High Church, stamp, Keble may have derived the idea of organizing a collection of verse around the church year. Even if he were totally unfamiliar with all of the preceding work in this vein, the existence of such work points to an undeniable interest in linking verse with the form and sequence of Christian worship, especially as ordered by the Prayer Book. The simultaneous appearance of Keble's volume and Reginald Heber's collection of hymns (of which, of course, Keble could not have been aware) suggests that the particular convergence of poetry with the ecclesiastical year was already in the air and accounts, at least in part, for the astounding success of Keble's collection. But it is Keble's volume that accounts for the flood of Victorian collections and anthologies based on the ecclesiastical year, and for the dominant organizational pattern of all English language hymnals, from the mid-nineteenth century to our own day. This is an influence that has gone largely unremarked, as has so much of Keble's work, but it has had wider repercussions in the actual religious life of the Christian community than even the far more celebrated and studied influence of Newman.

There remains one other work that casts an oblique light on Keble's formal strategy in *The Christian Year*, Wordsworth's series of *Ecclesiastical Sonnets*. The interest attached to this series in relation to *The Christian Year* stems as much from the authorship of the sonnets as from any similarities of form, but given Keble's known dedication to Wordsworth, it is unwise to pass over so signally religious a portion of Wordsworth's poetry.

Wordsworth's series of sonnets on church themes is almost exactly contemporaneous with Keble's composition of the poems in *The Christian Year*. The earliest sonnets in the series were written in 1820, and the first publication, under the title *Ecclesiastical Sketches,* occurred in 1822. Others were added in subsequent years up to 1842. The title *Ecclesiastical Sonnets* was substituted for *Sketches* in 1837, and additions were made as late as 1845. As formal influences, the *Ecclesiastical Sonnets,* then, are rather like Heber's collection of hymns for the Christian year: they bear evidence of a common interest in religious topics and, even more, in poems in a series designed to illustrate a larger religious theme. Wordsworth's sonnets are primarily historical. They trace the rise and progress of Christianity in Britain from the beginning to the nineteenth century. But there are also some sonnets on general religious topics, such as Baptism and other sacraments, that suggest that Wordsworth was himself striving towards a more than purely historical series. Above all, what is suggested by the simultaneous composition of the *Ecclesiastical Sonnets* and *The Christian Year* is an increasing preoccupation in orthodox Anglican circles with the idea of the Church itself, with the Church as both a human and divine institution, and with the Church as something more than the product of the Reformation, a continuing body from its first foundations in Britain to its present form in the established Church. This interest in the Church as an institution shows how ready certain circles were for a work like *The Christian Year*.

That the later Wordsworth found no difficulty in adapting his style and sentiments to religious purposes is another sign of the times. As he wrote in his early sonnet on Baptism:

> Dear be the Church that, watching o'er the needs
> Of Infancy, provides a timely shower
> Whose virtue changes to a Christian flower
> A growth from sinful Nature's bed of weeds!

From such sentiments and from the *Ecclesiastical Sonnets* sequence itself, one can perhaps view in a different light Wordsworth's observation that he wished he had written *The Christian Year* so that he could have written it better. Modern readers tend to see only the second part of that utterance with its negative assessment of Keble as poet. There is also the first part, however, an expression of genuine admiration from Wordsworth. Keble's genius lay not so much in writing Wordsworthian poetry—obviously

Wordsworth did that better—but in his adapting it to an external scheme familiar and accessible to all, a scheme that insured for his volume a far warmer public reception than Wordsworth enjoyed even with the *Ecclesiastical Sonnets*, let alone that which marked the *Lyrical Ballads.*

Appendix C

The Christian Year
in the Victorian Age

TO TRACE THE FULL Victorian response to *The Christian Year* would require a separate study, so frequent are the references and allusions to it throughout the nineteenth century. What follows is a brief summary of its dissemination in the age and mention of some of the notable persons who commented on it. In assembling the information and references that follow, I supplemented my own findings with those in the following works: Amy Cruse, *The Victorians and Their Reading* (Cambridge, Mass., 1935); B. M. Lott, "The Poetry of John Keble" (diss., London University, 1960); Raymond Chapman, *Faith and Revolt* (London, 1970); Brian W. Martin, *John Keble* (London, 1976); and C. J. Stranks, *Anglican Devotion* (London, 1961).

The publication history of *The Christian Year* provides a useful overview of its Victorian acceptance. Once the initial run of five hundred copies had sold out, Parker's issued a second edition within the year, and then an augmented edition in 1828, containing the poems added for the special services at the end of the Prayer Book. By 1837 there had already been sixteen editions. When Keble died in 1866, *The Christian Year* had gone through ninety-five editions. When the copyright expired in 1873, Parker's had published a total of 158 editions! None of these figures accounts for pirated American editions, nor for the flood of editions that issued from various publishers once the copyright had expired. It is safe to estimate that when the last regular edition was published just before the First World War, it must have brought the total of editions to well over two hundred since the first edition eighty-six years before, an average of considerably more than two editions a year for more than three generations. Accurate figures on number of volumes are impossible to come by, but it is known that the total sales of copyright editions numbered 379,000 in 1873, or approximately one copy for every sixty inhabitants of Britain. Richard Altick in *The English Common Reader* (Chicago, 1957) lists *The Christian Year* as a poetry bestseller; no other volume of verse in his list has a higher number of copies cited for it. If one assumes the same ratio of copies to population for the remainder of the century after the expiration of copyright, at least half a million copies would have been sold. Little wonder that J. C. Shairp in 1879 claimed that *The Christian Year* was the widest-selling book of poetry in the nineteenth century.

Of course statistics alone do not tell the full story. The works of Samuel Smiles or of Martin Tupper rival and collectively surpass Keble's in terms of sales figures, as of course do those of the hugely successful novelists like Dickens. But probably no single work surpasses *The Christian Year* in number of different separate editions in the same time span. In that regard, it may hold the all-time English-language record.

What is at least as telling as sales figures and number of editions is the quality of the readers' response to *The Christian Year*. When Amy Cruse wanted to suggest the flavor of the reading habits of the upper-middle class in the early Victorian period, she posited an imaginary Victorian young man named Edward who presented as a birthday gift to his fiancée Keble's *The Christian Year*, thinking to follow it in due course with a gift of the *Lyra Apostolica*. The young lady thought some of Keble's poems "sweetly pretty," even though her mother, an Evangelical, may have viewed the High Church volume at first with some distrust. But she too would be won over by the sincerity, piety, and sentimentalism of the collection.

That initial distrust from Evangelicals was wholly absent in the response of Keble's circle and of future Tractarians. Many, of course, had read the poems in manuscript and urged Keble to publish them, so that for the Keble circle, the publication made available to a wider audience what they had long treasured. As noted earlier, Newman came to know the poems so well that he mistakenly thought some Keble lines were his own. Newman's attitude towards *The Christian Year* became the prototype of the general Victorian attitude. Letters, autobiographies, reminiscences, and novels for the rest of the century teem with testimony to the way in which

The Christian Year became part of the fabric of Victorian life. Not only the Tractarians and their circle, not only the High Churchmen and the upper-middle classes generally, but also Low Churchmen, Evangelicals, dissenters, and non-Churchmen came to know and value *The Christian Year*. It is not surprising to find Charlotte Mary Yonge's May family, the principal figures in the series of novels beginning with *The Daisy Chain* (1856), all intimately acquainted with *The Christian Year* and given to quoting passages from it in times of emotion or stress, as does Owen in *Hopes and Fears* (1860), and perhaps not even surprising to come upon Guy and Richard in *The Heir of Redclyffe* (1854) undertaking to translate Keble's *Praelectiones Academicae*, though this latter degree of Keblemania would have been confined to a very select circle. Outside of High Church novels, one remembers that Thackeray's Pendennis was brought up on the verse, and "faint, very faint and seldom in after life Pendennis heard that solemn church music." Students of Victorian life additionally list among those who have left record of their love of *The Christian Year* such figures as Wordsworth, Thomas Arnold ("nothing equal to [it] exists in the language"), Oliver Wendell Holmes (it "makes one's heart a proselyte to the culture it grows from"), the Lyttleton, Cavendish, and Gladstone families, George Eliot ("fields of poesy lovelier than ever"), John Ruskin, Florence Nightingale, Matthew Arnold, John Morley (in *The Christian Year* "The Church of England finds her most affecting voice"), A. E. Housman ("Keble is a poet; there are things in *The Christian Year* that can be admired by atheists"), Robert Bridges, George Saintsbury ("he sometimes rises to a grandeur which Herbert hardly ever attains"), and of course numerous ecclesiastics, who doubtless shared the sentiments of Bishop Westcott that a verse of Keble was worth volumes of Tennyson.

In the rare cases in which *The Christian Year* was unknown to young Victorians it was almost always because of doctrinal opposition. Edmund Gosse, reared in the eighteen-fifties and sixties under the most austere religious fundamentalism, records in *Father and Son,* as evidence of his father's conscious effort to keep his son's mind free from High Church con-tamination, the fact that "of that famous volume [*The Christian Year*] I never met with a copy until I was grown up." He did of course eventually meet with it, for it would have been almost impossible for a Victorian not to. Witness Amy Cruse's account of Lady Cavendish's astonishment in 1864 upon learning that a friend did not know *The Christian Year:* she reported that the news made her "hair stand on end."

Less scrupulous dissenters than the Gosses encountered the volume earlier, and some did not hesitate to take issue with it on doctrinal grounds. As early as 1844, Anne Howard in *Mary Spencer: A Tale for the Times* (the title plays on the Tracts) has her heroine seek out theological "errors" in *The Christian Year,* and in her *Bampton Rectory* (1849), she devotes a long sequence to debating the merits of the volume. A comparable sentiment can be found in Lady Catherine Long's 1844 *Sir Rowland Ashton,* similarly subtitled *A Tale of the Times,* for she has her hero shown his errors in liking *The Christian Year,* a volume held to be doctrinally too Catholic. Later in the century, Ouida slightingly describes a politician as gaining the support of the clergy by quoting from *The Christian Year* in his campaign speeches. Such testimony points again to the widespread familiarity with *The Christian Year,* even among those who took issue with its High Church and Catholic leanings.

Still other dissenters were moved primarily by the verse, without undue concern for the doctrine. James Martineau, the celebrated Unitarian preacher, included some of the verses from *The Christian Year* in a Unitarian hymnal as early as 1840, and in due course, Keble verses found their way into hymnals of most denominations. Some survive in such collections to the present day, notably in Anglican hymnals; these are the last refuge of Keble the poet.

Victorians were unanimous in considering *The Christian Year* a work of major importance, and the great majority of them were equally convinced that it was a work of enduring poetic beauty and power. As late as 1891 R. W. Church could write that *The Christian Year* was "familiar wherever English is read," and Walter Lock in 1895 affirmed that *The Christian Year* would live as poetry as long as English is spoken. J. C. Shairp was convinced that *The Christian Year* and Newman's university sermons were the two enduring gifts to literature of the Oxford Movement; J. H. Overton said *The Christian Year* placed Keble among the immortals and that the volume would live as long as the Prayer Book. The abundance of editions up to 1914 and the appearance of various late nineteenth-century hagiographic works on Keble do indicate a continuing reverence, but the interest had begun falling off even as Church, Lock, and other late Victorians were writing. Owen Chadwick (in *The Victorian Church*) believes that by the nineties, the younger generation no longer knew *The Christian Year* virtually by heart as their elders did, though "families continued to recommend it, like the collect, for Sunday reading." In *Jude the Obscure* (1895), Hardy has his protagonist at Christminster (Oxford) encounter the shades of vanished Oxford worthies, and he captures in the depiction the mixture of reverence and yet increasing distance that the late-Victorian world felt toward Tractarianism and Keble's volume: "modern divines sheeted in their surplices, among whom the most real to Jude Fawley were the founders of the religious school called Tractarian; the well-known three, the enthusiast, the poet, and the formularist, the echoes of whose teachings had influenced him even in his obscure home." The three are of course Newman, Keble, and Pusey. A little later, two of the "shades" speak to him, the first being Newman who speaks of "converging probabilities," the second being Keble, who "no polemic, murmured quieter things," whereupon Hardy quotes two lines from Keble's poem for the Twenty-fourth Sunday after Trinity:

> Why should we faint, and fear to live alone,
> Since all alone, so Heaven has will'd, we die.

In addition to its impact on readers in the age, *The Christian Year*, as I have argued earlier, also exerted an influence of a practical kind on other volumes of verse and on collections of hymns. Such an influence is in the nature of the case impossible to "prove," and of course similar impulses would have been at work, such as Reginald Heber's collection of hymns and Wordsworth's increasingly liturgical sonnet series. But the enormous popularity of *The Christian Year* suggests that it was the primary influence in the large number of collections of poetry old and new based on the Church cycle, and in the vast number of hymnals composed wholly or in part on the basis of the liturgical year.

The most visible category of works influenced by *The Christian Year* are those whose titles are clearly derivative of the *Lyra Apostolica* but whose contents and arrangements follow all or some of the pattern of the Church year. Here the Keble connection seems unmistakable. Among such works listed in Appendix D, one can number the *Lyra Sanctorum* (minor festivals), *Lyra Sabbatica* (Sundays and Holy Days), *Lyra Eucharistica* (the Eucharist), *Lyra Liturgica* (the liturgical year). Even among those not based on the Church year as such, marks of a Kebelian organization can be discerned, as in the *Lyra Messianica* (poems on the life of Christ) or the *Lyra Seriorum* (poems for Sundays). Indeed, almost all *Lyra* titles, even secular ones, show a greater concentration on a single subject and a greater awareness of organization for its own sake than the *Lyra Apostolica* itself, all of which suggests the power of Keble's organizing principle.

There are many other works organized in ways similar to *The Christian Year* but not titled after the *Lyra Apostolica* or after *The Christian Year*, or titled to reveal their similarities only indirectly, or only in subtitle. I have not attempted to seek out all of these, but a few examples can stand for many.

As early as 1834 there appeared an anonymous volume titled *The Christian Seasons,* containing six long poems on the main divisions of the Christian year. Keble possessed a copy in his personal library, which is now at Keble College. The copy appears to have been a gift and a homage to the originator of the organization of poems by the Christian calendar. In 1841 Charlotte Mary Yonge assembled *The Child's Christian Year: Hymns for Every Sunday and Holy-Day,* to which Keble contributed four poems and a preface. It went through many editions and enjoyed wide popularity in the religious gift market. Keble's 1846 *Lyra Innocentium,* as noted earlier, combined the idea of a *Lyra* title with an organization at least partially based on the Church year. R. C. Trench's *Hymns for the Week, and Hymns for the Seasons* (1848) contained translations from the Breviary arranged in terms of the liturgical calendar, another instance of the convergence of several Tractarian interests.

In 1855 appeared *Dies Consecrati: Or, a New Christian Year with the Old Poets.* Here Keble's idea was employed in an anthology of devotional poetry, with selections extending back to the seventeenth century. In 1862 Christopher Wordsworth, nephew of the poet, published his *The Holy Year.* It is modeled strictly on the sequence in the Prayer Book, and it marks a melding of Tractarian and Evangelical influences. The hymns were written in a Wesleyan spirit of inculcating doctrine through hymnody. At the same time, Christopher Wordsworth announced in the preface that he sought inspiration from three sources: Scripture, the writings of antiquity, and the poetry of the ancient Church, sources that have a distinctly Tractarian ring. Two years after Wordsworth's collection appeared the anonymous *Hymns for Saints' Days.* The rest of the century produced many more such volumes, anthologies and original collections, to say nothing of the hymnals from all denominations, or the countless prose collections of sermons and meditations that reflect the liturgical year in their organization.

Rather like *Lyra* titles, which came to be applied so widely as to suggest an ignorance of the original source, collections of poems, hymns, and sacred songs in terms of the Christian year eventually became so common that one may assume many compilers were no longer consciously aware of the origin of the pattern, though new editions of Keble's volume were certainly always readily available throughout the century.

The Christian Year did not make the transition from a popular work to a classic one, as so many late Victorian admirers confidently assumed it already had. It passed instead from enormous popularity to almost total obscurity, soon after the First World War. Scholars continue to refer to it, especially those working in the fields of religious and ecclesiastical history, but not even all students of the Victorian age are any longer familiar with it or its history. Yet, a recent reissue of a late nineteenth-century American edition of it by an academic reprint house (Gale Research, 1975) and a recent wholly new issue of the work in England (Church Literature Association, 1977) may be signs not of a return to popularity but of a recognition of its historical importance, its value as an influence in literary and ecclesiastical history, and its special status as an index of Victorian taste and sentiment. These reprintings may even be the first signs signaling acknowledgment of its place as a minor classic.

Descendants of the *Lyra Apostolica*

FOLLOWING IS A LISTING of titles that appear to have been inspired, directly or indirectly, by the *Lyra Apostolica*. With one exception, I have found no comparable titles before the publication of *Lyra Apostolica* in book form. The British Library catalogue has a few titles from the seventeenth century, chiefly works in Latin, using the word *Lyra*, but none for more than a century and a half preceding the Tractarian collection. The only exception I have found is the 1832 Boston publication by the American hymnodist Lowell Mason (1792–1872) titled *Lyra Sacra*. This volume went through many later editions in America, but normally under the translated title of *The Sacred Harp*. It is virtually certain that the Tractarians did not know this work, especially not at the time the title *Lyra Apostolica* was adopted, which was not later than 1833. The existence of three independent works titled *Lyra Sacra,* and other duplicated titles in the list below, suggests that some post-Tractarians settled upon titles in ignorance of previously existing works, seeking chiefly a new adjective to modify the established title of *Lyra* for a collection of devotional poems. Mason's contemporaneous use of a *Lyra* title seems to parallel Reginald Heber's collection of hymns at the same time Keble was writing *The Christian Year*, that is, it is a case of independently converging interests.

Lyra titles fall into one of two categories, following either the original *Lyra Apostolica* volume or the form of Keble's adaptation in the *Lyra Innocentium*; that is, the title is cast either as *Lyra* followed by a modifying adjective (*Lyra Apostolica, Lyra Mystica, Lyra Anglicana*) or as *Lyra* followed by a genitive (*Lyra Innocentium, Lyra Sanctorum, Lyra Consolationis,* and so forth). The form of *Lyra* plus adjective is by far the more common.

Virtually all of the early imitations of the title were religious, either poems or hymns, but later this form of title passed into common currency and came to be attached to some unlikely subjects indeed, as in the *Lyra Nicotiana* or the *Lyra Piscatoria.* While most of the early titles seem to have been consciously inspired by the *Lyra Apostolica,* one must allow even here for accidental similarity, which may be the case with the early *Lyra Eboracensis,* for example, poems on the city of York. By the end of the century and the early part of the twentieth century, some *Lyra* titles must surely have been adopted without awareness of the 1836 original; yet, it is worth noting that, as late as the 1930s, *Lyra* titles of a distinctly religious cast (*Lyra Mystica, Lyra Martyrum*) were still being produced. Whatever else Tractarian devotional poetry did, it appears to have invested the Romantic lyre with an enduring religious aura.

The following list records only the first appearance I have found for a title, not subsequent editions, but many of the works listed went through numerous editions. I was not able to examine all of the titles listed, hence the designation "[unknown]" for the contents of some of them, and uncertainty in other cases as to whether the collection is original verse by one author or an anthology.

Year of publication	Title	Author, editor, translator	Contents, subject
1836	*Lyra Apostolica*	J. H. Newman et al.	Apostolic Church
1838	"Lyra Ecclesiastica" in *Thoughts in Past Years*	I. Williams	Church
1839	*Lyra Eboracensis*	Thomas Hollins	City of York
1840	*Lyra Urbanica*	Charles Morris	[Unknown]
1846	*Lyra Innocentium*	John Keble	Children
1847	*Lyra Memorialis*	Joseph Snow	Epitaphs
1849	*Lyra Czechoslovanska*	A. H. Wratislaw	Czech poetry

Year of publication	Title	Author, editor, translator	Contents, subject
	Lyra Catholica	Edward Caswall, ed. and trans.	Catholic hymnody
1850	*Lyra Sanctorum*	W. J. Deane	Minor Church festivals
1851	*Lyra Christiana*	Robert Montgomery	Christianity
1852	*Lyra*	Alice Cary	Original poems
	Lyra Hellenica	E. R. Humphreys, trans.	Contemporary British poetry into Greek
1856	*Lyra Anglicana*	B. Courtenay Gidley	Original verse on poetry
	Lyra Memorialis	Charles Neville	Graveyard
1859	*Lyra Germanica*	Catherine Winkworth, ed. and trans.	German hymns
1860	*Lyra Domestica*	Richard Massie, trans.	Religious
1861	*Lyra Sacra*	B. Wrey Saville, ed.	Hymns
1862	*Lyra Anglicana*	R. H. Baynes, ed.	English hymns
1863	*Lyra Sacra Privata*	Joseph Bush	Private devotions
	Lyra Eucharistica	Orby Shipley, ed.	Eucharist
1864	*Lyra Sabbatica*	Benjamin Gough	Sundays, Holy Days
	Lyra Messianica	B. Orby Shipley,	Life of Christ
1865	*Lyra Liturgica*	Frederick Oakeley	Holy Days
	Lyra Americana	George T. Rider, ed.	American poems of faith
	Lyra Anglicana	George T. Rider, ed.	English poems of faith
	Lyra Mystica	Orby Shipley, ed.	Sacred subjects
1866	*Lyra Fidelium*	S. J. Stone	Apostles' Creed
	Lyra Coelestis	A. C. Thompson	Heaven [anthol.?]
1867	*Lyra Britannica*	Charles Rogers	[Unknown]
	Lyra Silurum	W. Downing Evans	Original poems on nature
1867	*Lyra Elegantiarum*	F. Locker-Lampson, ed.	Vers de société
	La Lyre française	Gustave Masson, ed.	French poetry

Year of publication	Title	Author, editor, translator	Contents, subject
1868	*Lyra Sacra Americana*	Charles D. Cleveland	American sacred verse
	Lyra Devoniensis	J. Wollaston, ed.	Devon
1872	*Lyra Evangelica*	Robert Maguire	Hymns [anthol.?]
1875	*Lyra Viginti Chordarum*	J. Addington Symonds	Original poems
1878	*Lyra Hibernica Sacra*	William Macilwaine	Irish sacred verse
1880	*Lyra Bicyclica*	J. Grinnel	Cycling [anthol.?]
1885	*Lyra Regis*	Anon.	Old Testament anthol.
1886	*Lyra Consolationis*	Horatius Bonar	Hymns of sorrow
1888	*Lyra Christiana*	Jane Borthwick, ed.	Sacred verse
1890	*Lyra Consolationis*	Claudia F. Hernaman, ed.	Consolation
	Lyra Mancuniensis	Walter Hughes, ed.	Isle of Man
1891	*Lyra Heroica*	W. E. Henley	Verse for boys
1894	*Lyra Sacra*	Mary E. Kendrew	Original poems
1895	*Lyra Sacra*	H. C. Beeching	Devotion
	Lyra Piscatoria	Anon.	Fishing [anthol.?]
1896	*Lyra Hieratica*	R. E. Bridgett, ed.	Priesthood
	Lyra Celtica	Elizabeth A. Sharp and J. Matthay, eds.	Celtic poetry
1897	*Lyra Cyclus*	Edmund Redmond, ed.	Cycling
1898	*Lyra Nicotiana*	William G. Hutchinson	Tobacco
1899	*Lyra Frivola*	Alfred D. Godley	Light verse
1902	*Lyra Seriorum*	John A. Nicklin	Sundays
1904	*Lyra Amoris*	Gertrude H. Witherby	Love
1906	*Lyra Venatica*	J. Stanley Reeve	Hunting
	Lyra Gerhardti	Paul Gerhardt	Hymns
1909	*Lyra Evangelistica*	Arthur S. Cripps	Missionary
1911	*Lyra Nigeriae*	Edward C. Adams	Nigeria
	La Lyre d'Amour	Charles B. Lewis, ed.	French love poems

Year of publication	Title	Author, editor, translator	Contents, subject
1911 (cont.)	*Lyra Historica*	M. E. Windsor and J. Turral	British history
1913	*Lyra Yalensis*	Edward B. Reed	Yale
	Lyra Nordica	Giuseppe Finzi, ed.	Northern European verse
1914	*Lira Italica e Lira Nordica*	Giuseppe Finzi, ed.	Italian and Northern European verse
1918	*Lyra Hispana*	V. Gomez-Bravo	Spanish
1921	*Lyra Mutabilis*	Morley Roberts	Original poems
1922	*Lyra Levis*	Edward B. Reed	Humorous
1922–1927	*Lyra Graeca*	J. M. Edmonds, ed.	Greek lyric poems
1930	*Lyra Ebriosa*	Anon.	Popular ballads
1932	*Lyra Mystica*	C. C. Albertson, ed.	Mystical verse
1934	*Lyra Martyrum*	J. R. O'Connel, ed.	English martyrs
1942	*Lyra*	Alex Comfort and Robert Greacen, eds.	Modern lyric verse
1946	*Lyra Indica*	Avinasha-Chandra Vasu	India
	Lyra Romana Lyricorum	Anon.	Latin lyrics
1950	*Lyra Belgica*	Clark Stillman, ed.	Belgian verse

Notes

I. Introduction

1. T. S. Eliot, "Religion and Literature," in *Selected Prose,* ed. John Hayward (London, 1953), pp. 32-44.

2. In a later essay Eliot also elevated Herbert from the ranks of minor poets. See his "What Is Minor Poetry?" in *On Poetry and Poets* (New York, 1961), p. 42. Interestingly, Eliot here uses an argument for *The Temple* as a single unified work to substantiate his claims for Herbert's status as a major poet. My own arguments for more modest claims for Keble are based on the wholeness of *The Christian Year.* See Chapter III.

3. To take but the most prominent such reference work, the *Princeton Encyclopedia of Poetry and Poetics,* ed. Alex Preminger et al. (Princeton, 1974), has an entry for "Religion and Poetry" but none for the terms I am using here. A similar absence can be noted in the popular glossaries and handbooks of literary terms. The most helpful discussion I have found of the devotional form is Anthony Low, *Love's Architecture: Devotional Modes in Seventeenth-Century English Poetry* (New York, 1978), esp. pp. 1-11. My own definition of devotional poetry in terms of worship and ritual is posited on Evelyn Underhill's definition of worship as the "response of the creature to the Eternal." See *Worship* (1936; London, 1962), p. 13.

4. Helen Gardner, ed., *The Faber Book of Religious Verse* (London,

1972), p. 7. Gardner bases her definition of "religious" on an *OED* entry for "religion" as being the "recognition on the part of man of some higher unseen power as having control of his destiny, and as being entitled to obedience, reverence, and worship; the general mental and moral attitude resulting from this belief, with reference to its effect upon the individual or the community; personal or general acceptance of this feeling as a standard of spiritual and practical life." From this definition, as opposed to other *OED* definitions relating more specifically to confession of faith, she takes especially the concept of commitment as the "distinguishing mark separating the religious poem from the poem of metaphysical speculation, religious musing, or the poem of incidental apprehension of the divine." But she also arrived "at the criterion that a religious poem was a poem concerned in some way with revelation and with man's response to it." The idea of response allows her to "include poems that refuse commitment or express doubt more powerfully than affirmation." This is consistent with her views in *Religion and Literature* (New York, 1971). The absence in her anthology of virtually all of the poets in this book and the inclusion of relatively few Victorian poets of any kind is apparently the result of an aesthetic judgment rather than a failure of these poets to exhibit sufficient commitment. The matter of exclusion from the collection, however, is not discussed.

In the extensive and growing body of modern studies of religion and literature there is no notable agreement on exactly what constitutes a religious poem or on how the terminology is to be employed. I have not cited the many background studies in this field except where there is specific reference. For recent statements of contemporary approaches to religion and literature, see Vernon Ruland, *Horizons of Criticism* (Chicago, 1978), and Norman Reed Cary, *Christian Criticism in the Twentieth Century* (Port Washington, N.Y., 1975).

5. The triennial Oxford Prize for a "Poem on a Sacred Subject" was instituted in 1847 and first awarded in 1851. There were seventeen winning poems by the end of the century, all on biblical topics. Some typical titles include "St. Paul at Athens," "The Day of Pentecost," "King Saul," "Ruth," and the like. The only poet connected at all with Tractarian devotional poetry who wrote such a prize poem is Richard Watson Dixon, who won in 1863 with his "St. John on Patmos." See *Historical Register of the University of Oxford* (Oxford, 1900).

The Seatonian Prize for Sacred Poetry at Cambridge is much older than the Oxford Prize; it dates from 1750. The terms of this prize required that the poem be on the "Supreme Being." Christopher Smart won the prize five times in the 1750s, and John Mason Neale won it eleven times in the nineteenth century. See David B. Morris, *The Religious Sublime* (Lexington, Ky., 1972), pp. 126-130.

6. A large body of secondary literature exists on this topic. Two standard works that devote a good deal of attention to the nineteenth century and include reference to some of the works are Louis F. Benson, *The English Hymn* (Philadelphia, 1915), and J. B. Reeves, *The Hymn as Literature* (New York, 1921). A compact short introduction to the subject can be found in Arthur Pollard, *English Hymns,* Writers and Their Work series (London, 1960). An instructive study of the relation between hymnody and literature in selected authors is Martha Winburn English and John Sparrow, *Hymns Unbidden* (New York, 1966). A recent study of the Victorian hymn as indicator of social attitudes is Susan B. Tamke, *Make a Joyful Noise unto the Lord* (Athens, Ohio, 1978). Tamke mistakenly thinks Keble in *The Christian Year* wrote a collection of hymns but avoided calling it such to escape Anglican censure. For another illuminating treatment of Victorian hymns in a cultural context, see Lionel Adey, "Great Aunt Tilly's Beautiful 'ymns: A Victorian Sub-culture," *Wascana Review,* 12 (1977), 21-47.

7. Louis Martz, *The Poetry of Meditation* (1954; rev. ed., New Haven, 1962).

8. This verges again on hymnody, but as an example of Anglo-Saxon poetry influenced by liturgy without becoming hymnody, see Daniel G. Calder, *"The Fates of the Apostles,* the Latin Martyrologies, and the Litany of the Saints," *Medium Aevum,* 44 (1975), 219-224. There is increasing evidence too of a liturgical and Church calendar influence on Renaissance drama. See R. Chris Hassel, Jr., *Renaissance Drama and the English Church Year* (Lincoln, Neb., 1979).

9. R. W. Church, *The Oxford Movement* (1891; rpt. Chicago, 1970). Church's strong pro-Newman sympathies have long been recognized.

10. Raymond Chapman, *Faith and Revolt: Studies in the Literary·Influence of the Oxford Movement* (London, 1970). Chapman's study also contains an excellent appendix on "The Nomenclature of the Movement" (pp. 280-289).

11. While I have accepted the term Tractarian as the most fitting one for the first phase of the Oxford Movement, I have found it necessary to extend the term anachronistically backward before 1833 in order to accommodate theory and poetry prior to the Tracts but unmistakably part of the first phase of the Oxford Movement. For a view of the dating of the Movement that takes issue with Newman, see F. L. Cross, "The Myth of July

14, 1833," in his *John Henry Newman* (London, 1933), p. 162.

12. The major twentieth-century studies are: S. L. Ollard, *A Short History of the Oxford Movement* (London, 1915); Yngve Brilioth, *The Anglican Revival* (London, 1925); John Sparrow-Simpson, *The History of the Anglo-Catholic Revival* (London, 1932); N. P. Williams and Charles Harris, *Northern Catholicism* (London, 1932); Christopher Dawson, *The Spirit of the Oxford Movement* (London, 1933); Geoffrey Faber, *Oxford Apostles* (London, 1933); Owen Chadwick, *The Victorian Church,* 2 vols. (New York, 1966), and *The Mind of the Oxford Movement* (1960; rpt. Stanford, 1967); Horton Davies, *Worship and Theology in England,* vol. III, *From Watts and Wesley to Maurice, 1690-1850* (Princeton, 1961); David Newsome, *The Parting of Friends* (London, 1966); and Chapman, *Faith and Revolt.* For a full discussion of the literature on the Oxford Movement, see Howard W. Fulweiler, "The Oxford Movement, " in *Victorian Prose: A Guide to Research,* ed. D. J. DeLaura (New York, 1973), pp. 361-386. To ease the weight of footnotes, I have not documented references to well-known events in the Movement or in the biographies of the principals that are readily available in the secondary literature.

I became aware of Elva McAllester's pioneering work on Tractarian poetry too late to include reference to it in this study, but I was able to profit from her "The Oxford Movement and Victorian Poetry" (diss., University of Illinois, 1958), and from her unpublished anthology "Tractarian Trumpets: Verse of the Oxford Movement," which she kindly let me examine.

13. Reference to this relationship is made everywhere in the literature on the Movement, but the topic has not often been deeply explored. Two recent treatments of great value are Stephen Prickett, *Romanticism and Religion* (Cambridge, 1976), and Michael Bright, "English Literary Romanticism and the Oxford Movement," *Journal of the History of Ideas,* 40 (1979), 385-404.

14. A. M. Allchin, "Introduction," in S. L. Ollard, *A Short History of the Oxford Movement* (rpt.; London, 1963), p. 12.

15. I have adopted the increasingly common term "poetics" to describe Tractarian theory, intending to signify by it an aesthetics of poetry. The Tractarian position is sufficiently far-reaching to bid fair to be called an aesthetic, but most of their pronouncements are directed to poetry.

II. Tractarian Poetics

1. For an approach to the main Tractarian concerns, the reader may consult Owen Chadwick, *The Mind of the Oxford Movement* (1960; rpt. Stan-

ford, 1967). Chadwick organizes his selections from Tractarian writings under the three main headings of Faith, The Authority of the Church, and Sanctification, with many subordinate topics under each. He includes numerous selections from Tractarian poetry to illustrate his topics, for he recognizes the centrality of poetry to the Tractarian mind. See pp. 62-64.

2. See esp. Shairp's *Studies in Poetry and Philosophy* (Edinburgh, 1868); Lock's biography of Keble (London, 1893), and his edition of *The Christian Year*; and Church's history. For other sympathetic responses to Tractarian poetry in the age, see Appendix C.

3. Alba H. Warren, *English Poetic Theory, 1825-1865* (Princeton, 1950); M. H. Abrams, *The Mirror and the Lamp: Romantic Theory and the Critical Tradition* (1953; rpt., New York, 1958).

4. In addition to Stephen Prickett, *Romanticism and Religion* (Cambridge, 1976), and Michael Bright, "English Literary Romanticism and the Oxford Movement," *Journal of the History of Ideas,* 40 (1979), 385-404, see Lawrence J. Starzyk, *The Imprisoned Splendor: A Study of Victorian Critical Theory* (Port Washington, N.Y., 1977), esp. pp. 139-144, 151-152, 155-182; G. B. Tennyson, "The Sacramental Imagination," in U. C. Knoepflmacher and G. B. Tennyson, eds., *Nature and the Victorian Imagination* (Berkeley, 1977), pp. 370-390, and "Tractarian Aesthetics: Analogy and Reserve in Keble and Newman," *Victorian Newsletter,* no. 55 (Spring 1979), pp. 8-10. Patrick Parrinder, *Authors and Authority: A Study of English Literary Criticism and its Relation to Culture, 1750-1900* (London, 1979), treats Wordsworth and Coleridge and briefly Newman, but not any other Tractarians.

5. The article incorporates ideas and phrasings of an unidentified person who, according to Martin Svaglic, may have been William Palmer of Worcester. The essay was reprinted as "Prospects of the Anglican Church" in N, *Essays,* I, 265-308.

6. Svaglic provides this identification, A, p. 536.

7. J. T. Coleridge, *Memoir of the Rev. John Keble* (London, 1869), p. 247; Georgina Battiscombe, *John Keble* (London, 1964), p. 41. See also Prickett, pp. 91, 97-100. Prickett is unduly severe on Tractarian attitudes toward the poor, contrasting them unfavorably with Wordsworth's, but their poetry is as pious toward poverty as Wordsworth's, and there is evidence that the Bisley School, at any rate, was seriously concerned about the poor.

8. The full text reads: "To William Wordsworth, True Philosopher and Inspired Poet, who by the special gift and calling of Almighty God, whether he sang of man or of nature, failed not to lift up men's hearts to

the holy things, nor ever ceased to champion the cause of the poor and simple, and so in perilous times was raised up to be a chief minister, not only of sweetest poetry, but also of high and sacred truth—this tribute, slight though it be, is offered by one of the multitude who feel ever indebted for the immortal treasure of his splendid poems in testimony of respect, affection, and gratitude" (LP, I, 8; punctuation supplied). "Inspired poet" is E. K. Francis' translation of "vati sacro"; see *Praelectiones Academicae* (Oxford, 1844), I, iii, for the original Latin text.

9. See Prickett's chapter 2, pp. 34-69; subsequent references incorporated into text. For more light on Newman and Coleridge, see John Coulson, *Newman and the Common Tradition* (Oxford, 1970).

10. But see Owen Barfield, *What Coleridge Thought* (Middletown, Conn., 1971); J. Robert Barth, *Coleridge and Christian Doctrine* (Cambridge, Mass., 1969), and *The Symbolic Imagination* (Princeton, 1977). Prickett, pp. 57-60, cites Barfield, but he seems to miss the point of Barfield's carrying Coleridge's polarity into modern thought, which Barfield does with full awareness of the extent to which it runs counter to the modern temper.

11. Barfield, pp. 26-40. Other Barfield treatments of polarity of particular relevance here can be found in his *Romanticism Comes of Age* (rev. ed., London, 1960), and *Saving the Appearances* (New York, 1965).

12. The sense of myth Prickett is discussing here is best exemplified by the writers associated with the mythopoeic school of Barfield, C. S. Lewis, and J. R. R. Tolkien, though Prickett himself mentions no particular critics to illustrate his point.

13. O, pp. 148-162. The essay is titled "Copleston's *Praelectiones Academicae*" and was first published in the *British Critic* in 1814.

14. O, pp. 80-107; first published 1825 in the *Quarterly Review*. In discussing Keble's views in this essay, I have followed his use of the term "sacred poetry" rather than my own term "devotional poetry."

15. Conder (1789-1855) was a noted Congregationalist hymnodist and poet who later exhibited some High Church tendencies, producing such volumes as *The Choir and the Oratory* (1837), and *Hymns of Praise, Prayer, and Devout Meditation* (1856). Selections from his *Choir and Oratory* were published in 1838 under the Tractarian-sounding title *Harmonia Sacra*. See J, I, 256.

16. Warren, pp. 35-45; subsequent references incorporated into text. Geoffrey Tillotson has also examined the essay. See his "Newman's Essay on Poetry: An Exposition and Comment," in *Perspectives of Criticism,* ed. Harry Levin (Cambridge, Mass., 1950), pp. 161-195; reprinted in Tillot-

son's *Criticism and the Nineteenth Century* (London, 1951), pp. 147-187. Other treatments are: Alvan S. Ryan, "Newman's Concept of Literature," *University of Iowa Humanistic Studies,* 6 (1942), 119-175; and Edward Watson, "Newman and Aristotle's Poetics," *Renascence,* 20 (1968), 179-185. The essay is also frequently mentioned in full-length studies of Newman. For an especially insightful treatment that includes Keble as well, see Harold L. Weatherby, *Cardinal Newman in His Age* (Nashville, Tenn., 1978), pp. 264-274. Newman's essay itself is in N, *Essays,* I, 1-26; subsequent page numbers incorporated into text.

17. Tillotson, in Levin, p. 192n., suggested that Newman's essay shares views with Keble's 1825 "Sacred Poetry."

18. The earliest *OED* entry for this word in the sense of "characteristic spirit," "prevalent tone of sentiment," is from Francis Palgrave in 1851, who, however, almost certainly inherited it from Keble and the Tractarians, for they had been using it in this way as early as the 1820s. See J. T. Coleridge, *Memoir,* pp. 384-385; and Prickett, pp. 96-97.

19. T, 4, No. 80, pp. 1-83, and T, 5, No. 87, pp. 1-125; subsequent page references incorporated into text.

20. It is also the case that Williams conceived of the Tract as anti-Evangelical, and in it he directly attacked the Evangelical style.

21. See esp. Newman's note on "The Economy," A, pp. 299-301, and his *Arians of the Fourth Century* (N, *Ari*); see also Keble's sermon *Primitive Tradition* (London, 1839).

22. Robin Selby, *The Principle of Reserve in the Writings of John Henry Newman* (Oxford, 1975), p. 11. Selby's comparison is even apter than he realized; Keble had reservations about Origen because Origen had been condemned at the Second Council of Constantinople in 553, though the extent of the anathema is disputed. See Keble's Tract 89 (T, 6, No. 89).

23. See Tennyson, "Tractarian Aesthetics," pp. 9-10.

24. Isaac Williams, *The Autobiography of Isaac Williams,* ed. Sir George Prevost (London, 1892), pp. 88-91.

25. Ibid., p. 89. On Keble's conduct see note 27, below.

26. The *Disciplina Arcani* became Williams' favorite way of expressing the doctrine of Reserve and the basis for much of Williams' own poetry. An understanding of the *Disciplina* makes clear that Reserve is a more complex doctrine than mere reticence. On this matter and on typology, see Chapter V.

27. The classic illustration of Kebelian Reserve is the often told story of John Keble's hiding his copy of William Law's *A Serious Call to The Devout and Holy Life* (1728) in a drawer lest he be thought ostentatious to be seen

reading it or irreverent in letting it lie carelessly about. See Battiscombe, p. 73. The biographical literature on Keble abounds with instances of Reserve as a mode of personal conduct as well as a religious principle.

28. *Hymni Ecclesiae* (Oxford, 1836), pp. vi-viii. In 1838 Isaac Williams published his *Hymns from the Parisian Breviary.*

29. O, pp. 1-80; the essay was originally published in the *British Critic* in 1838.

30. Later in the essay Keble makes reference to the concept of Reserve: "Expression, *controuled and modified by a certain reserve,* [is] the very soul of Poetry" (O, p. 20; Keble's italics).

31. Here Keble is using *ethos* in an aesthetic as well as a social sense. The earliest *OED* citation for such a use is not until 1875.

32. T, 6, No. 89, pp. 1-186. This Tract was written as early as 1837 for one of Pusey's seminars. See Battiscombe, p. 214.

33. Newman, A, p. 29, discusses the centrality of Butler for Tractarian thinking, and Butler's name appears everywhere in the primary and secondary literature on Tractarianism. For Butler and Keble, see esp. Battiscombe, p. 54, and Prickett, pp. 107-109.

34. W. J. A. Beek, *John Keble's Literary and Religious Contribution to the Oxford Movement* (Nijmegen, 1959), p. 50. This valuable study is one of the few to make extensive use of Keble's writings outside the *Lectures on Poetry,* and it also contains a useful bibliography of Keble's works.

35. For more on Tractarians and typology, see Chapter V.

36. Abrams, p. 147.

37. Warren, p. 51.

38. Ibid., p. 65.

39. *Sehnsucht* itself may be a secularized theological yearning. It is noteworthy that this is the term C. S. Lewis uses to speak of his own early yearning for God before he understood what it was. See Lewis, *Surprised by Joy* (New York, 1955), p. 7.

40. Some other relevant passages from the *Lectures* are: early poets were put there by Providence to keep alive "some of those holier feelings and thoughts" until Christ's coming (LP, II, 198); "There is no richer fount of poetic inspiration than the unquenchable longing for some object which is absent" (II, 262); the ancient Hebrews did not need poetry because "they had God Himself" (II, 268); poetry is naturally associated with those "feelings that deeply affect humans and nothing affects us more than religious feelings" (II, 480).

41. Abrams senses this when he cogently observes: "The parallelism between the poetic theories of Keble and Freud may be taken as one more

evidence of the extent to which psychoanalysis is a secularized version of religious doctrine and ritual" (p. 148).

42. Warren, pp. 63-64.

43. So far as I know, Brémond does not cite Keble, but Brémond's *Prayer and Poetry* (1927) is a work strongly influenced by Romanticism and nineteenth-century literature. Henri Brémond (1865-1933) was a French Jesuit whose thought was much influenced by Newman and by the later Catholic modernists.

44. Keble himself would have been as dismayed by such a transformation of his doctrine as by finding it equated with the speculations of Freud.

45. Warren, p. 64, thinks Keble overstrains in his effort to salvage the "atheist" Lucretius as a religious poet, but I think Warren has again read Keble in the wrong spirit and failed to understand that Keble is saying Nature herself has redeemed Lucretius, who was writing more than he consciously knew. As Keble wrote in his poem for the Fourth Sunday in Lent, "Thoughts beyond their thoughts to those high bards were given."

46. Tennyson, "Sacramental Imagination," pp. 370-371.

III. Keble and *The Christian Year*

1. Georgina Battiscombe, *John Keble* (London, 1964), p. 104.

2. To cite but two examples, *Bartlett's Familiar Quotations* (14th ed., Boston, 1968), p. 567, gives four passages from *The Christian Year*, but one of them is the first stanza of "Abide with Me," which was written by Henry Francis Lyte; Michael Hardwick, *A Literary Atlas and Gazetteer of the British Isles* (Detroit, 1973), p. 70, lists Keble under Gloucestershire with the notice: "His principal work apart from hymns was *The Christian Year*, a briefly successful collection of sacred poems."

3. In addition to works on Keble and the Movement already cited, see Brian W. Martin, *John Keble: Priest, Professor and Poet* (London, 1976). Martin also considers Keble's poetry in relation to his theory and is especially strong on Keble's reflections of earlier poets like Milton; see pp. 119-167. Keble in relation to specifically Anglican devotional attitudes is treated by C. J. Stranks, *Anglican Devotion* (London, 1961), esp. pp. 236-266.

4. This remark is quoted extensively and in various formulations in the literature. See Battiscombe, p. 104. Mary Moorman, *William Wordsworth: The Later Years, 1808-1850* (Oxford, 1965), pp. 479-480, also records that Wordsworth thought Keble's verse "vicious in diction." For the general Victorian response, see Appendix C, below.

5. A. E. Housman, *The Name and Nature of Poetry* (New York, 1933), pp. 32-33.

6. Hoxie Neale Fairchild, *Religious Trends in English Poetry,* 4 (New York, 1957), 251. This massive survey contains a wealth of information and has observations on almost all the poets treated in the present study, but Fairchild's critical judgments are marred by an unrelenting hostility to Romanticism that renders him incapable of understanding the Tractarian enterprise.

7. Amy Cruse's term in *The Victorians and Their Reading* (Boston, 1935), p. 19.

8. Matthew Arnold, *Literature and Dogma,* in *Prose Works of Matthew Arnold,* ed. R. H. Super, 6 (Ann Arbor, Mich., 1968), 403. The Keble line that Arnold italicized appears in the poem for the "Sixth Sunday after Epiphany" (CY, p. 60).

9. Donald Davie, *A Gathered Church: The Literature of the English Dissenting Interest, 1700-1930* (New York, 1978), pp. 15-16.

10. For a contemporary illustrated guide to the Church year, see L. W. Cowie and John Selwyn Gummer, *The Christian Calendar* (Springfield, Mass., 1974).

11. In most modern usage Epiphany is counted as the season after Christmas, and Sundays up to Lent are now numbered in terms of their distance from Epiphany, thus absorbing the old pre-Lenten period of Septuagesima.

12. The poems for "Gunpowder Treason," "King Charles the Martyr," and "The Restoration of the Royal Family" were added to the third and subsequent editions to round out the sequence in the Prayer Book. They were not provided initially because they are not part of the universal Christian calendar. In the Victorian age the commemoration of the martyrdom of Charles I on January 30 was dropped from the Prayer Book to the considerable annoyance of Anglo-Catholics, who, however, continued to keep the day. The Lectionary is the table of Bible readings for the entire year; the Thirty-nine Articles are the Calvinist-inspired statement of principles and beliefs thàt generated Newman's Tract 90; the Tables of Kindred list family relations among whom marriage is forbidden.

13. See Appendix B on the antecedents of *The Christian Year.*

14. Charlotte Mary Yonge, *Musings over "The Christian Year," and "Lyra Innocentium"* (Oxford, 1871). This now scarce volume contains Yonge's own reminiscences of Keble, contributions from others related to his life and times, and Yonge's extensive individual commentaries on every poem in *The Christian Year.* It is thus a companion to a companion to the Book

of Common Prayer. Charlotte Mary Yonge was Keble's catechumen at Hursley, and her thinking on religious matters was always very close to Keble's own.

15. The First Sunday in Epiphany can never fall later than January 13.

16. James Anthony Froude, the younger brother of Hurrell Froude and himself a quondam Tractarian, made the comparison between Tennyson's poems and *The Christian Year*. See A. Dwight Culler, *The Poetry of Tennyson* (New Haven, 1977), p. 156.

17. B. M. Lott, "The Poetry of John Keble, with Special Reference to *The Christian Year* and His Contribution to *Lyra Apostolica*" (diss., London University, 1960), p. 210, notes that the Lectionary was changed in the nineteenth century, so that some of the correspondences are not so clear today as they once were in those poems where the readings for the day come from the Lectionary rather than from printed readings in the Prayer Book propers.

18. Margaret Oliphant, *Salem Chapel* (1863; London, 1907), pp. 53-54. Mrs. Oliphant is here certainly playing on the language of the Book of Common Prayer in the prayer for acceptance of the offering following the consecration of bread and wine: "We beseech Thee to accept this our bounden duty and service, not weighing our merits, but pardoning our offences." In the subsequent reference to the "Anglican lyre" she links *The Christian Year* to the other great Tractarian devotional collection, *Lyra Apostolica,* and in effect notes the frequency with which the idea of the lyre occurs in Tractarian poetry.

19. The other truth that Keble's poetry brought home to Newman was the doctrine of probability, which, as Newman himself notes in this passage, "runs through very much that I have written."

20. Similar points are made in other sympathetic Victorian commentaries, a good example of which is the Preface to Keble's *Miscellaneous Poems* (Oxford, 1869), pp. v-xxv, by G[eorge] M[oberly].

21. *Poetical Works of Wordsworth,* ed. Thomas Hutchinson and Ernest DeSelincourt (London, 1950), pp. 181-182.

22. Used as the motto for Keble's *Occasional Papers and Reviews.* The full passage reads: "In medio Ecclesiae aperuit os ejus, et implevit eum Dominus Spiritu sapientiae et intellectus" (In the middle of the Church he opened his mouth, and the Lord filled him with the Spirit of wisdom and understanding). I have not been able to trace the source. Keble's motto for *The Christian Year* was: "In quietness and confidence shall be your strength" (Isaiah, 30:15).

23. The only natural phenomenon missing from this catalogue is the

rainbow, but Keble frequently refers to it in other poems. See George Landow, "The Rainbow: A Problematic Image," in U. C. Knoepflmacher and G. B. Tennyson, eds., *Nature and the Victorian Imagination* (Berkeley, 1977), pp. 347-348. Keble's analogues are more or less consistent in *The Christian Year* but not so rigorously applied as to make possible any kind of allegory.

24. In the original manuscript "wishful" reads "wistful." Lock in CY records all such changes and variants from the manuscripts at Keble College. There was also a facsimile publication in 1878 of Keble's 1822 manuscript of most of the poems in *The Christian Year* and many sonnets dating from as early as 1810. The facsimile was titled after Keble's notation on the first page of the manuscript *Manuscript Verses, Chiefly on Sacred Subjects.* The facsimile was unauthorized and soon suppressed. Copies are now rare.

25. This is the phrasing from "A Catechism" in the Book of Common Prayer defining a sacrament.

26. The ten most frequent words in *The Christian Year*, with number of times they appear following each in parentheses, are: Love (227), Heart (182), Heaven (180), God (149), Earth (119), Lord (117), Light (98), World (95), Eye (92), High (89). Computed from the entries in *A Concordance to The Christian Year* (1871; rpt., New York, 1968).

27. Battiscombe, p. 113, quotes Newman: " 'In riding out today I have been impressed more powerfully than before I had an idea was possible with the two lines "Chanting with a solemn voice / Minds us of our better choice." I could hardly believe the lines were not my own and that Keble had not taken them from me. I wish it were possible for words to put down the indefinable vague and withal subtle feelings with which God pierces the soul and makes it sick.' " The original source is a letter from Newman to his sister Jemima in 1828; see *Letters and Correspondence of John Henry Newman,* ed. Anne Mozley (London, 1891), I, 183.

28. Wordsworth himself tried to do something of the same sort in the later "Ecclesiastical Sonnets," especially those that abandon the historical format of the "Ecclesiastical Sketches" to concentrate on Church rites and offices. It is noteworthy that the great bulk of these appeared after the publication of *The Christian Year* in 1827. See Appendix B.

29. Keble's remark that in *The Christian Year* he assumed the Church to be in "a state of decay" has been much quoted. See CY, p. xvii. One of his aims was to arrest this decay by revitalizing Church practices.

30. Zoar was Lot's city of refuge when God destroyed Sodom and Gomorrah.

31. Late Victorian Keble hagiographic works make much of the impact of Fairford Church on Keble's imagination, and in truth the church is an impressive late Gothic structure justly famed for its stained glass windows once believed to be by Dürer. See Yonge, *Musings,* pp. cxxxviii-cxlvii; J. G. Joyce, *The Fairford Windows* (London, 1872); W. T. Warren, *Kebleland* (Winchester, 1900); Oscar G. Farmer, *Fairford Church and Its Stained Glass Windows* (Fairford, n.d.).

32. The thirteenth stanza of this poem originally read: "O come to our Communion Feast: / There present, in the heart / Not in the hands, the eternal Priest / Will His true self impart." After repeated requests, Keble changed the third line just before his death to read: "As in the hands . . ." in order to make clear that he was not denying the doctrine of the Real Presence. See CY, p. 297, and J. T. Coleridge, *Memoir of the Rev. John Keble* (London, 1869), p. 163. The anti-Roman lines are actually very mild: "Speak gently of our sister's fall: / Who knows but gentle love / May win her at our patient call / The surer way to prove?"

33. Despite frequent Victorian comparisons of the two poets, modern critics have not found the subject rewarding, but see Elbert N. S. Thompson, *"The Temple* and *The Christian Year,"* PMLA, 54 (1939), 1018-1025; and Jean Wilkinson, "Three Sets of Religious Poems," *Huntington Library Quarterly,* 36 (1972-73), 203-226.

34. Lott, pp. 66-71. I have taken the statistical data from Lott but not the linkage of it with the stylistic imperatives of Reserve, which is my own interpretation.

35. George Saintsbury in the *Cambridge History of English Literature,* ed. A. W. Ward and A. R. Waller, 12, pt. 2 (Cambridge, 1917), p. 189; Housman, p. 33; David Cecil includes the two Keble poems I have mentioned in *The Oxford Book of Christian Verse* (Oxford, 1940).

36. Pusey was especially given to citing passages and lines in letters, and he testified that "scraps of *The Christian Year,* as they have occurred to me, have been a great comfort, and will be amid whatever He sees best to send" (quoted by Battiscombe, p. 113).

IV. Newman and the *Lyra Apostolica*

1. As the subsequent discussion makes clear, the idea and the first publication of the poems actually preceded the Assize Sermon that is taken to mark the beginning of the Movement.

2. The two poems added to the third and following editions were also originally printed in the *British Magazine,* one under the "Lyra" rubric

(No. 57; Newman's "The Call of David"), and one printed in April 1833 before the "Lyra" series began (No. 89; Keble's "The Winter Thrush").

3. Newman, *Letters,* I, 281. Frederic Rogers, afterwards Lord Blachford, was a lifelong supporter of the Oxford Movement.

4. The Prussian diplomat C. K. J. Bunsen (1791-1860) touched the Oxford Movement at several points, most notably in 1841 in the vexed affair of the Jerusalem Bishopric. Though Bunsen lent the volume of Homer, he later expressed intense dislike of the *Lyra Apostolica.* See Frances Baroness Bunsen, *A Memoir of Baron Bunsen,* I (London, 1868), 428. A further irony resides in the fact that Bunsen's 1833 collection of German hymns was eventually rendered into English by Catherine Winkworth under the title *Lyra Germanica.*

The Homeric motto for the *Lyra Apostolica* was in the same spirit as the biblical motto for the *Tracts for the Times,* which was, "If the trumpet give an uncertain sound, who shall prepare himself for the battle?" (I Corinthians 14:8).

5. A series of literary sketches of the early Church by Newman, published in book form in 1840, not to be confused with the *Library of the Fathers,* which was also a Tractarian undertaking, a multi-volume translation of writings of the Fathers launched in 1836.

6. Newman's later poetry was of course then unknown to Williams because it was unwritten, but it accounts in any case for less than half of his entire output of poetry and, except for *The Dream of Gerontius,* is far less well known than the poems from the *Lyra.* Most of the later poetry, even including *Gerontius,* is also much more derivative of previous writing, chiefly liturgical forms of prayer, than his *Lyra* poems. The most extensive treatment of Newman's poetry is Elizabeth Ann Noel, "An Edition of Poems by John Henry Cardinal Newman" (diss., University of Illinois, 1950). Noel discusses all editions of Newman's poems and prints all variant readings.

7. Isaac Williams, *The Autobiography of Isaac Williams,* ed. Sir George Prevost (London, 1892), p. 69; my italics.

8. The poems did first appear anonymously in the *British Magazine;* the lower-case Greek letters came in with book publication. Knowledgeable readers soon made the appropriate identifications, but no public linkage was made between letter and author until Newman's identification in the 1879 edition.

9. *Lyra Apostolica* (London, 1879), pp. vi-vii.

10. Meriol Trevor, *The Pillar of the Cloud* (London, 1962), p. 112, captures its quality in contrast to Newman's prose: "The sermons as literary

creations, are like an avenue of wonderful trees; the poems stark as bits of stone in a field."

11. Newman's poetry in the *Lyra* is also notable for offering a record of his incessant tinkering with his texts and his lifetime concern for doctrine. The subject is too complex, and ultimately too unrewarding, for pursuit here, but it should be noted that Newman continued to alter words and lines, usually for doctrinal reasons, throughout his career. The texts of *Lyra* poems as they appear in later editions of Newman's *Verses on Various Occasions* have frequently been altered to accommodate a point of doctrine Newman felt scanted in the original or to excise some doctrine he no longer held. The most celebrated, because comic, instance is the change wrought in the poem "Rest" (No. 52) from its *Lyra* appearances. The original poem is a reflection on the fate of the blessed dead in terms of the doctrine of the "Refrigerium," which was also occasionally the later title for this poem. The dead are depicted in Eden listening to the murmurings of the four-fold river. Later this was changed to a poem on Enoch and Elias, who were held to be more certainly in "Eden" than those who died in Christian times. Still later it was turned back into a poem on the dead but with the addition of the doctrine of Purgatory, so that the opening lines read: "They are at rest: / The fire has eaten out all blot and stain, / And, convalescent, they enjoy a blest / Refreshment after pain." Eventually Newman eliminated the convalescent pair and restored the poem to its original wording, leaving only and regrettably the word "hurries" for the four-fold river in place of the more fitting "murmurs." See H. C. Beeching's discussion, L, pp. lxv-lxvii; and Noel, pp. 182-183.

12. See G. B. Tennyson, "Tractarian Aesthetics: Analogy and Reserve in Keble and Newman," *Victorian Newsletter,* no. 55 (Spring 1979), p. 10.

13. As far as I know, the parallels between the two poems have not been noted, but they are striking. Hardy appears to be answering Keble's nature optimism or at least muting it. That Hardy knew Keble's work is certain. See Appendix C on the Victorian response to *The Christian Year.*

14. The dialogue is between the same two shepherds Arnold borrowed from Virgil—Thyrsis and Corydon.

15. This is an oddly unregarded Newman piece of some historical interest. Tillotson is familiar with it, as of course is Noel, but Noel's edition of Newman's poem prints only Newman's part of the collaboration and contains virtually no commentary on the poem. That it was not later reprinted by Newman is understandable in view of its anti-Catholic sentiments.

V. Isaac Williams: Reserve, Nature, and the Gothic Revival

1. For Williams' views on these matters and biographical details on Williams, see *The Autobiography of Isaac Williams,* ed. Sir George Prevost (London, 1892), and O. W. Jones, *Isaac Williams and His Circle* (London, 1971).

2. I except the Hampden Affair of 1836, in which the Tractarians opposed the appointment of R. D. Hampden as Regius Professor of Divinity, for this was an instance of the Tractarians taking the offensive. The estrangement between Keble and Thomas Arnold dates from the Hampden controversy and Arnold's bitter attack on the Tractarians as the "Oxford Malignants" in the *Edinburgh Review.*

3. The eventual winner was Edward Garbett, whose career confirmed the low Tractarian appraisal of his talents.

4. R. W. Church, *The Oxford Movement* (1891; rpt. Chicago, 1970), p. 58.

5. These were completed in 1849 and followed by many other prose works and some further poetry. See the bibliography of Williams's work in Jones, pp. 171-172.

6. Jones, pp. 32-34. Williams was, of course, also interested in continuity in religious practices, as is well illustrated by his Tract 86, titled "Indications of a Superintending Providence in the Preservation of the Prayer Book." It is this Tract showing Tractarian support for the Book of Common Prayer that has gained Williams some rare modern attention. See Horton Davies, *Worship and Theology in England,* III, *From Watts and Wesley to Maurice, 1690-1850* (Princeton, 1961), pp. 266-276. Elsewhere (III, 259), Davies describes Williams as "Pusey's faithful henchman."

7. See Dom Gregory Dix, *The Shape of the Liturgy* (London, 1945), pp. 15, 480-485. Dix says the earliest Western screens were originally designed to shield choirs and celebrants from drafts, but he acknowledges the later connection of the screen with the idea of veiling a secret. He maintains that the iconostasis (also referred to as the *ikonostasion*) serves by intention to *prevent* the Orthodox laity from seeing the consecration, whereas the Western screen, though marking a barrier, explicitly *enables* the congregation to see the consecration. He finds the same differing intentions in the Western Elevation of the Host as opposed to the Orthodox secreting of the Host until the "Great Entrance" following a hidden consecration. Timothy Ware, *The Orthodox Church* (Harmondsworth, Eng., 1963), pp. 276-280, asserts, somewhat unconvincingly, that the iconostasis does *not* "make the people feel cut off from the priest in the sanctuary," and "in any

case, many of the ceremonies take place in front of the screen." It is doubtful that Isaac Williams would have been aware of all the arguments in the case, but there is no doubt that his attitude toward the screen is distinctly that of "veiling" and hence has affinities with Orthodoxy. Much the same is true of Pugin, who was the most vocal Victorian proponent of the screen. His *Chancel Screens,* however, did not appear until 1851. Pugin's treatment makes clear that the distinction between chancel screens and rood screens is a purely technical one. Rood screens are simply chancel screens that are topped by a crucifix (rood).

8. Earl Miner, Prefce, *Literary Uses of Typology,* ed. Earl Miner (Princeton, 1977), p. ix.

9. George Landow, "Moses Striking the Rock: Typological Symbolism in Victorian Poetry," in Miner, pp. 315-344, esp. pp. 342-344. See also Landow, *Aesthetic and Critical Theories of John Ruskin* (Princeton, 1971), pp. 329-356; "The Rainbow," in U. C. Knoepflmacher and G. B. Tennyson, eds., *Nature and the Victorian Imagination* (Berkeley, 1977), pp. 341-369; "Bruising the Serpent's Head: Typological Symbol in Victorian Poetry," *Victorian Newsletter,* no. 55 (Spring 1979), pp. 11-14; and *William Holman Hunt and Typological Symbolism* (New Haven, 1979), esp. pp. 7-17, 186-187.

10. Once again, the Protestant difficulty with pre-Reformation materials may have caused intellectual contortions. Typological and figural elements had long been used in Protestant hymnody, but there appears to have been a reluctance to link these with patristic and medieval practice.

11. *Thoughts in Past Years,* p. vii; subsequent references incorporated into text.

12. I am not positing a causal relation. Pugin's *Contrasts* appeared first in 1836, and was revised and expanded in 1841. He could not have known Williams' early poetry like "The Ancient and Modern Town," since *Thoughts in Past Years* did not appear until 1838. The coincidence of interests is merely another indication that many minds were moving in the same direction at this time. My point is that Isaac Williams was in the forefront of the movement toward the Gothic.

13. It is almost impossible to establish primacy among many of these Tractarian interests, since all the Tractarians were exchanging ideas, fertilizing each others' minds, and responding with a sense of excitement and discovery to the riches of the Church, but Williams was surely among the first to discover the Breviary. He and Keble read it in 1829 when Sir George Prevost brought the four volumes of the Parisian Breviary back from a trip to France. See Williams, *Autobiography,* pp. 36-37. Another

important source of this kind of interest has long been recognized as residing in William Palmer of Worcester's *Origines Liturgicae* (1832). Hitherto unnoted in this connection was the publication in 1837 of *Ancient Hymns from the Roman Breviary,* translated and edited by Richard Mant, at that time Bishop of Down and Connor. Mant (1776-1848) left Oxford before the Tractarian Movement began, but he appears to have independently shared some of the Tractarians' interests. Apart from his translations, the most striking parallel lies in his two-volume work, *The Holydays of the Church* (1828-1831).

14. Since Eastlake's *History of the Gothic Revival* (1872), the literature on this subject has grown enormously. Particularly relevant here are Kenneth Clark, *The Gothic Revival* (1928; 3rd ed., London, 1962); George L. Hersey, *High Victorian Gothic* (Baltimore, 1972); Georg Germann, *Gothic Revival in Europe and Britain* (Cambridge, Mass., 1973). For the relation of architecture to worship and the influence of the Oxford Movement, see G. W. O. Addleshaw and Frederick Etchells, *The Architectural Setting of Anglican Worship* (London, 1948), esp. pp. 203-210. For the impact of the Ecclesiological Society, see James F. White, *The Cambridge Movement* (Cambridge, 1962). White (p. 24) has also uncovered the interesting information that Isaac Williams was a committee member of the Oxford Society for Promoting the Study of Gothic Architecture, founded in March 1839. Other committee members were: J. R. Bloxam, Newman's curate; Francis A. Faber, Frederick Faber's brother; and J. B. Mozley, Tractarian and brother of Thomas Mozley, author of the *Reminiscences,* containing much information on the Tractarian years. Ordinary members included Newman, John Ruskin (then an undergraduate), and William Palmer.

15. It is difficult to ascertain when the Tractarian practice of dating by the liturgical calendar and especially by saints' days came in, but the impetus seems to have come initially from *The Christian Year.* Williams, *Autobiography,* p. 53, dates the revival of serious Church observance of saints' days as 1832. Eventually the practice became a hallmark of the true Tractarian and appeared in publications and correspondence. Many of the Tracts and many prefaces to other Tractarian works are dated by reference to the Church calendar. Bishop Shuttleworth of Chichester found the practice so irritating he sent out letters dated "The Palace, Washing Day."

16. *The Baptistery* (3rd ed., Oxford, 1846), p. viii; subsequent references incorporated into text.

17. *The Altar* (London, 1847), pp. v-vi; subsequent references incorporated into text. Three years later Williams did not feel obliged to offer a rationale for versifying the creation of the world, perhaps because he was

confident that no one would object to so obviously biblical an undertaking. But in his volume on that theme, *The Seven Days, or The Old and New Creation* (1850), Williams does provide an "Argument" and "Notes" for each of the seven days, and these are as heavily patristic as his preface to *The Altar* or his presentations in the Tracts. *The Seven Days* contains just under 400 pages of Spenserian stanzas retelling the story of creation. It was Williams' penultimate volume of verse and the last one published in the Tractarian period to 1850. In his final volume of poetry, *The Christian Seasons* (1854), he returned to a liturgically based plan.

18. The best illustration is in the work of the pre-eminent Tractarian architect Butterfield. See Paul Thompson, *William Butterfield: Victorian Architect* (Cambridge, Mass., 1971), esp. pp. 27-41, and illustrations.

VI. Tractarian Postlude

1. The fullest account of the religious novel in the age is now Robert Lee Wolff, *Gains and Losses: Novels of Faith and Doubt in Victorian England* (New York, 1977).

2. The classic illustration is the response of Tractarians to *Loss and Gain* that Newman had "sunk below Dickens," a sentiment gleefully conveyed to Newman by Faber (Meriol Trevor, *The Pillar of the Cloud* [London, 1962], p. 421), Presumably the Tractarians mellowed on religious issues in fiction in the fifties, when the novels of Charlotte Mary Yonge began appearing.

3. *Lyra Innocentium* (Oxford, 1846); subsequent references incorporated into text. Keble's title inspired a now-lost painting by the pre-Raphaelite Charles Collins to the 1852 Royal Academy Exhibition.

4. For the career of the Wordsworthian child in the age, see U. C. Knoepflmacher, "Mutations of the Wordsworthian Child of Nature," in U. C. Knoepflmacher and G. B. Tennyson, eds., *Nature and the Victorian Imagination* (Berkeley, 1977), pp. 391-425.

5. These five do not exhaust all possibilities, but they best cover the spectrum of Tractarian concerns. For a broad sampling of the religious verse of the age, including the authors cited here, see Alfred H. Miles, ed., *The Poets and Poetry of the Nineteenth Century*, vols. 11-12 (London, 1906).

6. On Hawker, see S. Baring-Gould, *The Vicar of Morwenstow* (London, 1886); C. E. Byles, *The Life and Letters of R. S. Hawker* (London, 1905); and Piers Brendon, *Hawker of Morwenstow* (London, 1975).

7. See Tennyson, "The Sacramental Imagination," in Knoepflmacher and Tennyson, pp. 379-380; and Charlotte Mary Yonge, *John Keble's Parishes* (London, 1898), p. 113.

8. R. S. Hawker, *Cornish Ballads,* ed. C. E. Byles (London, 1894), p. 49.

9. See J. Silvester, *Archbishop Trench* (London, 1891); and J. Bromley, *The Man of Ten Talents* (London, 1959).

10. Trench was serving his first curacy under H. J. Rose at Hadleigh during the time of the Hadleigh Conference that helped launch the Oxford Movement, but Trench himself was not a participant. See Bromley, p. 51.

11. R. C. Trench, *Poems* (12th ed., London, 1899), p. 162.

12. See John Edward Bowden, ed., *Life and Letters of Frederick William Faber* (London, 1869); Ronald Chapman, *Father Faber* (London, 1961); and Raleigh Addington, ed., *Faber: Poet and Priest* (Cowbridge, Wales, 1974).

13. For Protestant purposes it was necessary to change two lines in the third stanza. These originally read: "Faith of our Fathers! Mary's prayers / Shall win our country back to thee." In Protestant versions they read: "Faith of our Fathers! Good men's prayers / Shall win our country all to thee." See J, I, 363.

14. F. W. Faber, *Hymns* (London, 1861), p. xvii. This contains a reprint of the Preface to the 1849 edition. Faber also refers to the "refined and engaging works of Oxford writers," that is, Tractarian devotional poetry, and its absence from English Catholic writing. See also J, I, 361-362.

15. Addington, p. 13. See also Brian W. Martin, "Wordsworth, Faber, and Keble: Commentary on a Triangular Relationship," *Review of English Studies,* 26 (1975), 436-442.

16. J, I, 214-215.

17. Edward Caswall, *Masque of Mary* (London, 1858).

18. Eleanor A. Towle, *John Mason Neale, D. D.: A Memoir* (London, 1906); and A. G. Lough, *The Influence of John Mason Neale* (London, 1962). See also James F. White, *The Cambridge Movement* (Cambridge, 1962). In 1843 Neale collaborated with Benjamin Webb, another founder of the Camden Society, to translate Durandus' *The Symbolism of Churches and Church Ornaments,* and he was also active in the reestablishment of Anglican religious orders.

19. Lawrence J. Starzyk, *The Imprisoned Splendor: A Study of Victorian Critical Theory* (Port Washington, N.Y., 1977), p. 162. Starzyk's entire chapter six, "Poetry and the New Spiritual Cult," pp. 155-182, is especially relevant here.

20. Eliot, "Religion and Literature," in *Selected Prose,* ed. John Hayward (London, 1953), p. 32.

VII. Postscript: Christina Rossetti and Gerard Manley Hopkins

1. Hoxie Neale Fairchild, *Religious Trends in English Poetry*, 4 (New York, 1957), 292.

2. Raymond Chapman, *Faith and Revolt: Studies in the Literary Influence of the Oxford Movement* (London, 1970), pp. 170-197.

3. William Michael Rossetti, ed., *The Poetical Works of Christina Georgina Rossetti* (London, 1904); subsequent references incorporated into the text. William Michael Rossetti's edition is now being superseded by R. W. Crump's *The Complete Poems of Christina Rossetti* (Baton Rouge, La., 1979), but as of this writing her edition had reached only the first of a projected three volumes. The first volume contains only a small portion of Christina Rossetti's devotional poetry, hence this edition could not be cited for the present study.

4. Christina Rossetti's devotional poetry appeared in various individual volumes of verse and in her many prose works of devotion. It was gathered together under various headings in the volume *Verses* (1893). In general, she wrote more devotional poetry as she aged, but the chronology is complex, and it is to be hoped that the Crump edition will make it clearer than William Michael Rossetti's edition does.

5. Chapman, p. 173, mentions her favorable citation of Williams. Lona Mosk Packer, *Christina Rossetti* (Berkeley, 1963), p. 7, notes that, although no fervent admirer of Keble, the young Christina Rossetti did compose pencil drawings in the margins of an edition of *The Christian Year* owned by her sister Maria.

6. Wendell Stacy Johnson, *Gerard Manley Hopkins: The Poet as Victorian* (Ithaca, N.Y., 1968); Allison G. Sulloway, *Gerard Manley Hopkins and the Victorian Temper* (New York, 1972); subsequent references to Sulloway incorporated into the text.

7. Dolben's verse is a further illustration of how strong the Tractarian influence was at Oxford during Hopkins' early years there. See Robert Bridges, ed., *The Poems of Digby Mackworth Dolben, with a Memoir* (rev. ed., Oxford, 1916); and his *Three Friends* (London, 1932). See also Martin Cohen, ed., *Uncollected Poems of Digby Mackworth Dolben* (Reading, Eng., 1973).

8. I make no attempt here to canvass the huge body of secondary literature on Hopkins' poetry and poetic theory, but I note that some of the recent research by Jerome Bump into the medievalist character of Hopkins' poetics has a number of striking points of contact with Romanticism and, by implication, with Tractarianism. See especially his "Art and

Religion: Hopkins and Savonarola," *Thought* 50 (1975), 132-147; and "Hopkins, Pater, and Medievalism," *Victorian Newsletter,* no. 50 (Fall 1976), pp. 10-15.

9. Claude Colleer Abbott, ed., *The Correspondence of Gerard Manley Hopkins and Richard Watson Dixon* (London, 1935), p. 99.

10. *The Poems of Gerard Manley Hopkins,* ed. W. H. Gardner and N. H. MacKenzie (4th ed., London, 1967), pp. 94-95; subsequent references incorporated into text.

Index

261

Index